Building a Community, Having a Home

WORKING AND WRITING FOR CHANGE
Series Editors: Steve Parks, Cristina Kirklighter, & Jess Pauszek

The Writing and Working for Change series began during the 100th anniversary celebrations of NCTE. It was designed to recognize the collective work of teachers of English, Writing, Composition, and Rhetoric to work within and across diverse identities to ensure the field recognize and respect language, educational, political, and social rights of all students, teachers, and community members. While initially solely focused on the work of NCTE/CCCC Special Interest Groups and Caucuses, the series now includes texts written by individuals in partnership with other communities struggling for social recognition and justice.

Books in the Series
CCCC/NCTE Caucuses
History of the Black Caucus National Council Teachers of English by Marianna White Davis
Listening to Our Elders: Working and Writing for Social Change by Samantha Blackmon, Cristina Kirklighter, and Steve Parks
Building a Community, Having a Home: A History of the Conference on College Composition and Communication edited by Jennifer Sano-Franchini, Terese Guinsatao Monberg, K. Hyoejin Yoon

Community Publications
PHD to PhD: How Education Saved My Life by Elaine Richardson

Building a Community, Having a Home

A HISTORY OF THE CONFERENCE ON COLLEGE COMPOSITION AND COMMUNICATION ASIAN/ASIAN AMERICAN CAUCUS

Edited by
Jennifer Sano-Franchini
Terese Guinsatao Monberg
K. Hyoejin Yoon

Parlor Press
Anderson, South Carolina
www.parlorpress.com

Parlor Press LLC, Anderson, South Carolina, USA
© 2017 New City Community Press
Printed in the United States of America on acid-free paper.

S A N: 2 5 4 - 8 8 7 9

Library of Congress Cataloging-in-Publication Data on File

1 2 3 4 5

978-1-60235-926-0 (paperback)
978-1-60235-927-7 (PDF)
978-1-60235-928-4 (ePub)

Working and Writing for Change Series
Edited by Steve Parks

Cover photograph by Chad Shomura
Cover design by Jennifer Sano-Franchini
Interior design by Elizabeth Parks, elizabethannparks@gmail.com

Parlor Press, LLC is an independent publisher of scholarly and trade titles in print and multimedia formats. This book is available in paper, cloth and eBook formats from Parlor Press on the World Wide Web at http://www.parlorpress.com or through online and brick-and-mortar bookstores. For submission information or to find out about Parlor Press publications, write to Parlor Press, 3015 Brackenberry Drive, Anderson, South Carolina, 29621, or email editor@parlorpress.com.

CONTENTS

IX   ACKNOWLEDGMENTS

XI   VOICES FROM THE CCCC ASIAN/ASIAN AMERICAN CAUCUS
Dominic Ashby, Holly Bruland, Karen Ching Carter, Stuart Ching, Jerry Won Lee, Peter Mayshle, Jolivette Mecenas, Iswari Pandey, Charlyne Sarmiento, Mira Shimabukuro, Hui Wu, Morris Young

XX   THE STAND
Lawson Fusao Inada

1   INTRODUCTION: RE/ARTICULATIONS OF HISTORY, RE/VISIONS OF COMMUNITY
Terese Guinsatao Monberg, K. Hyoejin Yoon, and Jennifer Sano-Franchini

31   CHAPTER ONE: TAKING TIME FOR FEMINIST HISTORIOGRAPHY: REMEMBERING ASIAN/ASIAN AMERICAN INSTITUTIONAL AND SCHOLARLY ACTIVISM
Jennifer Sano-Franchini

68   CIRCULATION ESSAY: THE PRESENCE OF ASIAN/ASIAN AMERICAN SCHOLARS IN *COLLEGE COMPOSITION AND COMMUNICATION* (1950–2010)
Phuong Minh Tran, with a foreword by K. Hyoejin Yoon

79   CHAPTER TWO: "TO ESTABLISH A HOME WITHIN A HOME": AN INTERVIEW WITH LUMING MAO
Chanon Adsanatham

87 CHAPTER THREE: "DEVELOPING PROFESSIONAL RELATIONSHIPS AND PERSONAL FRIENDSHIPS": AN INTERVIEW WITH MORRIS YOUNG
Robyn Tasaka

95 CHAPTER FOUR: FOSTERING OUR EFFORTS TO "WRITE IN THE SPACES LEFT": STORIES OF EMERGENCE IN ASIAN AMERICAN RHETORIC
Terese Guinsatao Monberg and Haivan V. Hoang

115 CIRCULATION ESSAY: THE IMPACT OF ASIAN AND ASIAN AMERICAN SCHOLARSHIP AS A PRODUCTIVE, CONTESTED SITE
Linh Dich

119 A COLLECTION OF IMAGES AND ARCHIVAL DOCUMENTS

169 CHAPTER FIVE: A SURVEY OF RESEARCH IN ASIAN RHETORIC
Reflections on "A Survey of Research in Asian Rhetoric"
Bo Wang

184 CIRCULATION ESSAY: RACIAL IDENTITIES, VISUAL REPRESENTATIONS, AND PERFORMATIVE CAPACITIES: RHETORICAL PRODUCTION(S) OF/BY ASIANS/ASIAN AMERICANS IN HAWAI'I
Scott Ka'alele, Edward Lee, and Michael Pak, with K. Hyoejin Yoon

200 CHAPTER SIX: GLOBALIZATION AND THE TEACHING OF WRITTEN ENGLISH
Reflections on "Globalization and the Teaching of Written English"
Paul Kei Matsuda

216 CHAPTER SEVEN: WHAT DOES THE FIELD OF WRITING ASSESSMENT NEED? OR, HOW ASIAN AND ASIAN AMERICAN RHETORIC CAN HELP WRITING ASSESSMENTS WORK BETTER
Asao B. Inoue

228   CIRCULATION ESSAY: BUILDING ON RECENT RESEARCH FROM AAAC MEMBERS TO ADVOCATE FOR SECOND LANGUAGE INTERNATIONAL STUDENTS
Jolivette Mecenas

236   CIRCULATION ESSAY: RISKS AND AFFORDANCES: THE NAMING OF THE ASIAN/ASIAN AMERICAN CAUCUS
Lehua Ledbetter

240   APPENDIX A: ASIAN/ASIAN AMERICAN CAUCUS, 2016

243   APPENDIX B: TIMELINE OF SCHOLARSHIP AND ACCOMPLISHMENTS

255   APPENDIX C: BIBLIOGRAPHY OF ASIAN/ASIAN AMERICAN RHETORIC AND COMPOSITION

269   APPENDIX D: ASIAN/ASIAN AMERICAN PUBLICATIONS IN COLLEGE COMPOSITION AND COMMUNICATION (1950–2010)
Phuong Minh Tran

277   CONTRIBUTORS

Acknowledgments

Thank you to Samantha Blackmon, Cristina Kirklighter, and Steve Parks of Writing and Working for Change, which established the exigency for our caucus to work on this collection. We acknowledge NCTE and CCCC for their generous support of the Writing and Working for Change project and this book. A special thanks to Steve Parks for his encouragement, flexibility, patience, and advice during the production of this manuscript. Finally, thank you to the reviewers, who provided valuable and generative feedback.

We are also grateful to the members of the Asian/Asian American Caucus (AAAC) for trusting us to re-narrate this history of our caucus, and for their many contributions to making and telling the histories that are the foundations of this project. Chanon Adsanatham, Dominic Ashby, Holly Bruland, Karen Ching Carter, Stuart Ching, Linh Dich, Scott Ka'alele, Lehua Ledbetter, Edward Lee, Jerry Won Lee, Haivan V. Hoang, Lawson Fusao Inada, Asao B. Inoue, LuMing Mao, Paul Kei Matsuda, Peter Mayshle, Jolivette Mecenas, Michael Pak, Iswari Pandey, Charlyne Sarmiento, Mira Shimabukuro, Robyn Tasaka, Phuong Minh Tran, Bo Wang, Hui Wu, and Morris Young provided invaluable contributions to this collection, and we acknowledge members who have helped in perhaps less visible ways. We thank, in particular, Jolivette Mecenas for pointing us to "Racist Love," and for her substantial contributions in imagining the outline for this collection in its early stages. We are thankful to Asian American poet Lawson Fusao Inada, who shared his experiences working in NCTE in the 1970s.

And, finally, heartfelt thanks to the participation of caucus members at the 2014 and 2015 AAAC meetings during which we collectively reflected on this history and how it might shape the histories we make going forward.

Voices from the CCCC Asian/Asian American Caucus

Dominic Ashby, Holly Bruland, Karen Ching Carter, Stuart Ching, Jerry Won Lee, Peter Mayshle, Jolivette Mecenas, Iswari Pandey, Charlyne Sarmiento, Mira Shimabukuro, Hui Wu, Morris Young

Almost all teacher–scholars in rhetoric and composition attend the Conference on College Composition and Communication, but not all of them show up at the caucuses, the mostly hidden gems of the large annual convention. The Asian/Asian American Caucus is such a treasure that blesses emerging scholars through their connections with established scholars. My first encounter with the caucus was in 1997, when it was called the Asian Caucus, without "Asian American" in the name. At the time, the organizer of the yearly business meeting was a group of first generation immigrants teaching and researching ESL/EFL. In other words, the Asian Caucus was the meeting where ESL/EFL teachers and researchers met and were connected to other scholars beyond it, regardless of their race or skin color. The 1997 CCCC saw me wandering around the Convention Center in Phoenix to come across Xiaoming Li, author of *"Good Writing" in a Cross-Cultural Context*, who introduced me to the Asian Caucus and to Helen Fox, author of *Listening to the World: Cultural Issues in Academic Writing*, and Carol Severino, a co-editor of *Writing in Multicultural Settings*, among others.

The 1997 meeting was held at 6:00 p.m. on Friday, the same time as now. It was the third anniversary of the Asian Caucus led by Nancy Lay of City College of New York. The meeting was the first time and place that I met more than twenty English professionals, originally from Asia, all at once since I came to the U.S. As an ABD from Texas Christian University, I was excited yet I felt like I had been in China, or Hong Kong, or somewhere in Asia, heartily familiar but unaccountably different—our skin color looked alike, but we all spoke in English. It was a different world from TCU, where most English faculty and students were middle-class Caucasian Americans. As a newbie, I felt the warmth of welcome from the chair, Nancy, and seasoned professionals, such as George Xu, LuMing Mao, and others. With keen interest, I watched others speak about issues and participate in planning in an encouraging casual environment. At the end of the meeting, we all went to an Asian restaurant for dinner. I don't remember if anybody got drunk; but I do remember that everybody was happily busy with talking. It was at the 1997 Asian Caucus meeting that I began friendships with Xiaoming Li, LuMing Mao, and others. The meetings afterwards introduced me to Paul Kei Matsuda, Morris Young, Xiaoye You, and more. The Asian/Asian American Caucus continues to inspire me with new energies from new and young people; its people continue to give me aspirations for better teaching and research.

Hui Wu

At the outset of my career, the Asian/Asian American Caucus was the cornerstone of my professional life. In one context, it was an invaluable professional resource that enabled me to gather in both solidarity and dialogue with colleagues committed to shared causes; to receive mentoring and then, later, to support mentorship; and to advocate as part of a collective for students of color studying the English language arts throughout primary, secondary, and higher education. In another more personal context, the caucus was—and continues to be—a home in a profession and institution that, if not for spaces and places like the caucus, I could not call home otherwise. In his 2004 guest-edited volume of *College English, Rhetorics from/of Color*, Victor Villanueva, Jr., reminds us: "*Memoria* calls and pushes us forward. *Memoria* is a friend of ours. We must invite her into our classrooms and our scholarship" (19). I believe that cultural memory—which we recover in scholarship, which we affirm through shared struggle, and which we inhabit through the stories of elders—inspires us to imagine both individually and collectively. It binds us to our pasts and summons and pushes us toward the work that still needs to be done.

Stuart Ching

My first AAAC meeting was in New York, 2007. I was a graduate student at University of Hawai'i at Mānoa, and had presented with fellow graduate students from my program. I had won a Scholars for the Dream Award the year before, at the Chicago meeting, and Morris Young came to my presentation. How awesome was it for me as a grad student to look out into the audience and see, not only that we had an audience, but also that people whose work I was currently reading were in attendance! AAAC prioritizes supporting Scholars for the Dream awardees.

Robyn Tasaka invited me the caucus meeting. CCCC can be so daunting and overwhelming for new people. Meeting AAAC members made my goals legitimate; these were people who sincerely wanted me to succeed. Being a part of the AAAC made CCCC seem smaller and a lot friendlier. But importantly, AAAC meetings have inspired many discussions, collaborations, and publications in which it has been an honor for me to participate. All of the minority caucuses are so important to the mission of CCCC and to the intellectual work that we in Composition and Rhetoric do as a whole; I'm proud to participate as an AAAC member.

Jolivette Mecenas

I have been attending CCCC long enough (since 1992) to remember a time before Asian Americans had their own caucus. As a graduate student my work focused on the literacy and rhetorical practices of Asian Americans and I hoped to find colleagues doing similar work in my professional networks. I was aware of the Black Caucus, and was even invited to the Latino Caucus, as it was named at the time, by my friend Renee Moreno who noted that Gail Okawa, a Japanese American scholar from Hawai'i, was a member. And then I noticed the Asian Caucus meeting on the 1995 CCCC program. There was no description of the session, just the title, "Asian Caucus." What did that mean? Was Asian being used in an analogous way to Black or Latino? Why not Asian American or Asian American/Pacific Islander, which had official license as a U.S. Census category then? Or if the organizers were trying to be political or inclusive of pan-Asian ethnicities, why not "Yellow" Caucus? The confusion on my part was enough to keep me from attending the session and later programs only reinforced my belief that the Asian Caucus was not for me since it seemed to offer topics on Asian rhetorics or ESL teaching. This iteration of the Asian Caucus existed from 1995–98.

However, things began to change when LuMing Mao took over as organizer for the Asian Caucus and in 1999 we began to explore the "Asian

American text." This meant examining the range of writing by Asians and Asian Americans and what this might tell us about their rhetorical and literacy practices. But this also meant examining ourselves as "texts" within the organization and the field of composition and rhetoric: what did it mean to be an Asian or Asian American scholar–teacher in this discipline? I think for many of us this is still a central question, especially when we continue to see a relatively small number of Asian and Asian American scholars in CCCC. While we have certainly grown and we have benefited from a broader effort to make work by scholars of color more visible and to mentor scholars of color within the organization, we still need to reach out to ensure that those new to the field can find their place among us.

Morris Young

I attended my first AAAC meeting in 2009 in hopes of dialoguing with others who were addressing Asian and Asian American rhetorical traditions and practices in their teaching. At the time, I was teaching undergraduate rhetoric courses at the University of Hawai'i at Mānoa, a location that heightened my awareness of the need for presenting rhetorical perspectives beyond the Greco–Roman traditions in which I had primarily been trained. As a Caucasian ("haole") doctoral student, I was concerned that my presence at the business meeting might be an intrusion, but a friend in the Caucus convinced me to attend, reminding me that the group's stated purpose is to support scholarship "by and/or about Asian and Asian American language practices, rhetorics, and literacy education," emphasizing the space within the Caucus' mission for non-Asian scholars such as myself. I was welcomed warmly and encouraged by several members to pursue the goal of addressing Asian and Pacific rhetorical traditions in the classroom. At the meeting, I listened to editors' and authors' perspectives on and aspirations for the recently published collection, *Representations: Doing Asian American Rhetoric*, backstories that offered insight into how I might frame this text in my own classrooms. I also appreciated learning about exciting dissertations, book projects, and collections in progress that will be wonderful resources for scholarship and teaching. While I have not since been a regular attendant at the AAAC business meetings, I have remained a member of the listserv so that I might keep abreast of issues pertaining to this important scholarly community.

Holly Bruland

I chose to study comparative rhetoric as my area of concentration in graduate school, with a particular focus on East Asian rhetorics. My dissertation topic deals with Japanese rhetoric, and I have also done some research on the rhetoric of Zen Buddhism. So, given my research interests, it seemed like I should be involved with the AAAC, to meet others who might be doing similar research. In addition, my friend Chanon, also studying at my university, invited me to attend the meeting. I enjoyed the meeting, and I plan to continue attending. I wasn't sure what the agenda of the caucus would be, so I was interested in finding out more about what the group is focused on and to get a sense of how I might participate.

I identify as white, of German descent (my mother is German). Because my research topic is Japanese rhetoric, a lot of people look at me and ask, what led you to study that? Most often the question is genuine, but I also encounter folks who are questioning whether I can do this kind of research legitimately. So, I feel I have to stay sensitive to issues of orientalism and cultural appropriation, and be very upfront about them. Doing so is just good research practice anyway, so really those sorts of questions help me out a lot in the long run. I believe strongly that the rhetorical tradition as widely taught in the United States needs more exposure to other rhetorics, a goal many people in the AAAC have worked hard to make happen, and one that continues to be a work in progress. I hope to be a productive part of this intellectual movement, and that my research can further broaden our discipline's perspectives on non-Euro–American rhetorics.

Dominic Ashby

I appreciate being a part of the AAAC because it provides me the opportunity to appreciate, but also challenge and interrogate, the very narrative categories of "Asian" and "Asian American." My interest in interrogating these categories is rooted in my experiences growing up in Los Angeles, where racial discrimination and conflict were everyday occurrences at the middle school I attended. At the time, Asian gangs were being established, growing, and quickly gaining notoriety in the Los Angeles area. The gang culture trickled down to the middle schools and, in some cases, the elementary schools. I was by no means a gangster, but at our school, identifying as "Asian" and sticking together with other "Asians" was in many ways a means of survival. In other words, I never chose to be Asian. And my experience is by no means unique.

Although subscribing to categorical Asianness in my youth was to a certain extent empowering, today I see racial/national/ethnic/geographic categories, including ones like "Asian" and "Asian American," as always tenuous, sometimes arbitrary, and often hegemonic. Scholars in the AAAC have done incredible work in the last couple decades, helping to challenge the hegemony of categorization in a variety of ways, directly and indirectly, and I think it will be a continued priority as we move forward.

Jerry Won Lee

I attended the AAAC meeting at CCCC 2012 because, as a new face at the convention, I knew I wanted to become involved. Attending AAAC was a logical choice as I hoped to be able to connect with a group of people that had some common history and life experience as me. At my first meeting, I experienced a cohesive group that was committed to providing a climate in which all AAAC members and newcomers felt that they belonged, and that each individual had much to contribute to the field of English writing and rhetoric. I felt that AAAC's intent is to not only fulfill the purpose of CCCC, but also build connections among all scholars by making visible the perspectives and scholarly works of Asian Americans.

Karen Ching Carter

My learning and intellectual work in Asian/Asian American rhetoric has taken place primarily in/with Asian/Asian American communities, and in my classroom. My experiences working with the Chicago Civic Leadership Certificate Program (CCLCP), for instance, allowed me to understand the value of enacting community-based approaches to Asian American rhetoric. Such approaches are central to understanding the nuances of Asian/Asian American communities, their diverse forms of cultural production, and unrecognized examples of rhetorical action. For example, my students in the CCLCP—a community-based writing course in which first-year students fulfill writing requirements with a community nonprofit—used ethnographic methods as they worked with organizations like the Pui Tak Center and the Chinese American Service League (CASL) to develop such projects as an oral history project for long time members of the Pui Tak community, a feature story for the CASL's volunteer newsletter, a computer literacy handbook for the Community Technology Center, and online feature stories of community events.

By working with these non-profits and their surrounding communities, students were exposed to various forms of knowledge production and sites of research. As a result, they developed sophisticated inquiries that aimed not to pathologize or marginalize the communities they were working with—a common concern in traditional service-learning courses, but to develop questions that emerged from their community. My students' engagement with their communities of practice and use of ethnographic methods were central in disrupting the Western contemporary rhetoric that first shaped our perceptions of the traditional writing classroom and what constituted civic engagement. These approaches are furthermore valuable for developing critical pedagogies that challenge traditional understandings of civic engagement in rhetoric and composition programs and, more broadly, how non-school literacy practices and Asian/Asian American rhetorical action are valued. I look forward to engaging AAAC scholars and teachers who are interested in community-based learning and research in discussions about how I might build more opportunities for community-based learning in my classroom.

Charlyne Sarmiento

I went to an AAAC business meeting at CCCC because I guess I was 1) curious, and 2) lonely. I didn't know many people in our area, in our field—heck! in the country—and I was feeling quite marginalized, so I thought maybe, just maybe, fingers crossed. Morris was very nice to invite me, of course, and I was delighted to meet Terese and Paul Kei and Stuart, and I thought: wow! I can belong here. It was a wonderful moment for me.

Peter Mayshle

The year I went to my first AAAC meeting in Chicago, I had recently started my PhD coursework, but I was really still trying to decide if I wanted to complete the degree. I was looking for community, and my advisor mentioned the CCCC caucuses. So I went, hoping to find kindred spirits, potential mentors, and people who understood the difference between middle-class, Asian international students, and Asian Americans, in their transnational, generational, diasporic, multilingual, pan-ethnic, racialized complexities. What I found was a small group, but it was enough—what I needed at the time to re-center and return to Madison, where I was the only API [Asian Pacific Islander] graduate student in our Comp/Rhet program.

These scholars would become a strong collective of mentors and colleagues, sponsors of my own scholarship on the uses of writing by Japanese Americans to redress mass incarceration during World War II. Through their work and words, they would remind me of the importance of historicizing Asian American rhetoric, applying culturally-relevant frameworks, and attending to the complex interplay of culture, oppression and resistance in the making of Asian American rhetorics. And while some reminding is of course done from afar, there is something powerful about literal pats-on-the-back, kind comments, and nodding heads we experience in each other's presence.

Mira Shimabukuro

Since arriving to the U.S., my relationship with Asia and Asians has been harder to define than before. While in Nepal, it was common to think of Asia as the largest continent on earth and identify people in the region as citizens of a state. One was either Chinese, Indian, Indonesian, or something like that. When terms like Asian or non-Western were used in relation to Europe or North America, it was to denote the complex contours of Asia's engagement with them, and their engagement with things Asian.

A little over a decade in the U.S., and that relationship has been complicated. Asia, Asian, and Asian American denote a complex geo-cultural identity, almost always racially charged. The terms are also often deployed to produce a homogenized image of Asians, irrespective of their location or loyalty, subsuming all geopolitical and other terms of relations. Personally, that makes my being Asian tricky, even impossible—Asian in the purely geopolitical sense, and anything but Asian from other obvious lenses. This is not to record any envy of my friends who are more easily recognized as Asian, but a reflection on the problem of coming together. Could Asia and Asian be wrested away from that homogenizing move and used to counter it? Increased visibility of diverse work and people within Asia and Asian America would be a step in that direction. AAAC couldn't have come into being at a better time.

Iswari Pandey

WORKS CITED

Fox, Helen. *Listening to the World: Cultural Issues in Academic Writing.* Urbana: NCTE, 1994. Print.

Li, Xiao-Ming. *"Good Writing" in Cross-Cultural Context.* Albany: State U of New York P, 1996. Print.

Mao, LuMing, and Morris Young, eds. *Representations: Doing Asian American Rhetoric.* Logan: Utah State UP, 2008. Print.

Severino, Carol, Juan C. Guerra, and Johnnella E. Butler, eds. *Writing in Multicultural Settings.* New York: Modern Language Association, 1997. Print.

Villanueva, Victor. "Memoria is a Friend of Ours: On the Discourse of Color." *Rhetorics from/of Color.* Spec. issue of *College English* 67.1 (2004): 9–19. Print.

The Stand*

Lawson Fusao Inada

I am somewhere
where I have decided to stand.

There has been long
maneuvering,

having been staked to a land,
sowing in the heat,

moving huge tools
in an absurdity of moon.

Chanting, my own
tune in the machinery,

I find the chanting soothes
That sweet voice is ruined.

I move now,
sifting pavements through my feet,

sweat in the eyes, a horizon.
Sun turns the wheat.

---

*   Republished with the author's permission.

Braced to my spine,
I resume the chanting—

utterances in a sound
octaves older than my own.

INTRODUCTION
Re/Articulations of History, Re/Visions of Community

Terese Guinsatao Monberg, K. Hyoejin Yoon, and Jennifer Sano-Franchini

> " . . . the project of writing as a subject who remembers is not exclusively a matter of finding better modes of representing or renarrating those 'histories'. . . . It is also to retrieve in places other than official history a repertoire of forms of memory, time, or counterhistory . . . and to rearticulate them in culture in ways that permit practices of subject and community not strictly governed by official modes."
>
> —Lisa Lowe, *Immigrant Acts: On Asian American Cultural Politics*

> "The willful desire to claim a 'memory that is only sometimes our own,' the unremitting imperative to rearticulate cultural memory, is fundamental to Asian American rhetoric."
>
> —Haivan V. Hoang, *Writing Against Racial Injury: The Politics of Asian American Student Rhetoric*

Building a Community, Having a Home: A History of the Conference on College Composition and Communication Asian/Asian American Caucus aims to re-narrate history and "rearticulate cultural memory," as Lowe and Hoang state in the epigraphs, by locating the contributions of Asian and Asian American teacher-scholars within the history of the National Council of Teachers of

English (NCTE), the Conference on College Composition and Communication (CCCC), and the discipline of rhetoric and composition more broadly. This collection is part of Writing and Working for Change, a project that seeks to document the historical importance of NCTE/CCCC caucuses, special interest groups, and task forces in transforming NCTE, CCCC, and rhetoric and composition. The Writing and Working for Change committee, consisting of Samantha Blackmon, Cristina Kirklighter, and Steve Parks, envisioned narratives that might begin to "shift what counts as an historic moment" ("Writing and Working"). History is not always made, they note, "when an article or book is published" but also "when formally marginalized individuals form into collectives, enabling them to have a greater influence within our profession" ("Writing and Working"). As such, the history narrated in this collection traces the diverse ways in which Asian and Asian American teacher–scholars in NCTE and CCCC have contributed to the discipline, whether by forming into collectives that would enable political change within these organizations and educational practice more generally, or through scholarship, mentorship, and other forms of institutional work.

Our approach to historicizing the work of Asians and Asian Americans in rhetoric and composition consisted of looking to both official and unofficial representational regimes for excavating and rearticulating this history. As Lisa Lowe has theorized, history is narrated and carried forward through horizontal, vernacular channels that challenge the sanctioned authority of more hierarchical, dominant, "official representational regimes" (113). The task of historiography, then, is to look for histories in those channels often overlooked and to rearticulate those histories "in ways that permit the practices of subject and community not strictly governed by official modes" (127). This mode of historiography allowed us to acknowledge the multiple layers, subject positions, and forms of work that Asian and Asian American teachers, scholars, administrators, and activists have played across and over time in rhetoric, composition, and literacy studies—whether they were formally affiliated with the caucus or not. We saw, in other words, how the writing of this history was not only contingent on communities whose existence was readily documented but also on communities whose formation may have been more imagined,[1] loosely

---

[1] Imagined in Benedict Anderson's sense of the term, where members may "never know most of their fellow members, meet them, or even hear of them, yet in the minds of each lives the image of their communion" (6). The sense of an imagined community also calls forth Royster and Kirsch's idea of "critical imagination," which imagines the longer view of a stream when only traces may be visible (81).

defined, undocumented, or precluded. Through attention to horizontal channels and traces of this institutional memory, we aim to bring into focus what Jacqueline Jones Royster calls "the long view," a historical narrative that illuminates "institutional, collective patterns in broad scope" (*Traces* 83).

Because our work on this project was guided by a deep responsibility to narrate a history that would be generative for the caucus and its members, key to our task of "rearticulating cultural memory" was the need to center a space where the writing of history and the potential for community coalesce. More importantly, we argue that a history that acknowledges the alliances, unexpected connections and coalitions, gaps, setbacks, and silences is necessary for building a form of *alternative institutional memory* that remains useful for sustaining a scholarly, organizational, activist, and racial community that is persistently open to re/vision and useful for caucus members. We situate the caucus as a space where a longer continuum of past and present alternative institutions[2] related to Asians and Asian Americans might become visible. Situating this particular history of the caucus as one that forwards alternative institutional memory acknowledges the deep and sometimes dispersed histories of communities that change over time but remain committed to a consistent agenda of racial justice in many forms—scholarly, organizational, and activist. And because history and community are recursively shaped through storytelling that defies linearity, taking responsibility for our institutional memory kept us conscious of the ways this edited collection—as a text or artifact—has longevity and how it might continue to be read, carried forward, and offer potential for ongoing re/vision, a method of engagement that Jacqueline Jones Royster and Gesa Kirsch term "social circulation" (23).

REARTICULATING FOUNDINGS AS RE/VISIONS

In curating this collection, our commitments to feminist rhetorical studies, to a methodology of listening, and to the rhetorical work of sustaining the collective, communal spirit of our caucus were all crucial to our process. We exercised *critical imagination*, a form of listening that, according to Royster and Kirsch, "not only justifies going beyond anointed research methods, sources, and published scholarship but actually mandates that researchers engage their topics in multiple ways, using dialectic and dialogic approaches and

---

2   Our understanding of alternative institutions is informed by scholarship on the visible and invisible institutions that people of color have created and sustained over time. See, for example, work by Shirley Wilson Logan, Vorris L. Nunley, Reva Sias and Beverly Moss, Kendall Leon, Qwo-Li Driskill, and Mira Shimabukuro.

imagining ways in which historical subjects might have left traces of a stream in places where we may not have looked, looked closely enough, or may have overlooked" (79). It was important to provide context to moments marked as historically significant (in the normative sense) and to unpack why certain moments are often more visible in our history than others. This question prompted us to listen for moments that we might call sustaining threads: the seemingly small, often unseen fibers that critically shape the direction and subsistence of a movement, organization, or collective. For example, the evidence of Asians and Asian Americans participating in NCTE as early as the 1930s demonstrates a consistent, sustained effort to work against structural forms of oppression built into our disciplinary habits and formations. And these efforts, some less visible than others, are threaded through the work of caucus members and the caucus as a collective body even today.³

To make this alternative institutional memory more visible, and to make room for its further potential, our collection speaks back to "founding" texts and documents, looking to the diverse ways in which Asian and Asian American teachers and scholars in NCTE and CCCC have formed collectives and enabled political change within our organization and our profession. Emphasizing this continuum of work over time is in line with feminist researchers who, as Hui Wu argues, see collectivity as "a primary value in selecting subjects and materials as well as in considerations of transformative powers of feminist research" (89). These collectivities radiate out of the AAAC into other realms and other collectivities, such as the Asian American Movement, the Students' Right to Their Own Language Movement, the emergence of Asian American literary studies, and ongoing movements in transnational studies, writing assessment, cultural rhetorics, and digital rhetorics. In looking for these affiliations and alliances, we have only begun to account for a history that has not always been documented. As a project grounded in listening, community memory, and reflexive historiography, we have worked to consciously make room for the variety of contributions Asian and Asian American teachers and scholars have made, thereby helping to displace the narrative of individual exceptionalism—even though many of those contri-

---

3   Throughout this introduction, we refer to the caucus both as a community and as a collective. We see these ideas as interconnected but not necessarily interchangeable. While a community serves to create a sense of belonging and inclusion among members with shared subjectivities, concerns, or interests, we see a collective as a group of members who come together and position themselves more explicitly as enacting rhetorical, scholarly, or institutional agency. Again, sometimes these directly coincide; other times these are layered or clustered and networked.

butions are not (yet) present in this history. Leaving the historical narrative open, in other words, recognizes the caucus as a sedimented space, which Lisa Lowe reminds us "is an emblem for history as excavation rather than projection, simultaneity rather than sequential time, and collective geography rather than individual biography" (125).

Early efforts to begin listening to our legacies were undertaken by Jolivette Mecenas, Mira Shimabukuro, and Jennifer Sano-Franchini. One interview granted, another denied because of the project's connection to NCTE, a trip to the NCTE Archives, and a collection of breadcrumbs led Mecenas and Sano-Franchini to Frank Chin and Jeffery Paul Chan's 1972 publication "Racist Love," a powerful, if polemical, intervention into the official narrative of the organization. The essay was prompted by Chin and Chan's service on the 1971 Textbook Review Committee for NCTE's Task Force on Racism and Bias in the Teaching of English. "Racist Love," and the archives surrounding it, document how Asian Americans have participated in historical interventions that include but also reach beyond institutional, scholarly, and cross-caucus activism.

At the same time, uncovering this set of "founding" documents raised many questions for us regarding what it would mean to mark or claim this (or any) moment as a founding moment. Throughout the process of rearticulating our caucus histories, caucus members recognized the importance of marking founding moments but resisted and complicated the idea of "foundings," a word that carries colonialist overtones and tends to overshadow the smaller moments and sustaining threads that go unnoticed and unmarked, partly because traditional measures don't see them as significant. For this reason, we prefer to use the term "re/visions," a term that resonates with Morris Young's work on Asian American narratives and, in the context of this particular project, emphasizes the ongoing work of sustaining collectivities over time.[4] What we hope this collection subsequently narrates is a caucus shaped by multiple, different moments of being "founded," re/visioned, or becoming, some of which have yet to be rearticulated.

As LuMing Mao recounts in his interview in this collection, prior to 1999, the "Asian Caucus" provided an intellectual space for scholars of

---

4   Young writes: "Re/vision is a way to bring in multiple voices, to connect the public and personal, to view uncertainty as possibility, to work, as [Nancy] Sommers suggests, 'between the drafts.' This trope is particularly important to people of color whose visions of America are often 'between the drafts' and in the margins rather than being a commonly told tale in America" (*Minor Re/Visions* 8).

"Asian" rhetoric and scholars and teachers in the field then defined as English as a Second Language (ESL). In an effort to broaden the focus and make the group more relevant to what we then called minority scholars [c.f. Omi and Winant], Mao and Young shifted the focus to support scholars of Asian descent as well as scholars pursuing research on the meaning-making practices of Asians/Asian Americans. This re/vision of the caucus resonated with other CCCC initiatives, like the Scholars for the Dream Travel Award Program, which supports and mentors emerging scholars from historically underrepresented groups. It was under the collaborative leadership of Mao and co-chair Morris Young that the current manifestation of the caucus was born in 1999, in Young's words, "to explore the 'Asian American text'" (Young, in this volume). The caucus served as a collectivity for emerging scholarship on Asian/Asian American rhetoric, much of it published in the 2008 landmark collection *Representations: Doing Asian American Rhetoric*, edited by Mao and Young.

The publication of *Representations* marks several important moments and shifts in our history. Since Mao and Young's 1999 re/vision and renaming of the Asian/Asian American Caucus, our members have had many discussions about the affordances of pursuing scholarship on Asian/Asian American rhetoric, composition, and literacy studies, of marking our work explicitly with the term "Asian/Asian American," and of doing this work as people racially marked as Asian/Asian American. Thus, it was particularly significant for our members when *Representations* received honorable mention for the Modern Language Association's 2009 Mina P. Shaughnessy Prize. In addition to recognizing the value of our work, the award also affirmed the collegial space created by Mao and Young, a space that Stuart Ching characterizes as a "unique spac[e] in which cultural memory, as an epistemological standpoint, informs professional activity" (89). As the first extended articulation of "Asian American rhetoric," *Representations* provides a selective snapshot of an emerging landscape and collective. Situating *Representations* as a re/visionary moment in our history permits a more horizontal view of the caucus, rendering visible the many members who have helped build and who continue to sustain this epistemological space—a narrative that counters the more vertical view of "founding" narratives. The bold use of the singular "rhetoric" in Mao and Young's subtitle, *Doing Asian American Rhetoric*, intentionally signals both the diversity within this growing body of work and the enactment of a strategic essentialism. Reviews of *Representations* note this defining tension and view the collection as engaging a broad range of concerns and perspectives that suggest future paths for Asian American rhetoric (Summers; Mejía). And as some of the essays in this collection demonstrate, caucus members find the work in *Representations* useful for situating and affirming their work and for carrying the conversations forward. It is within this larger narrative that we situate the publication of *Representations* as a significant moment of re/vision, preceded by and followed by other sustaining threads and possibilities.

BROADENING THE LANDSCAPE: ALLIANCES, SUSTAINING THREADS, AND SOCIAL/HISTORICAL CIRCULATIONS

As Sano-Franchini's work in the NCTE Archives teaches us, Asians/Asian Americans have been present in the organization at least as early as the 1930s, and many of them, like Lawson Fusao Inada, Gail Y. Okawa, and Min-Zhan Lu formed alliances with other caucuses and sub-disciplines in their struggle to both, in the words of Jacqueline Jones Royster and Jean C. Williams, "write in the spaces left" and to open the field. For this reason, we find it important to situate landmarks in our history, like the publication of *Representations*, in relationship to these alliances. Doing so brings into focus a larger landscape of work that has made it possible for this history to be made and written. In other words, as a caucus and as a discipline, our view of the landscape—our ongoing historical narrative—must include the continuum of work on Asian and Asian American rhetoric like Hui Wu's work in feminist historiography and Xin Liu Gale's response to Cheryl Glenn's work on Aspasia. We might also look for work that forged paths for us, including work by Okawa, Lu, Shirley Wilson Logan, Jacqueline Jones Royster, Malea Powell, Victor Villanueva, Geneva Smitherman, Keith Gilyard, as well as studies in third world feminisms—scholarly alliances that Mao and Young also recognize. Recognizing these disciplinary alliances as sustaining threads encourages us to imagine a broader community that is always in motion but persistently positioned to interrogate "the ways in which racial formation clings onto language, literacy, and rhetorical education" and to collaboratively work against these formations (Hoang 163).

Just as important as the scholarly alliances across the discipline are the scholarly alliances that have been built within the caucus itself. In this collection, for example, we intentionally feature scholarly areas in which caucus members have been doing important research in the years following the 1999 re/vision of the AAAC, often crossing disciplinary boundaries in order to get the discipline to remember and account for the perspectives of Asians and Asian Americans. Highlighting this work here supplements the diverse and groundbreaking scholarship on Asian American rhetoric published in *Representations,* a collection that carves out a space to articulate and illustrate Asian American rhetoric in its many forms. In dialogue with that work, this collection includes some of the other areas of scholarship in rhetoric, composition, and literacy studies to which Asians and Asian Americans are contributing. Chapters by Bo Wang, Paul Kei Matsuda, and Asao B. Inoue, for example, are included in this collection because they highlight the kinds of work *beyond* Asian American rhetoric within which Asian/Asian American teachers and scholars have made significant scholarly and institutional contributions. These contributions have not only impacted the discipline's understandings of Asian rhetoric, second language studies, and writing assessment, but also our understandings of mentorship, collegial support, and institutional and disciplinary leadership. More importantly, this work is connected to the community of scholars that formed alliances within the AAAC because of Mao and Young's 1999 re/vision of the caucus.

The histories we rearticulate here also recognize that alliances are built not just once, but repeatedly over time. Echoes of early coalition building can be seen in the recent history of our caucus. The Scholars for the Dream network (established 1993), a CCCC mentoring workshop for women of color (2002), and conversations with NCTE leadership on the findings of the NCTE Task Force to Advance and Support Members of Color (2008) are all examples of coalition building across the race-based caucuses. AAAC members have also worked to build scholarly alliances within the caucus. Under the leadership of Haivan V. Hoang and Nancy Linh Karls (2005–10), in particular, the caucus began to establish more formal infrastructures designed to foster emerging areas of study, facilitate peer mentoring, create more opportunities to collaborate, and develop an online presence. Cross-caucus workshops and panel presentations might not always be foregrounded as such in the history of CCCC conference programs, but they have had a consistent presence and have become a priority in recent years. This work of strengthening networks that support scholarship and activism, and foster a sense of community are important sustaining threads of our institutional memory.

The annual caucus meetings themselves have historically provided a space for institutional and scholarly activism, and members have made use of that space explicitly. This is where the invisible work of making community and history coalesce. It was in the caucus meetings that Sano-Franchini was emboldened to take on the editing of *Building a Community*. Mao and Young first engaged the future contributors of *Representations* in a caucus meeting, and more recently prompted caucus members to think about contributing to a collected volume on Asian and Asian American primary texts. Caucus meetings (and the networks developed there) serve as a vehicle for what Royster and Kirsch call "social circulation," a process through which our scholarly, activist, and institutional legacies might be "carried on, changed, reinvented, and reused" not just within the caucus but also "across generations, across time, and across space" (101). Generative discussions during and after these meetings produce themes for conference panels and new lines of research.

This process of social circulation has been especially important with a growing caucus membership and the inclusion of more and more Asian/Asian American scholars in the field. As is probably true of other NCTE/CCCC caucuses and special interest groups, our business meetings serve as a reflective space where members collaboratively take stock of our community as scholars, teachers, and professionals; build a vision; and strategize next steps. It was through this process that we recollected both our history and our collectivity as a caucus. As Jennifer Sano-Franchini and Jolivette Mecenas uncovered important pieces of our history, we circulated this knowledge through conference presentations and caucus discussions. Additionally, in 2012, we conducted a survey of members' priorities, the results of which evinced two main questions that the membership prioritized and wanted to explore: 1) How do material, historical, political, and disciplinary, conditions shape the work of Asian/Asian American scholars? 2) What is the status of the work of Asian/Asian American scholars and how does it impact the field? These concerns encapsulated caucus members' desire to understand the place of Asian/Asian American rhetoric and the work of Asian/Asian American scholars in the broader landscape of discussions and discourses in composition and rhetoric. Other important outcomes from this social/historical circulation were collective strategies for how to position our work, build a stronger institutional presence, and "push back against the existing limits of our field and organizations to insure a broader sense of common responsibility and humanity [is] recognized" (Blackmon, Kirklighter, and Parks, *Listening* 1).

Particularly relevant to this collection is the caucus activity surrounding the annual sponsored session at CCCC. Implemented in 2014, the sponsored session makes visible scholarly and institutional activity of various standing groups; it also represents the collective work and will of caucuses, special interest groups, committees, and coalitions. We see the sponsored session as one way to document our current and emerging priorities, functioning over time as a working history and a method for building community alliances. Thus we thought it important to include a slice of that working history in this collection. To reflect the energy of those sessions and conversations, we curated what we call "circulation" essays: selections from the 2015 sponsored session, "Asian/Asian American Scholarship in Rhetoric and Composition: Risks and Rewards." In doing so, we hope the collection illustrates how this sponsored session, in particular, brought together senior and junior scholars from our caucus to reflect on the state of Asian/Asian American scholarship in rhetoric, composition, and literacy studies. Many of the authors are graduate students or early-career scholars who are able to provide different lenses on issues that resonate and recur in the discipline, while also furthering the work of other AAAC members. These circulation essays help us see what questions are worth asking and re-asking, and they shed light on what we may take for granted—our familiar assumptions or patterns of discourse, inquiry, and methods.

While many of the chapters in the book could be discussed in these terms, as markers of how social circulation occurs in the caucus, we wanted to specifically make space for this work, these voices, and our recent history. As selections of papers presented at that 2015 sponsored session, these contributions are shorter and less formal. In the true spirit of the word "essay," they are attempts to discover and engage. These brief circulation essays are interspersed among the longer chapters of the collection as a way to illustrate an ongoing conversation, to give credit to works in progress, and to highlight questions as they are being asked. But we include them also to affirm a model of scholarship that allows for the developing scholar in contrast to the "finished" scholar we sometimes assume behind a publication. These circulations essays document our current, living history, and suggest future directions for Asian/Asian American scholars. By including these re/visions of the caucus into social circulation with more established histories, we envisioned a scholarly conversation that would enable our caucus "to see how the past can reach into the present and how the close at hand might reach toward the distant and further away, thus helping all of us to imagine a future worth working toward as a more inclusive enterprise" where "the whole idea of continuity and change takes on ever-new possibilities" (Royster and Kirsch 101).

ATTENDING TO THE LEGACIES OF "RACIST LOVE"

> "Attending doesn't stop with these epistemologically rich memories of widely varied and sometimes fleeting moments of intersubjective receptivity. Attendance is vigilant, not passive. One must 'apply oneself,' must 'stretch one's mind,' must be 'consequent of' what has come before and 'follow' with something new."
>
> — Mira Shimabukuro, *Relocating Authority: Japanese Americans Writing to Redress Mass Incarceration*

To illustrate what becomes visible when we decenter "foundings" and prioritize instead the many sustaining threads of our history, we return to the legacy of "Racist Love." Chin and Chan originally composed "Racist Love" as a position paper presented to (and rejected by) NCTE after serving on the 1971 Textbook Review Committee. Upon their assessment that no Asian or Asian American writers were represented in the literary anthologies they reviewed, Chin and Chan indicted the "American literary canon and all of the organizations, not just NCTE but MLA for 'gross negligence'" (Mecenas, "A Career" 39). Sano-Franchini's chapter in this collection focuses on the NCTE Archives pertaining to "Racist Love," including NCTE's response. But for our purposes here, we want to follow what it means to move "Racist Love" from a founding moment to one of re/vision by connecting the difficult and groundbreaking legacies surrounding "Racist Love" to issues relevant to our caucus today. We chose "Racist Love" as a representative example because it is one that we can follow in our recent history, as it came up during the writing of this collection. But this idea of "attending," in Shimabukuro's sense of the word, is relevant to all moments that might be marked as "foundings," revealing the larger collective and often invisible activities that precede, surround, and follow historical moments often deemed as significant.

While many caucus members were familiar with Chin and Chan's collaborative work on the edited collections of Asian American literature—*Aiiieeeee!* and *The Big Aiiieeeee!*, published in 1974 and 1991 respectively[5]—few

---

5   While "Racist Love" was published by Chin and Chan, *Aiiieeeee!* and *The Big Aiiieeeee!* were co-edited with Lawson Fusao Inada and Shawn Wong. In introducing this wider, deeper tradition in *Aiiieeeee!*, Chin, Chan, Inada, and Wong write: "In the 140-year history of Asian America, fewer than ten works of fiction and poetry have been published by American-born Chinese, Japanese, and Filipino writers. This fact suggests that in six generations of Asian–Americans there was no impulse to literary or artistic expression.

knew that the arguments asserted in those anthologies had been published earlier in "Racist Love."[6] This is not surprising given that "Racist Love," as Mecenas notes, was published outside of the discipline of rhetoric and composition. Subsequently, when referenced by Asian American scholars over the years, its connection to our discipline is not always apparent. It is important to note that, after writing "Racist Love," Chin and Chan sought to establish an Asian American literary canon *outside* of the disciplinary spaces represented by NCTE and MLA because these spaces would not have been productive for this kind of extended intervention. If it were not for a collective of writers and scholars in literature and ethnic studies seeking to shift the landscape, "Racist Love" and the anthologies that followed may not have been published.

Positioning "Racist Love" within this larger interdisciplinary history evinces the alignment of the caucus more explicitly with the Asian American Movement (AAM), and the legacy of coalition building within the Asian American community and across racial groups to demand relevant curriculum, shared governance, and political power.[7] And this connection to the AAM demonstrates a legacy of work by Asians/Asian Americans that spans disciplines. We don't know, for example, how many Asian/Asian American scholars may have been part of our history with NCTE/CCCC but turned, instead, to other disciplinary homes. In other words, the number of Asians/

The truth is that Asian–Americans have been writing seriously since the nineteenth century and writing well" (xxi).

6   This body of work, framed as loud disruption, has been groundbreaking but it was a strategy that also brought critique. To do justice to the ways this work has been taken up, debated, and engaged by countless Asian American scholars is beyond the scope of this introduction and edited collection.

7   Chin and Chan's visceral critique of literature textbooks and the literary canon comes out of a deeper context: an emerging discipline of Asian American literature and literary studies and the 1968–69 protests at San Francisco State, which led to the formation of the first College of Ethnic Studies in the United States (Mecenas "A Career"). Listening to Chin and Chan's agenda against the backdrop of the 1960s–70s Asian American Movement (AAM), we hear several overlapping political motives: one, the drive to recognize those who had long been U.S. citizens without negating their Asian heritage—an attempt to challenge the image of the Asian as "forever foreign" in the U.S. imagination, according to Mia Tuan; second, the drive to acknowledge the American citizenship of Chinese, Japanese, Korean, and Filipino immigrants who had been living in the U.S. since the late 1800s and early 1900s, as a way to claim political leverage, civil rights, and belonging; and third, the drive to be more collectively identified in a pan-Asian formation to signal and mobilize solidarity, to leverage collective political power, and effect social change.

Asian Americans in our disciplinary history may have been impacted by the context that prompted "Racist Love." And this legacy may continue to have an impact on our caucus today as we reflect on voices that may get lost when disciplinary boundaries are viewed as narrow rather than expansive. The history surrounding "Racist Love" reveals, in part, processes through which disciplinary assumptions and structures are formed and reformed and prompts us to think about ways to continually re/vision the disciplinary formations and assumptions that impact the caucus, its members, and the communities we stand for, and with, in our work.

At the same time, in claiming "Racist Love" as a significant historical moment for our caucus, we recognize an uncomfortable inheritance of both the institutional context that provoked Chin and Chan's reactions and the gendered and nationalist rhetorical strategies they resorted to in order to talk back, intervene, and shift the conversation(s). The rhetorical strategies evident in "Racist Love" signal defiant non-cooperation and resistance, necessary strategies, in that context, to be heard and to push back against the sexism and racism that conspired to emasculate not just representations of but also whole communities of Asian/Asian American men throughout history. But as a result, women become not only largely absent in their view of Asian American literature but are, in significant ways, antithetical to the entire project of Asian American cultural studies.[8] Feminist scholars in Asian American Studies have responded to the ways in which Chin and Chan's "Racist Love" denigrates and subordinates the presence of women in Asian American literature, while also recognizing the importance of this intervention (c.f. Lee; Chu). Along the same lines, the nationalist strategy used by Chin and Chan, necessary in that historical moment, raises commonly heard concerns about which ethnic group gets to represent "Asian America" in the context of the United States.[9]

---

8   The Maxine Hong Kingston/Frank Chin debate has, for decades, continued to produce important methodological discussions about what it means to write literature and history, discussions that are deeply relevant to rhetoric, composition, and literacy studies. Also, for anthologies of writing by Asian American women see, for example, Lim, Tsutakawa, and Donnelly's *The Forbidden Stitch,* or the Asian Women United of California's *Making Waves* and *Making More Waves.*

9   For example, Chin and Chan claim that by the late 1960s, Japanese American writers had been more favorably received than Chinese American writers, and that Asian and Asian American women writers were even more embraced by "racist love." While this line of reasoning has been heavily critiqued for defining the term Asian American in a particularly nationalist and gendered way, we see the relevance of these politics in our

In other words, while "Racist Love" has the potential to expand the ways we might imagine the caucus and its affiliated communities, it also potentially limits how we imagine those affiliations. Following feminist scholars in Asian American Studies, we recognize and honor the impact that Chin and Chan have had in building a discipline and making room for more of us at the table. Chin and Chan's stance toward institutional racism embedded within English studies demonstrates the need (and impact) of asserting an intellectual and activist stance for the larger community. We recognize their contributions to our larger alternative institutional memory. But we also had to ask ourselves, how would we choose, in this particular moment, to sit with, respond to, or move on from "Racist Love" and the difficult parts of its legacy? What possibilities might we imagine that would allow us to build on its positive, radical intervention, without furthering other forms of oppression? How might we shape the rhetorical strategies, historiographical accounts, and narratives of Asian/Asian American leadership to come? As Monberg and Yoon suggest in "Ruptures, Wounds, Possibilities," presented at the AAAC sponsored session at CCCC 2014, we must continue to listen carefully for the echoes of sexism and nationalism in our scholarship and in our evolving understanding of the caucus and the collectives we are building through this work.

In this history of the caucus, then, we resist and work against familiar narrative constructions in historiography. We wanted to move beyond the immediately visible, and to see the worth of asking whether the efforts of other caucus members or kindred spirits may have gone and, perhaps, continue to go undocumented and unacknowledged. We made special efforts to listen for (and to evoke) the voices of *women* who have shaped the history of the Asian/Asian American Caucus. As Hui Wu argues, "feminist rhetorical historiography requires us to become research agents who bring transformations to dominant research practices and interpretive frameworks. It must not only emphasize women as an additional historical subject but also pose methodological challenges to predominant theoretical models" (85–86). We see in Sano-Franchini's chapter in this collection Asian/Asian American women who have taken on leadership roles in NCTE and CCCC, and made scholarly interventions in their research that Sano-Franchini argues were also activist. We had to move out of the shadow of Chin and Chan's legacy,

---

latest analysis of the caucus history, where members were concerned about over- and underrepresentations of various constituencies, including different ethnic groups, genders, and emerging voices.

which had the potential to obscure the visibility and work of other Asian Americans, especially women, "behind the podium" throughout our history (Monberg, "Listening" 89). And recovery work like that in Sano-Franchini's chapter affords us the opportunity to transform our understanding of our history and inheritance.

Mao and Young cite Chin and Chan's rhetoric as a move toward "an Asian American cultural nationalism" and "what might be considered an early definition of Asian American rhetoric" (8). We find it compelling that thirty-five years after the publication of "Racist Love" (outside of the discipline), this nationalist strategy was useful and necessary (within the discipline) to make room for Asian American rhetoric. And as Mao and Young imply, we must continue to expand and complicate early definitions and paradigms. With caucus members predominantly asserting their identification as Asian and/or Asian American, we need to expand our understanding of the boundaries between these terms, to highlight their cultural, geopolitical, and nationalist constructedness, to question the purposes they serve, and to consider ways these boundaries can be redrawn. Furthermore, as we work across caucuses, identity categories, and intersectionalities, we need to be able to acknowledge and respond to an array of horizontal tensions. Larger decolonial frameworks can help us make sense of relationships between immigrants and natives, settler and indigenous populations. Recent work by caucus members contributes to our understanding of these horizontal relationships that remain situated in histories of structural oppression (Young "Native Claims"; Mecenas "Beyond"; Carpenter and Yoon; Sano-Franchini, Tasaka, and Ledbetter; also Lee, Pak, and Kaʻalele in this collection). But we need to continue to make progress in these areas and look, in particular, to the work of indigenous scholars so we might flesh out the affinities and tensions of racial and national identity when analyzed through the lens of sovereignty or survivance (King; Lyons; Powell; Byrd).

Finally, as a model for community building, situating "Racist Love" within our history has brought forward the collaborative workings, legacies, and movements behind this act of defiance. Situated in this way, the legacy of "Racist Love" has the potential to make visible the important ongoing work of rebuilding community and re/visioning our caucus—work that many members do in collaboration, and that often sets the stage for these big moments to come to fruition. It takes time and a community to get to these big moments. But it also takes people like Chin and Chan who use those opportunities to push back. And we embrace all of this work as part of our history and possible future. Chin and Chan's stance asserted the power of the humanities—language, literature, and writing pedagogy, in particular—as "an important arena in which to fight racism" (Lee 7). Finally, "Racist Love," provides a concrete instance where Asian/Asian Americans have made waves and demanded justice and have reshaped the knowledge that exists about them and their writing. While not the only form of activism, "acting ill-mannered" can make an impact (Mecenas, "A Career"). By reclaiming both an activist and scholarly genealogy, our institutional memory re-affirms a commitment within our caucus to sustain a community that is socially conscious and concerned with questions of equity and social justice at its core.

A RECURSIVE MAP OF A LIVING HISTORY: THE STRUCTURE OF THE BOOK

The sustaining threads of this collection come from informal conversations and more formal interviews with AAAC leaders, forms of written correspondence, archival documents, academic essays, and conference presentations. As we listened across these threads, we made a special effort to shed some light on the important work that often remains invisible: the work of building community, the labor of preparing caucus meetings, coordinating initiatives, designing sponsored sessions, bringing people together, and making histories. Taken together, this living history represents a slice of the organizational work that Sano-Franchini calls institutional activism, which has supported an Asian/Asian American presence within NCTE, CCCC, and the larger discipline.

To emphasize the recursive nature of our listening over time, we designed the layout of the book to purposefully reflect the processes of social circulation that we alluded to earlier in this introduction. We view this collection as a form of history-making that is intended to build a community that also sees itself as a collective, positioned for greater rhetorical and political agency. The individuals included are purposefully diverse in terms of where they are in their academic careers, their areas of scholarship, and the types of work that they do, as well as their gender, ethnicity, and other identifications. Readers will also find a range of styles, discourses, tones, genres, and perspectives. We view each contribution as a re/vision and opening up of possibilities for Asian/Asian American community in rhetoric and composition.

The opening chorus, "Voices from the CCCC Asian/Asian American Caucus," is intended to frame the book and the history of the CCCC AAAC as a collaborative effort, including reflections and recollections by Dominic Ashby, Holly Bruland, Karen Ching Carter, Stuart Ching, Jerry Won Lee, Peter Mayshle, Jolivette Mecenas, Iswari Pandey, Charlyne Sarmiento, Mira Shimabukuro, Hui Wu, and Morris Young. These voices direct themselves both inward toward the caucus and its impact on members, as well as outward, toward larger institutional and political issues that impact the caucus, the scholarship of our members, and members' varied approaches to bringing about institutional change. These perspectives are intended to demonstrate complexity, diversity, and even tensions within the caucus; while all who have contributed to this chorus are current AAAC listserv members, they come from a wide range of backgrounds, speak from a wide range of ethnic, racial, and cultural positions, work from a wide range of academic interests, relate to the AAAC in a range of different ways, and include those at varying places in their academic careers, including graduate students, junior faculty, senior faculty, and those who have chosen to leave academia for a different path. These contributions furthermore reflect the diverse experiences, backgrounds, and concerns of caucus members, serving to remind us that a history of the AAAC necessarily comprises numerous voices and experiences, many of which may not fit the conventions of a neat, linear historical narrative.

This collection continues to subvert the notion of linear history as it weaves across temporalities, bringing together memory from separate historical moments. Thus, the more contemporary voices from the caucus are followed by Lawson Fusao Inada's poem "The Stand," originally published in 1975.[10] As Sano-Franchini's chapter in this volume shows, Inada was an active member of NCTE for many years, and he actively participated in coalition building that worked toward institutional change. In the context of this volume, "The Stand" signifies the ways in which the issues and concerns that continue to be taken up by the caucus and its members are locatable amongst a much longer history of Asian/Asian American collective action, both within and beyond NCTE. We place both "Voices from the CCCC Asian/Asian American Caucus," and Inada's "The Stand" before our introduction to emphasize the recursive relationship between history and community within and beyond NCTE/CCCC and across generations.

---

10   "The Stand" was also previously published in *The Big Aiiieeeee!: An Anthology of Chinese American and Japanese American Literature*, edited by Frank Chin, Jeffery Paul Chan, Lawson Fusao Inada, and Shawn Wong in 1991.

Following our introduction, the first chapter of the book is Jennifer Sano-Franchini's "Taking Time for Feminist Historiography: Remembering Asian/Asian American Institutional and Scholarly Activism," an engaging microhistory that follows NCTE's initial and subsequent actions and reactions to Chin and Chan's participation in the Task Force on Racism and Bias in the Teaching of English. She documents the effect "Racist Love" had on NCTE administrators, highlighting a change in attitude—or at least a self-consciousness and wariness—around representations of Asian Americans within organizational materials. Sano-Franchini also documents as-yet unknown, or at least underappreciated, participation of Asian/Asian American women in the NCTE organization in the 1960s and 70s, profiling three women: San-su C. Lin, Shizuko Ouchi, and Doris C. Ching. These women were undoubtedly a part of the historical, disciplinary conversations that preoccupied writing teachers during the period. Their publications and institutional service engages with the better-known work of contemporaries like Geneva Smitherman and Mina Shaughnessy, and was later elaborated upon in the work of Min-Zhan Lu and others. This recovery work redefines our understanding of the history and community of Asian/Asian Americans in the broader NCTE organization, and helps us to locate our ongoing engagement in the discipline within a richer legacy of activists and change agents.

Corresponding nicely with Sano-Franchini's work in the archives, we include a circulation essay from our 2015 sponsored session. The piece by Phuong Minh Tran, "The Presence of Asian/Asian American Scholars in *College Composition and Communication* (1950–2010)," reviews 60 years of back-issues of *College Composition and Communication* and catalogs the publication of pieces by and about Asians/Asian Americans (see Appendix D). Tran's findings summarize the shifts in focus by Asian/Asian American scholars throughout the decades, from the teaching of composition and ESL, prominent in the discipline's formative years, to more structurally-situated, identity-directed issues. Tran's essay also raises questions about archival research methods, and the importance and challenges of doing recovery work based on identity.

The two chapters that follow are interviews with LuMing Mao and Morris Young, interviewed by Chanon Adsanatham and Robyn Tasaka, respectively. In these transcribed interviews, Mao and Young speak firsthand about their 1999 revitalization and renaming of the "Asian Caucus" to the "Asian/Asian American Caucus." They share their re/visions of the caucus, including an emphasis on mentorship, collaboration, and ensuring that Asian and Asian American voices are heard at CCCC. Adsanatham opens his interview by describing Mao's contributions to the field of rhetoric and composition, and Tasaka's introduction speaks particularly to the recurring theme of mentorship, as she reveals how Young, along with the AAAC and its members, have directly contributed to her development as a scholar in Asian American rhetoric. Taken together, these two interviews signal how the presence of Asians and Asian Americans at CCCC began shifting and growing under the leadership of Mao and Young.

In "Fostering Our Efforts to 'Write in the Spaces Left': Stories of Emergence in Asian American Rhetoric," past AAAC co-chairs Terese Guinsatao Monberg and Haivan V. Hoang tell "stories of emergence," sharing their experiences as graduate students and young scholars of color at CCCC who, at different moments, transitioned to leadership roles as junior faculty and co-chairs of the AAAC. Monberg and Hoang's essay demonstrates how forms of institutional memory are constructed through stories, memories, and collaborative reflection. By interweaving their own caucus histories with a larger history of the caucus and the discipline, they reflect on the difficulties that come with situating oneself in a field that did not yet exist. Their "stories of emergence," also highlight shifts in the ways that the broader discipline has talked about Asians and Asian Americans—shifts that resulted from Asian/Asian American scholars asserting their rhetorical agency. We also hear the sustaining threads of organizational/administrative interventions in these stories as Monberg and Hoang illustrate the significance of mentorship and support in the development of their scholarly identities, whether via the Scholars for the Dream network before the AAAC was established, or through the AAAC. As co-chairs with successive terms following Mao and Young's re/vision of the AAAC, Hoang and Monberg furthermore provide insight into how the caucus and its goals have evolved and been sustained over time.

Linh Dich's circulation essay, "The Impact of Asian/Asian American Scholarship as a Productive, Contested Site," provides further narrative and reflection on the evolution of the caucus and the productive tensions implicit in the naming of Asian/Asian American scholarship and the caucus itself. Dich's essay exemplifies the process of social circulation that went into assembling this collection as she refers specifically to caucus meeting discussions prompted by this very project. Dich's contribution provides a glimpse into an alternative form of institutional memory by looking at the work performed in caucus meetings, by looking backward and forward, and by reflecting on how history and community coalesce.

Following Dich's essay on productive tensions between Asian and Asian American scholarship, we turn to Bo Wang's "A Survey of Research in Asian Rhetoric." Originally published in the 2004 summer issue of *Rhetoric Review*, this piece provides a glimpse of the state of Asian rhetoric at that time, and helps historicize the scholarship in Asian rhetoric, showing retrospectively how far the field has moved forward in the past decade. For instance, Wang describes key characteristics and concerns of research in Asian rhetoric as of 2004: "that is mindful of the logic of Orientalism, that studies Asian rhetoric in its own cultural and political contexts, that appropriates Asian rhetoric for Western contexts, and that applies Asian rhetorical traditions to the study of pedagogical issues." In this chapter, Wang surveys five prominent scholars in Asian rhetoric—Vernon Jensen, Mary Garrett, XiaoMing Li, Xing Lu, and LuMing Mao—about the state of the field. It is worth noting that this group of scholars indicates a strong emphasis on Chinese rhetoric, especially classical Chinese rhetoric, which is in some ways illustrative of what Asian rhetoric scholarship looked like at the time. The scholars interviewed by Wang additionally discuss the impact of Asian rhetoric research on the study of Western rhetoric, as well as the future of the field; for instance, Garrett calls for more contemporary rhetorical work, while Jensen suggests that we not neglect Southeast Asia, and that there should be more attention paid to cross-ethnic rhetorics within Asian communities. Wang herself has since extended on this work, having produced a significant body of scholarship on Chinese feminist rhetoric and historiography.

We continue to illustrate productive tensions by looking forward to emergent work on forms of Asian/Asian American rhetoric taking shape and focused on Hawai'i. In "Racial Identities, Visual Representations, and Performative Capacities: Rhetorical Production(s) of/by Asian/Asian Americans in Hawai'i," K. Hyoejin Yoon introduces selections from papers presented at our 2015 sponsored session by Scott Ka'alele, Edward Lee, and Michael Pak. These three emerging scholars explore the conflicts and contradictions of identity, especially masculine Asian/Asian American and Hawaiian identity in the richly multi-ethnic context of Hawai'i. Building on work by Morris Young and LuMing Mao, Tomo Hattori and Stuart Ching, and Jolivette Mecenas, these selections by Lee, Pak, and Ka'alele elaborate on the intersections of native and "local," "Asian/Asian American" language and identity, and how racial structures are tied to place. These new voices bring a self-conscious sensibility on global, multi-ethnic, and multi-linguistic cultures. Moreover, Yoon's introductory and concluding remarks situate their selections within larger interdisciplinary frameworks, demonstrating how previous work in Asian American rhetoric allows them to enter the conversation at a different point than, for example, Monberg and Hoang did as graduate students. At the same time, as Yoon suggests, these selections point to particularly important challenges for Asian/Asian American scholars, and the historically informed reliance on nationalist discourses of belonging predominantly informed by scholarship on Asian/Asian Americans on the continental United States.

Following the thread of global movements, nationalist discourses, and linguistic diversity, Paul Kei Matsuda's chapter, "Globalization and the Teaching of Written English," explores the diverse varieties of English emerging in the context of globalization. More specifically, Matsuda discusses how the English language has changed shape and become more diverse through accelerated forms of globalization, which is shifting understandings of nationalism and national identity. At the same time, Matsuda points out that "the teaching implications of world Englishes has been less than clear." In response, Matsuda discusses approaches for taking the diversity of world Englishes into consideration in the teaching of writing, particularly as many students negotiate a range of language and cultural differences. In the context of globalization, Matsuda situates English as an Asian language, illustrating how caucus members are leading pedagogical innovations in rhetoric, composition, and literacy studies.

Asao B. Inoue's chapter likewise illustrates pedagogical and administrative innovation amidst changing waves of globalization by centering on writing assessment practices. In "What Does the Field of Writing Assessment Need? Or, How Asian and Asian American Rhetoric Can Help Writing Assessments Work Better," Inoue outlines his WPA work on race and writing assessment, synthesizing his studies of writing assessment practices with Hmong students at California State University, Fresno. Inoue uses these studies to make a strong case for better inclusion of scholars of color in writing assessment research, as well as for the relevance of scholarship on race, racism, and cultural studies to writing assessment scholarship and practice. In addition to raising significant questions that implore scholars from all racial backgrounds in rhetoric and composition to take steps in combating racism in assessment practices, Inoue also reminds us that racial formations are always shifting, requiring continual attention to our institutional practices. As much as we need more space for inclusion, we also need more among us to do the work of inclusive scholarship. Through this argument, Inoue provides another compelling case for how Asian Americans can—and have—effected change in the broader discipline.

The research in Matsuda's and Inoue's chapters is carried forward by research shared by Jolivette Mecenas in her circulation essay, "Building on Recent Research from AAAC Members to Advocate for Second Language International Students." Mecenas explicitly calls attention to Inoue's work on race and writing assessment discussed in this collection, and Linh Dich's work on the increasing presence of international students on U.S. college campuses. Together, they help us to see how racial formations result, sometimes unexpectedly, from institutional priorities for revenue generation. Mecenas shows how the work of writing programs and administrators may need to change in response to these new demographic populations, which along with the anticipated dominance of Spanish-speaking students in the next decades, brings the issue of language diversity squarely into the provenance of U.S. writing instruction and the field of rhetoric and composition in ways that have until recently been cordoned off as ESL instruction or a matter of foreign languages. Mecenas builds upon recent research undertaken by AAAC members in two areas: 1) the responsibilities of writing program administrators concerning second language writers (Matsuda, Saenkhum, and Accardi), and 2) racial formation theory as methodology for writing assessment research (Inoue; Inoue and Poe). As a circulation essay, Mecenas' paper illustrates how critical the caucus has been in fostering new scholarship that responds to specific contexts, including shifting institutional priorities that create new racial formations in WPA work.

In the final circulation essay, "Risks and Affordances: Naming the Asian/Asian American Caucus," Lehua Ledbetter echoes caucus discussions around the name of the caucus. In the spirit of feminist historiography, Ledbetter asks, what is missing, dropped out, or erased in the naming of the AAAC? While the term articulates a positive, collective political identity that creates a coherent presence within CCCC and calls forth the intentional naming of the Asian American Movement, Ledbetter cites our 2014 caucus discussion and calls us to examine how the naming of the caucus may function to include, exclude, or complicate members' positionalities as well as our political visions and scholarship. Rather than attempting to resolve the fissures and inadequacies that such naming inevitably creates, Ledbetter calls us to expand our understanding of the risks, dangers, and affordances of naming practices through Asian/Asian American, indigenous, feminist, and queer rhetorics. We find it apt to close the collection with an essay that resonates with caucus discussions we have had while writing this history. Increasingly, caucus members are calling for us to open ourselves up again to critique and engagement; not to synthesize into one identity, history, or rhetoric, but rather to disperse and branch out into the many possibilities of the caucus as a home, a hub of institutional and disciplinary activism, a scholarly collective, a nationalist and transnationalist community. Work by many caucus members—Eileen Lagman, Jerry Won Lee, Shui-Yin Sharon Yam, and others—is moving us in these expansive directions.

The appendices that follow are additional steps toward documenting a living history of the AAAC as an ongoing collective effort. "Appendix A: Asian/Asian American Caucus, 2016," is a snapshot of current AAAC members based on listserv subscription as of March 2016. "Appendix B: Timeline of Scholarship and Accomplishments" is a chronological list that was produced collaboratively with the AAAC. This timeline highlights a number of disciplinary and scholarly moments that are not always reflected in historical narratives, including changes of leadership within the caucus, featured sessions at conferences, and awards. The disciplinary moments included within this list have been collected through a review of past CCCC convention programs, along with self-reporting via the caucus listserv and conversations with caucus members. As a result, the timeline does not comprehensively list all accomplishments by AAAC members; however, it is a step toward what can potentially become a larger resource for those interested in Asian and Asian American scholarship in rhetoric and composition. Looking over time, two patterns are visible: 1) the Scholars for the Dream Award has been a consistent supporter of Asian/Asian American scholars and work, and 2) work by Asian/Asian American scholars and surrounding Asian/Asian American issues seem to gain wider disciplinary support, with increasing numbers of featured conference presentations including Asian/Asian American scholars in recent years. However, we also note the timeline's inherent limitations: as a reflection of academia at large, it tends to privilege particular forms of knowledge production and does not include the many other kinds of important work done by the caucus and its members, including various forms of activism, advocacy work, mentorship, teaching, and alliance building. "Appendix C: Bibliography of Asian/Asian American Rhetoric and Composition" is a working bibliography of scholarship by and affiliated with the caucus and its mission. Appendix D, as noted earlier, is part of Phuong Minh Tran's research on Asian and Asian American publications that appear over 60 years of back-issues of *College Composition and Communication.*

This collection offers a multifaceted look at how Asian and Asian American teacher–scholars have contributed to NCTE and CCCC over time and how these contributions have oftentimes had activist underpinnings, challenging the existing political structure of the institution. Beyond establishing a disciplinary presence for AAAC, this work enables multiple layers of community—layers that are necessary for the becoming of a community that is re/visionary and complex like the membership it represents, and that engages tensions and ruptures, acknowledges wounds, and comes together to move forward. Still, the collection represents just a selection of the diverse work being done by caucus members.[11] Despite these spaces, however, this collection represents some of the significant work that has been and is currently being done by Asian/Asian American teachers and scholars in NCTE and CCCC. If there is one thing to take away from this introduction, it is that, as a caucus, we are not founded by one single narrative. Rather, we have multiple beginnings, re/visions, accommodations, resistances, and sustaining threads. While the archives are relatively quiet on this account, we do have publications, and the stories of the people who have been active in/with the caucus. This collection attempts to represent the conversations that have taken place over time, some resulting in published or archived written documents, and others not.

The collection would not be complete without a brief look forward. As we've worked on this collection, caucus members have reflected on where we've been and where we might go next. So, in closing, we take a moment

11   As many historiographers have noted, histories—and archives—are inevitably distinct from the realities they purportedly represent, limited by ideology, convention, and the narrative form. As de Certeau said, "in current usage 'history' connotes both a science and that which it studies—the explication which is *stated* and the reality of *what has taken place* or what takes place" (21). In "holding to the idea of discourse and to its fabrication," he asks, "doesn't language not so much implicate the status of the reality of which it speaks, as posit it as that which is other than itself?" (21). Thus, there is still room to examine the participation of Asians and Asian Americans in NCTE and CCCC in a variety of time periods that are only briefly mentioned in this collection, particularly before the 1960s and between the 1980s and late 1990s. There have been Asian/Asian American NCTE presidents like Beverly Chin and Yvonne Siu-Runyan, as well as influential scholars in the discipline like Min-Zhan Lu and Gail Y. Okawa who have shaped the work of Asian/Asian American scholars and teachers in significant ways, yet whose stories are not told here. Much more could also be said about the community-based work done by Asian/Asian American teacher–scholars in rhetoric and composition.

to listen for possibilities, offering sustaining questions for re/visioning the caucus and for reconceptualizing a community that foregrounds alliances, unexpected connections and coalitions, redefining the categorical terms we use to understand ourselves:

How might we continue to foster a space that addresses tensions and ruptures, gaps, setbacks, and silences? How might we thoughtfully foster complexity within the caucus, in terms of intersectional and marginalized identities, cross-racial and cross-ethnic engagement, and the rhetorics of Asians/Asian Americans within the context of transnationalism?

How might we intervene in disciplinary conceptions of "important contributions" in relation to the work that we do? Asian/Asian American scholarship in rhetoric and composition is often represented as an esoteric subspecialty in the discipline, and this is particularly visible in the discipline's publication history. How might we intervene in the ways our work is positioned and represented in the discipline?

How might we develop sustaining threads that continue to attend to our disciplinary presence? What other layers of community are necessary for establishing this presence? What can the caucus do to support existing and emerging leaders to take on more high-profile positions in the organization? As Young notes in Tasaka's interview with him, we have yet to have an Asian/Asian American CCCC Chair. How can we promote an institutional literacy for Asian/Asian American professionals?

Such questions continue to make visible the work of sustaining a community, varied modes of social circulation, and how the writing and unfolding of history interconnect. We offer this history as one telling, one collection of stories about the Asian/Asian American Caucus at CCCC, one history within the larger history of Asians/Asian Americans who have been active in both CCCC and NCTE. There are many more stories to excavate, many more stories to be told, and we hope that others will continue this work, filling in the gaps and complicating the narrative of our histories through either official or unofficial channels of rearticulation.

WORKS CITED

Anderson, Benedict. *Imagined Communities: Reflections on the Origin and Spread of Nationalism.* London: Verso, 2006. Print.

"Asian/Asian American Scholarship in Rhetoric and Composition: Risks and Rewards." Conference on College Composition and Communication. Tampa Marriott Waterside, Tampa, FL, 19 March 2015. Sponsored by the Asian/Asian American Caucus.

Asian Women United of California, eds. *Making More Waves: New Writing by Asian American Women.* Boston: Beacon Press, 1997. Print.

—. *Making Waves: An Anthology of Writings by and about Asian American Women.* Boston: Beacon Press, 1989. Print.

Blackmon, Samantha, Cristina Kirklighter, and Steve Parks. *Listening to Our Elders: Working and Writing for Change.* Philadelphia: New City Community Press; Logan: Utah State UP, 2011. Print.

—. "Writing and Working for Change: Recognizing the Collective Work of Teachers within and across Diverse Identities." *National Council of Teachers of English.* 2011. Web.

Byrd, Jodi A. *The Transit of Empire: Indigenous Critiques of Colonialism.* Minneapolis: U of Minnesota P, 2011. Print.

Carpenter, Cari M., and K. Hyoejin Yoon. "Rethinking Alternative Contact in Native American and Chinese Encounters: Juxtaposition in Nineteenth-Century U.S. Newspapers." *College Literature* 41.1 (2014): 7–42. Print.

Chan, Jeffery Paul, Frank Chin, Lawson Fusao Inada, and Shawn Wong. *The Big Aiiieeeee!: An Anthology of Chinese American and Japanese American Literature.* New York: Signet, 1991. Print.

Chin, Frank, and Jeffery Paul Chan. "Racist Love." *Seeing Through Shuck.* Ed. Richard Kostelanetz. New York: Ballantine Books, 1972. 65–79. Print.

Chin, Frank, Jeffery Paul Chan, Lawson Fusao Inada, and Shawn Wong. *Aiiieeeee!: An Anthology of Asian-American Writers.* Washington, D.C.: Howard UP, 1974. Print.

Ching, Stuart. "Cultural Memory in the Classroom Public Space." *English Journal* 101.1 (2011): 89–90. Print.

Chu, Patricia P. *Gendered Strategies of Authorship in Asian America.* Durham: Duke UP, 2000. Print.

De Certeau, Michel. *The Writing of History.* Trans. Tom Conley. New York: Columbia UP, 1992. Print.

Driskill, Qwo-Li. *Asegi Stories: Cherokee Queer and Two-Spirit Memory.* Tucson: U of Arizona P, 2016. Print.

Gale, Xin Liu. "Historical Studies and Postmodernism: Rereading Aspasia of Miletus." *College English* 62.3 (2000): 361–86. Print.

Gilyard, Keith, ed. *Race, Rhetoric, and Composition.* Portsmouth, NH: Boynton/Cook-Heinemann (CrossCurrents Series), 1999. Print.

Hattori, Tomo and Stuart Ching. "Reexamining the Between-Worlds Trope in Cross Cultural Composition Studies." *Representations: Doing Asian American Rhetoric.* Ed. LuMing Mao and Morris Young. Logan: Utah State UP, 2008. 41–61. Print.

Hoang, Haivan V. *Writing against Racial Injury: The Politics of Asian American Student Rhetoric.* Pittsburgh: U of Pittsburgh P, 2015. Print.

Inada, Lawson Fusao. "The Stand." *The Big Aiiieeeee!: An Anthology of Chinese American and Japanese American Literature.* Ed. Frank Chin, Jeffery Paul Chan, Lawson Fusao Inada, and Shawn Wong. New York: Signet, 1991. 601. Print.

Inoue, Asao B. "Grading Contracts: Assessing Their Effectiveness on Different Racial Formations." *Race and Writing Assessment.* Ed. Asao B. Inoue and Mya Poe. New York: Peter Lang Publishing, 2012. Print.

Inoue, Asao B. and Mya Poe. *Race and Writing Assessment.* New York: Peter Lang Publishing, 2012. Print.

King, Lisa. "Competition, Complicity, and (Potential) Alliance: Native Hawaiian and Asian Immigrant Narratives at the Bishop Museum." *Native/Asian Encounters.* Spec. issue of *College Literature* 41.1 (2014): 43–65. Print.

Lagman, Eileen. "Moving Labor: Transnational Migrant Workers and Affective Literacies of Care." *Literacy in Composition Studies* 3.3 (2015): 1-24. Web.

Lee, Jerry Won. "Transnational Linguistic Landscapes and the Transgression of Metadiscursive Regimes of Language." *Critical Inquiry in Language Studies* 11.1 (2014): 50-74. Print.

Lee, Rachel C. *The Americas of Asian American Literature: Gendered Fictions of Nation and Transnation.* Princeton: Princeton UP, 1999. Print.

Leon, Kendall. "La Hermandad and Chicanas Organizing: The Community Rhetoric of the Comisión Femenil Mexicana Nacional." *Community Literacy Journal* 7.2 (Spring 2013): 1–20. Print.

Lim, Shirley Geok-lin, Mayumi Tsutakawa, and Margarita Donnelly, eds. *The Forbidden Stitch: An Asian American Women's Anthology.* Corvallis:

Calyx Books, 1989. Print.

Logan, Shirley Wilson. *Liberating Language: Sites of Rhetorical Education in Nineteenth-Century Black America.* Carbondale: Southern Illinois UP, 2008. Print.

Lowe, Lisa. *Immigrant Acts: On Asian American Cultural Politics.* Durham: Duke UP, 1996. Print.

Lu, Min-Zhan. "An Essay on the Work of Composition: Composing English Against the Order of Fast Capitalism." *College Composition and Communication* 56.1 (2004): 16–50. Print.

—. "From Silence to Words: Writing as Struggle." *College English* 49.4 (1987): 437–48. Print.

—. "Professing Multiculturalism: The Politics of Style in the Contact Zone." *College Composition and Communication* 45.4 (1994): 442–58. Print.

—. "Redefining the Literate Self: The Politics of Critical Affirmation." *College Composition and Communication* 51.2 (1999): 172–94. Print.

Lyons, Scott Richard. "Rhetorical Sovereignty: What Do American Indians Want from Writing?" *College Composition and Communication* 51.3 (2000): 447–68. Print.

Mao, LuMing, and Morris Young, eds. *Representations: Doing Asian American Rhetoric.* Logan: Utah State UP, 2008. Print.

Matsuda, Paul Kei, Tanita Saenkhum, and Steven Accardi. "Writing Teachers' Perceptions of the Presence and Needs of Second Language Writers: An Institutional Case Study." *Journal of Second Language Writing* 22 (2013): 68–86. Print.

Mecenas, Jolivette. "A Career of Acting 'Ill-Mannered': An Interview with Jeffery Paul Chan on Reviewing Textbooks for NCTE and Teaching Ethnic Studies (Because it is Good for People)." *Listening to Our Elders: Working and Writing for Change.* Ed. Samantha Blackmon, Cristina Kirklighter, Steve Parks. Philadelphia: New City Community Press; Logan: Utah State UP, 2011. 28–44. Print.

—. "Beyond 'Asian American' and Back: Coalitional Rhetoric in Print and New Media." *Representations: Doing Asian American Rhetoric.* Ed. LuMing Mao and Morris Young. Logan: Utah State UP, 2008. 198–217. Print.

Mejía, Jaime Armin. "Ethnic Rhetorics Reviewed." *College Composition and Communication* 63.1 (2011): 145–61. Print.

Monberg, Terese Guinsatao. "Listening for Legacies or, How I Began to Hear Dorothy Laigo Cordova, the Pinay behind the Podium Known as FANHS." *Representations: Doing Asian American Rhetoric.* Ed. Mao,

LuMing and Morris Young. Logan: Utah State UP, 2008. 83–105. Print.

Monberg, Terese Guinsatao, and K. Hyoejin Yoon. "Ruptures, Wounds, Possibilities: Asian/Asian American Disciplinary History and Scholarship." Conference on College Composition and Communication. JW Marriott, Indianapolis, IN, 20 March 2014. Sponsored by the Asian/Asian American Caucus.

Nunley, Vorris L. *Keepin' It Hushed: The Barbershop and African American Hush Harbor Rhetoric.* Detroit: Wayne State UP, 2011. Print.

Okawa, Gail Y. "Letters to Our Forebears: Reconnecting Generations Through Writing." *The English Journal* 92.6 (2003): 47–51. Print.

—. "Re-seeing Our Professional Face(s)". *The English Journal* 88.2 (1998): 98–104. Print.

—. "Resurfacing Roots': Developing a Pedagogy of Language Awareness from Two Views." *Language Diversity in the Classroom: From Intention to Practice.* Ed. Geneva Smitherman, Victor Villanueva, and Suresh Canagarajah. Carbondale: Southern Illinois UP: 2003. 109–33. Print.

Omi, Michael and Howard Winant. *Racial Formation in the United States: From the 1960s to the 1990s.* New York: Routledge, 1994. Print.

Powell, Malea. "Rhetorics of Survivance: How American Indians Use Writing." *College Composition and Communication* 53.3 (2002): 396–434. Print.

Royster, Jacqueline Jones. *Traces of a Stream: Literacy and Social Change Among African American Women.* Pittsburgh: U of Pittsburgh P, 2000. Print.

—. "When the First Voice You Hear Is Not Your Own." *College Composition and Communication* 47.1 (1996): 29–40. Print.

Royster, Jacqueline Jones, and Gesa E. Kirsch. *Feminist Rhetorical Practices: New Horizons for Rhetoric, Composition, and Literacy Studies.* Carbondale: Southern Illinois UP, 2012. Print.

Royster, Jacqueline Jones, and Jean C. Williams. "History in the Spaces Left: African American Presence and Narratives of Composition Studies." *College Composition and Communication* 50.4 (1999): 563–84. Print.

Sano-Franchini, Jennifer, Robyn Tasaka, and Lehua Ledbetter. "Hawai'i's 'Remix' Culture: Engaging Postcolonialism and Settler Colonialism in Discussions of Copyright and Intellectual Property." *Cultures of Copyright.* Ed. Dànielle Nicole DeVoss and Martine Courant Rife. New York: Peter Lang, 2014. Print.

Shimabukuro, Mira. *Relocating Authority: Japanese Americans Writing to Redress Mass Incarceration.* Boulder: UP of Colorado, 2015. Print.

Sias, Reva E. and Beverly J. Moss. "Rewriting a Master Narrative: HBCUs and Community Literacy Partnerships." *Reflections: A Journal of Public Rhetoric, Civic Writing, and Service Learning* 10.2 (2011): 21–51. Print.

Smitherman, Geneva. *Talkin and Testifyin: The Language of Black America*. Detroit: Wayne State UP, 1977. Print.

Summers, Sarah. "Book Review: *Minor Re/Visions: Asian American Literacy Narratives as a Rhetoric of Citizenship; Reading Chinese Fortune Cookie: The Making of Chinese American Rhetoric; Representations: Doing Asian American Rhetoric*." *Journal of Language, Identity, and Education* 9.4 (2010): 282–85. Print.

Villanueva, Victor, Jr. *Bootstraps: From an American Academic of Color*. Urbana: NCTE, 1993. Print.

—. "'Memoria' Is a Friend of Ours: On the Discourse of Color." *College English* 67.1 (2004): 9–19. Print.

—. "On the Rhetoric and Precedents of Racism." *College Composition and Communication* 50.4 (1999): 645–61. Print.

Wu, Hui. "Historical Studies of Rhetorical Women Here and There: Methodological Challenges to Dominant Interpretive Frameworks." *Rhetoric Society Quarterly* 32.1 (2002): 81–97. Print.

Yam, Shui-Yin Sharon. "Education and Transnational Nationalism: The Rhetoric of Integration in Chinese National and Moral Education in Hong Kong." *Howard Journal of Communication* 27.1 (2016): 38-52. Print.

Young, Morris. *Minor Re/Visions: Asian American Literacy Narratives as a Rhetoric of Citizenship*. Carbondale: Southern Illinois UP, 2004. Print.

—. "Native Claims: Cultural Citizenship, Ethnic Expressions, and the Rhetorics of 'Hawaiianness'." *College English* 67.1 (2004): 83–101. Print.

CHAPTER ONE

Taking Time for Feminist Historiography: Remembering Asian/Asian American Institutional and Scholarly Activism

Jennifer Sano-Franchini

> "Whatever we currently know about rhetorical history as a disciplinary landscape is situated on a larger terrain of developed and undeveloped possibilities."
>
> — Jacqueline Jones Royster, "Disciplinary Landscaping, or, Contemporary Challenges in the History of Rhetoric" (148)

In the spring of 2010, Cristina Kirklighter, Samantha Blackmon, and Steve Parks contacted the Conference on College Composition and Communication (CCCC) Asian/Asian American Caucus (AAAC) in search of members willing to work with them on Writing and Working for Change, an NCTE-funded, cross-caucus project intended to document and preserve a history of the organization that includes the collective work of teachers from across diverse identifications. Kirklighter, Blackmon, and Parks sought volunteers who would interview our caucus' "founding members," and manage archival documents relevant to the caucus. Jolivette Mecenas agreed to interview Jeffery Paul Chan, her former professor at San Francisco State University. Mira Shimabukuro agreed to interview Frank Chin. I said I would serve as "historical archivist representative" for the AAAC, responsible for cataloging caucus-related documents from the NCTE Archives Index.

At the time, I was a graduate student and new caucus member, having attended my first caucus business meeting in 2009. I knew little about the caucus, and nothing about its history. That summer, I took Malea Powell's seminar on Historical Methodologies in Rhetoric Studies, where we read and talked about the archive as a physical, material, and institutional space, and about archival research as an embodied experience. We discussed the archive as hermeneutic authority, and how, according to Derrida, "the archontic power, which also gathers the functions of unification, of identification, of classification, must be paired with what we will call the power of *consignation* [...] the act of assigning residence or of entrusting so as to put into reserve (to consign, to deposit), in a place and on a substrate, [...] the act of *consigning* through *gathering together signs* (10). From Powell's work, I learned to see the "physical space of an archive" as a "deliberate institutional cataloging of memory," and I came to understand that archives can reshape how we make sense of ourselves (116).

I was inspired by Gail Okawa's work on American internment camps, noting how she described her experiences doing historical and archival work in ways that were insistently relational. She noted gaps in her grandfather's written record; how she stayed with friends when she visited Kilauea Military Camp, the first facility where her grandfather was imprisoned; and how tips and guidance from others—internees, their families, and people who attended her research talks—guided her work to new people, new places, and unexpected directions. My experience of the current project was similar.

Unsure of where to start, I consulted Powell, who suggested that I ask Kirklighter if I could accompany her and Blackmon on their upcoming trip to the NCTE Archives in July of that year. Kirklighter agreed, and on July 19, 2010, I drove from East Lansing, Michigan, to Urbana, Illinois to meet them. Powell also suggested that I consult caucus co-chairs, Terese Guinsatao Monberg and Stuart Ching, for direction. Monberg suggested that I speak with Jolivette Mecenas, who had already interviewed Jeffery Paul Chan, and that I ask Mecenas if Chan had mentioned any names, documents, or keywords that I might look out for at the archives.

"'Racist Love.' Look for 'Racist Love,'" she said.

Kirklighter, Blackmon and I spent three short days in Urbana, getting set up and digging. I was placed behind four, slim boxes labeled "Asian-American Publications."

"There're your boxes!" I heard someone chirp.

Over the three days, we pored over old, typewritten correspondence, black and white photos, photocopied news clippings, bibliographies, newsletters, magazines, and past convention programs. I searched for any mention of an Asian/Asian American Caucus. I looked intently for any mention of Frank Chin, Jeff Chan, or "Racist Love." And at the end of each day, Kirklighter, Blackmon and I debriefed over dinner, sharing what we found and how we felt, talking through exciting discoveries and disappointing gaps. Kirklighter and Blackmon helped me to understand both the impetus and significance of the Writing and Working for Change project. I learned that founding members of some of the other caucuses who had been working in NCTE in the 1960s and 1970s had mentioned Frank Chin and Jeff Chan's names. It was also in Urbana that I learned that Frank Chin had refused Shimabukuro's invitation for an interview, deriding NCTE as "a well-meaning but racist outfit."

"Whoa, really?"

I *had* to learn what happened with Frank Chin at NCTE.

LOOKING FOR ASIAN/ASIAN AMERICAN INSTITUTIONAL ACTIVISM: FRANK CHIN, JEFFERY PAUL CHAN, AND "RACIST LOVE"

In 1969, the NCTE Task Force on Racism and Bias in the Teaching of English, headed by Director Ernece B. Kelly, was established to address the issue of racism in school textbooks. A news clipping at the time reports, "Nonwhite minorities are still not adequately represented in educational materials now being used in schools, according to the National Council of Teachers of English." More specifically, the NCTE asserted, "anthologies used as basic texts should contain more than token representation of the works of nonwhite minority group members. The minority groups should be represented in a fashion which respects their dignity and mirrors their contribution to American culture, history, and letters." To address this problem, the NCTE Task Force on Racism and Bias worked across scholarly communities recruiting American Indian, Black, Chicanx, and Asian/Asian American teachers and scholars to review anthologies of literature. They invited "minority publishers" to set up booths at the NCTE Convention, and made special arrangements for "presses run by minority persons and specializing in minority individuals," allowing per-book charges that would make their presence at the Convention more feasible, to name a couple of examples.

At this time, the Task Force contacted Asian American authors and literary scholars Jeffery Paul Chan and Frank Chin to be part of the Textbook Review Committee. Chan and Chin would later become renowned editors, with Lawson Fusao Inada and Shawn Wong, of two critical texts in early Asian American literary studies: *Aiiieeeee!* (published in 1974) and *The Big Aiiieeeee!* (published in 1991). Chan recounts in his interview with Mecenas, "We were there to review literary anthologies that were used in freshman and sophomore comp classes and to determine whether in fact they represented fairly or they represented at all ethnic minorities' cultural contributions in literature. Our job was very easy because [...] Frank [Chin] and I [determined] there were no Asians in any of the texts" (Mecenas 38). On the Textbook Review Committee, Chin and Chan opted to forgo the criteria provided for reviewing the books, and instead, as Chan put it, "produced a fairly massive screed on the whole idea of any kind of representation of Asian American literature" through a position paper that would later become known as "Racist Love" (Mecenas 39). In this controversial and contested essay, Chin and Chan argue that "Asian American" literary texts, including those published in anthologies at the time, perpetuated what they called "racist love"—a pattern of Asian American self-contempt based on "acceptable stereotypes" such as that of the "model minority" and the emasculated Asian male. Furthermore, they contend: "The vehicles of this illusion are education and the publishing establishment" (Chin and Chan 67).

While, notably, the NCTE Archives does not include a copy of "Racist Love," there is evidence—pieces of a conversation—that show how the organization responded. In a letter dated July 14, 1971, NCTE Executive Secretary Robert Hogan wrote to his attorney, Philip C. Zimmerly, laying out the chain of events involving Chin and Chan and the Task Force on Racism and Bias:

> Another muddy one.
>
> We had a Task Force of people meeting here two or three weeks ago concerned with the treatment of minority groups in conventional textbooks, particularly American literature textbooks at the college level.
>
> Two of the participants were representing Asian-Americans. During their time here they drafted an "Asian-American" position paper. They left a copy behind.
>
> I was troubled by parts of it and wrote to them in that connection.

This "'Asian-American' position paper," "Racist Love," was meant to be published by NCTE, but Hogan expressed that he was hesitant to publish the paper, and his lawyer confirmed: "stick to your guns and refuse to print the materials [position paper] you sent me" (Zimmerly).[1] Hogan's primary concern was the possibility that NCTE might be held legally liable for distributing "Racist Love," should Eileen Whalen, editorial representative at Houghton Mifflin, get fired not long after—presumably as a result of—Chin and Chan's critique. Hogan wrote to Chin and Chan to this effect, and Chin and Chan responded sardonically, in a letter dated July 9, 1971:

> Check with your attorney and I think you'll find your fears are unfounded. Virginia Lee was interviewed as the authoress of the novel, THE HOUSE THAT TAI MING BUILT, which featured Chinese and Chinese-American characters and a San Francisco Chinatown setting. She was interviewed on tape by a writer who announced himself as a writer, and photographed by a photographer, with the understanding that the material would be made available to scholars of Chinese-America and used. In fact, the material has been used, not only by us, who gathered it, but by Kai-yu Hsu in his introduction to the Asian American anthology to be released this year by Houghton Mifflin Company.
>
> The material quoted is about her writing and her subject matter and the Chinatown background used in her novel...not her character. Within the realm of literary criticism it is fair, in fact, it is the function of literary criticism to question the intelligence and the competence of the author under discussion. And our paper is literary criticism.
>
> As to the letter. Letters become the property of the addressee and are theirs to publish, file away, or destroy as they please. Ellen Whalen[2] has

---

[1] These review essays were meant to be published in NCTE's *Searching for America*, edited by Ernece B. Kelly. Included in place of "Racist Love" is an essay by Chinese scholar Kai-yu Hsu.

[2] As Mecenas explains, "Racist Love" ends with an early call "for mainstream publishers to acknowledge language variety in minority literature as a function of self-determination." Here, Chin and Chan refer to a letter from Whalen where she requests "that the title of [Chan's] contribution to the first anthology of Asian American literature be revised." Mecenas continues, "The title of the story is 'Auntie Tsia Lays Dying,' and the editor requests to change "Lays" to "Lies" in order to reflect word usage in Standard American English. 'Racist Love' ends with a scathing, personal attack on the editor, who is identified by name in the original manuscript." (32).

nothing more to say about her letter, since it doesn't belong to her but to Jeffery Chan. That's the law. So this letter is now yours. And I pooh pooh your worrying about that last satirical tag getting Ellen Whalen fired. If she does get the can it won't be because of anything in the paper. There's no case to get on. But if you're real uptight about it…that tag, you can substitute the word "bleep" for those words you feel are too charged and offensive.

Jeffery and I had a good time that week

The very tone of this letter reflects Chan's assessment that, "We were being poor guests." He continues in his interview with Mecenas, "of course, that was our whole point, I think. It was going to be bad mannered, ill-mannered" (40). In other words, their "plan of attack" was strategic in both tone and context, as Chan acknowledges that he and Chin saw NCTE as a large venue from which they could launch their position regarding Asian American literature (40). This confrontational stance subverts the very stereotypes Chin and Chan denigrate in "Racist Love."

Perhaps as a result of these interactions, NCTE collected a number of periodicals and clippings mentioning Frank Chin, including two (mostly negative) reviews of Chin's play, "The Chickencoop Chinaman" (Barnes; Novick) and several issues of *Bridge: The Asian American Magazine*, two of which included "Who's Afraid of Frank Chin, or Is It Ching?" and "Chin vs. Ching, Part II" a series of debates between Frank Chin and Frank Ching, managing editor of *Bridge*. These debates illustrated the kinds of tensions and outright disagreements that existed within the Asian/Asian American community at the time.[3] It is not precisely clear why these documents were

3   The debates between Chin and Ching centered largely on the similarities and differences among Asians and Asian Americans; for example, while the purpose of *Bridge* was to draw connections between Chinese Americans and Chinese in China (Wei 115), such efforts were criticized by Chin who argued that "Americanized Chinese who've come over in their teens and later to settle here and American born Chinaman have nothing in common, culturally, intellectually, emotionally," and that "the writing of Americanized Chinese is just as racist as white writing, when it deals with Chinese America" (qtd. in Wei 115). In response, Ching asserted, "within the Chinese–American community there are many who were born and raised in this country and many others who were born and raised abroad. We recognize the differences in experiences and attitudes between them. But you cannot exclude the foreign-born Chinese–Americans and say you have nothing in common with them. Your father is a foreign-born Chinese–American. You have at least that much in common" (qtd. in Wei 115-6). At the center of Chin's politics was a resistance to stereotypes about Asian Americans, including that of the perpetual foreigner. As

preserved and archived. Was it thought that such documents might be useful to NCTE, should they find themselves in legal trouble? Were the documents meant to show that there were members of the Asian/Asian American community who disagreed with Chin and Chan's views about stakes and boundaries of Asian American literature? Could the documents serve as evidence that Chin's character was simply rash, argumentative, and confrontational? Or were NCTE administrators genuinely interested in understanding who Frank Chin was and the nature of his work?

For several years, Chin continued to participate in NCTE, showing how confrontational politics *and* convention participation can represent a dual strategy for some. Though there were most likely some who did not appreciate Chin's work on the Textbook Review Committee, there were others involved with NCTE who were interested in what he had to say: in 1975, Chin was a convention luncheon featured speaker for the CCCC at the Sixty Fifth Annual NCTE Convention in San Diego, California.[4] In a Convention Wrap-Up, it was noted that Chin "charged that 'culturally deprived' white teachers 'bring up my kids to be culturally deprived'":

> We are taught to look on ourselves as Chinese-Americans, Japanese-Americans. . . It's what we're taught to call white people that bothers me. We're taught to call them Universal Man, Just Plain Folks, human beings, just writers, just people. So that our people go around aspiring to become human beings. When I grow up I want to become a human being. It's a code word for white.

Chin was later invited to be a speaker at a two-day pre-convention workshop in November 1977, titled, "Racism and Sexism Awareness: New Strategies for the Language Arts," arranged by The Council on Interracial Books for Children.[5] His literary work was often included in bibliographies of Asian American texts.

---

a result, he pushed for seeing Asian Americans as a distinct group with their own distinct culture, aesthetics, and intellectual and literary traditions. At times, this agenda would mean rejecting any connection to Asian cultures.

4   No title was listed for Chin's talk.

5   The issue of Asian/Asian American representation in literature was taken up by others, and it appeared in the titles of such panels as, "The Minority Presence in Literature: Asian," with speakers John Tateishi, Lawson Fusao Inada, and N. V. M. Gonzalez. There was also at least one panel that focused on working with students of Asian descent: "Working with Vietnamese and Cambodian Children," with speakers Nguyen Hy Quang, Sadae Iwataki, and Robert Kaplan.

Despite their contested politics within the Asian American movement, Chin and Chan's participation on the Task Force's Textbook Review Committee is one relatively well-documented example of institutional activism that, I argue, set the stage for how NCTE would engage Asian/Asian American concerns in the years to come. When I say "institutional activism," I refer to the ways in which individuals participate in collective action, working to open up institutional space for perspectives not yet adequately included. I use the word "activism" to refer to a wide range of strategic and collective efforts made to intentionally effect political change within institutional structures. By "political change," I mean shifts in existing power structures that have historically silenced, marginalized, misrepresented, and/or misunderstood the needs and concerns of particular identity formations—in this case, Asian Americans. Usually this change is constituted by a shift in power dynamics, whether in terms of opening up access to resources, opening up avenues for voices that have been unheard, or opening up means for agency and self-determination.

Despite the pervasive myth of the "model minority"—which includes the perception of Asians/Asian Americans as apolitical assimilationists who are able to achieve socioeconomic success within an oppressive social order—Asian/Asian American activism and political organizing has taken place for some time, most often associated with the Asian American civil rights movement of the late 1960s and 1970s.[6] To be sure, Asian/Asian American rhetoric and composition scholars have studied Asian/Asian American activism, documenting the legacies of Asian/Asian American political organizing and demonstration. For instance, I think of Haivan V. Hoang's work on solidarity rhetoric in the Vietnamese American Coalition (VAC), Jolivette Mecenas' essay about her own participation in the Kearney Street Workshop, Terese Guinsatao Monberg's research on the Filipino American National Historical Society (FANHS), and Mira Shimabukuro's work on Japanese American resistance during mass incarceration.

Here, I build on the works of Hoang, Mecenas, Monberg, and Shimabukuro, exploring Asian/Asian American activism within our own professional organizations of NCTE and CCCC. Generally, people conceptualize activism

---

6   It is worth noting that the Asian American Movement was taking place concurrently with Chin and Chan's service on the NCTE Task Force on Racism and Bias in the Teaching of English. Therefore, Chin and Chan worked in the context of Asian American politics at the time, drawing connections across NCTE and the Asian American Movement.

in terms of public protest and demonstration. Less often, however, is the word "activism" attached to the kinds of work we ourselves are compelled to do as Asians and Asian Americans in rhetoric and composition—despite much of this work constituting forms of political intervention. My task in this chapter, then, is to ask, what does it mean to look at our own participation in our discipline's professional organizations like NCTE and CCCC as forms of activism? What does it mean to shift conceptions of activist work beyond (and with) public protest and demonstration to interventions internal to organizations as well? In asking such questions, I think of Kendall Leon's work on the *Comisión Femenil Mexicana Nacional (CFMN)*, where she argues that we ought to see seemingly small, mundane organizational activities—such as writing marginalia and stapling documents together—as examples of a Chicana rhetorical methodology that strategically pushes at existing configurations of power. Like Leon, I am interested in bringing to the fore some of the behind-the-scenes work that functions to politically transform institutions like NCTE, and that then goes on to effect public educational policy.

For example, in its first year, the NCTE Task Force on Racism and Bias in the Teaching of English composed the "Criteria for Teaching Materials in Reading and Literature." According to a Task Force brochure, this document was "adopted in 1970 by the Board of Directors as NCTE policy," one year prior to Chan and Chin's visit to NCTE; however, after their visit in 1971, the document was revised in terms of how it framed the experiences of Asian and Asian Americans. While it is not clear who proposed these revisions, one might surmise that perhaps because of Chin and Chan's "attack," folks in the organization were compelled to think about Asians and Asian Americans differently. To illustrate, the earlier version of the "Criteria for Teaching Materials in Reading and Literature" stated:

> Of all the minority groups in the United States, the non-white minorities (American Indians, Blacks, Chicanos, Puerto Ricans, et al.), more than any others, suffer crippling discrimination in jobs, housing, civil rights, and education. *Other non-white minorities (e.g., Asians) while not subject to the same kind of economic and social oppression* often face a school curriculum which in their terms is culturally impoverished (emphasis added).

In response to this depiction of Asian/Asian American experience, a document titled, "Proposed changes in the 'Criteria for Teaching Materials in Reading and Literature,'" identifies how this earlier version of the "Criteria" not only evoked the Asian American model minority myth, but also problematically ordered marginalized groups by degree of oppression, pitting them against one another: "The statement invites pointless comparison of the relative degrees of discrimination between several colored minorities. Moreover, it seems to respond to that invitation by asserting that Asian-Americans have enjoyed preference and little economic or social oppression."[7] The writer suggests revisions clarifying that Asian Americans are indeed among the groups that "suffer crippling discrimination in jobs, housing, civil rights, and education, and face a school curriculum which in their terms is culturally impoverished." These revisions were implemented in a later version of the document.

There were other Asian/Asian American contributors who would directly continue in this vein. For example, John B. Lum of the San Francisco Unified School District later provided additional feedback on "Criteria for Teaching Materials in Reading and Literature." In a letter date stamped December 17, 1971, Lum describes the kinds of covert racism long experienced by Asians/Asian Americans:

> I would like to point out that racism in the urban areas was perfected by racist elements on Asian-Americans. Urban racism, as we now know it, was first perfected on the Asians, and is now, in turn, being used on other out-groups. I think that I have enough evidence to back up what I have just said with a great amount of authority. The point is, then, that one of the Asian-Americans' 'contributions' to America is their being victims of marginal racism, a type of racism that sometimes is so covert that it is impossible to combat.

Lum continued to work with NCTE in later years. On May 25, 1977, he shared with Sandra Gibbs, NCTE Director of Minority Group Affairs and Special Projects, copies of TACT/ESAA (The Association of Chinese Teachers/Emergency School Aid Act) Newsletter, which aimed "to further cross-cultural understanding within the San Francisco school district through the development and distribution of curriculum materials related to Chinese Americans, and through other activities such as workshops, conferences, and the publication of newsletters." As result, Gibbs wrote to Joe Huang of TACT/ESAA requesting thirty additional copies of a newsletter, and permission to reprint a section on Chinese American Resources for an upcoming NCTE workshop.

---

7 It is indicated on this document that it was prepared for presentation to the Board of Directors on November 25, 1971.

At around the same time, Lawson Fusao Inada, preeminent Asian American poet, and, with Chan, Chin, and Shawn Hsu Wong, co-editor of *Aiiieeeee!* and *The Big Aiiieeeee!*, was consulted by the Task Force for the 1975 Spring Institution on "Teaching Minority Literatures At All Levels" in Santa Barbara. For this event, Inada put together "A Selected Bibliography on Asian American Literature." This bibliography included fundamental texts in Asian American literary studies like *Aiiieeeee!* and *Roots: An Asian American Reader*.[8] As Haivan V. Hoang explains, *Roots* was an early effort to recover Asian American experiences, a response to "the need to strategically legitimize such perspectives within academe, especially when Asian American studies was in its infancy" (67). At the bottom of the bibliography developed by Inada is a reference to the Chinese Media Committee in San Francisco, an organization established in 1969 that worked toward more responsible representations of Chinese in the media (Fong).

Inada continued to be an active contributor to NCTE, and he later worked with Roseann Duenas Gonzalez (Chair), Rafael Castillo, John Gardenhire, Kris Gutierrez, Linda Hogan, Gwendolyn Alexander, and Sandra E. Gibbs to develop a 1986 policy titled, "Expanding Opportunities: Academic Success for Culturally and Linguistically Diverse Students." He was affiliated with what would become the NCTE Rainbow Strand, participated in the Whole Language Movement, and served on the 1995–96 Task Force on Involving People of Color in the Council, which articulated a set of strategies in governance, leadership, and program planning, including mentorship and scholarship programs for supporting people of color. Inada also served on the Conference on English Education Nominating Committee and reviewed articles for *College English*.

As the archives show, Asian and Asian American teachers and scholars constituted a small but important presence within NCTE between the late 1960s and 1970s.[9] Inada recalls, "Sometimes, I'd say hello to young adult author Laurence Yep, while he was signing books, and down the hall might be a panel of teachers from Hawaii, so for 'Asian Americans,' as I recall, that was about it" ("Letter to the author"). Several of them spoke out against the lack of

---

8   A copy of *Roots* (edited by Amy Tachiki et al.) can be found in the NCTE Archives.

9   Another Asian/Asian American participant in NCTE during this period was Jeannie Chin, Director of the CIBC Asian American Children's Book Project, who spoke at a workshop on August 8, 1977.

Asian American voices and stereotypical and misinformed representations of Asian Americans in discussions of language, reading, and literacy.

What's more, Asian/Asian American institutional activism in NCTE often took place as Asian/Asian American teacher–scholars worked with colleagues from other systemically marginalized backgrounds to enact institutional change, forming collectives that would have greater institutional impact. Inada remembers, "back in the '70s and 80s, I was *part* of developments, and took part in planning, implementation. So there were two Latina professionals, Kris Gutierrez and Roseann Gonzalez, a lone Navajo educator, Suzanne Benally, and me—reps of the West, working with members of the Black Caucus, in conjunction with Dr. Sandra Gibbs, a 'pioneer' in NCTE administration" ("Letter to the author"; emphasis in the original). Indeed, Asians/Asian Americans in NCTE contributed to how individuals from across the organization would understand the relevance of Asian issues to the larger cause of combatting racism and inequality in the teaching of English. In her presentation on the early history of the Latino/Chicano Caucus, Carlota Cardenas Dwyer recounts, "Our network of contacts grew and grew—our panels of consultants similarly multiplied [...] From Lawson Inada we learned the bitter emotional toll a presidential Executive Order had on a population of American citizens who discovered the bitter limitations of their presumed equality."

The impact of Asian/Asian American institutional activism in NCTE is visible in a letter from John Maxwell, Deputy Executive Director of NCTE, to Marjorie Farmer of the School District of Philadelphia, dated August 22, 1980, about a decade after Chin and Chan shared "Racist Love" with NCTE. Specifically, the letter shows how even though "Racist Love" was rejected from publication by NCTE, Chin and Chan's arguments about the distinctions between Asian and Asian American, alongside the contribution of folks like Lum and Inada, allowed for an increasingly nuanced way of imagining Asian/Asian American identity that would have a direct impact on institutional policy. In the letter to Farmer, Maxwell relays Robert Hogan's concern about how Asians and Asian Americans were being represented in a piece of "proposed legislation":

> I passed along a working draft of the proposed legislation by way of keeping Alan Purves and Bob Hogan informed. Bob responded affirmatively but worried quite a bit about the statement regarding Asians[...]

I gather [...] there was concern among Asian American members that people not be led to believe Asian Americans don't suffer discrimination. Bob feels it would be at least awkward to include the point you've made, given the prior concern expressed to and within the Task Force.

I must confess that, on looking more closely at your sentence, I notice that you begin by talking about groups and then talk about "certain Asian–Pacific immigrants," possibly confusing subsets with all of given groups. Even if the discussion of Asian Americans is important to keep, it's probably more precise to say something like this: 'Some immigrants, more noticeably among Asian–Pacific groups, seem exempt from this pattern, having had the advantage of early instruction in English in their homelands.'

On this point, I'm struck by some language from the [U.S. Department of Education] proposed regulations on Title VI of the Civil Rights Act which says, according to estimates by [the National Institute of Education] and [National Center for Education Statistics], the 'overwhelming majority' of the three and a half million limited-English-proficient children of school age are born in this country. It would follow from this, then, that only a minuscule minority receive bilingual instruction in their homelands.

A closer analysis of this letter and the rhetorical moves deployed by Maxwell provides compelling evidence for how the activist efforts by folks like Chan, Chin, Inada, and Lum had real impact on institutional policy: Maxwell describes how he showed Hogan the proposed legislation, explaining that Hogan "responded affirmatively but worried quite a bit about the statement regarding Asians." Maxwell then says that Hogan feels it would be "awkward" to include a particular point "given the prior concern expressed to and within the Task Force." Maxwell goes on to agree with Hogan, explaining how the generalization about Asians/Asian Americans could be more nuanced, providing the language: "Some immigrants, more noticeably among Asian–Pacific groups, seem exempt from this pattern, having had the advantage of early instruction in English in their homelands." It is worth noting, however, that Maxwell follows this point with a reflection and refutation: "*On this point, I'm struck* by some language from the [...] proposed regulations on Title VI of the Civil Rights Act which says, [...] the 'overwhelming majority' of [...] limited-English-proficient children of school age are born in this country" (emphasis added). Maxwell goes on to rationalize what this point means for the claim being made, explaining, "It would follow from this, then, that only a minuscule minority receive bilingual instruction in their homelands." In other words, Maxwell provides some possible language for revising the proposed legislation, before reflecting on and refuting that language he provided. In so doing, Maxwell seems to walk us through his thought process, illustrating how he, perhaps, was given cause to reflect on this issue as result of Asian American members expressing concern to Hogan, who went on to express this concern to Maxwell, who then expressed the same concern to Farmer.

It is easy to overlook how the sorts of behind-the-scenes acts, in which Chan, Chin, Inada, and Lum took part, contribute to long-term impact toward critical social change; however, the changes that the profession has seen with regards to racist language, attention to stereotypes in representations of Asian Americans, and more inclusive attitudes toward traditionally marginalized groups seems to have roots in some of the moments collected here. Indeed, it can be argued that despite the legitimate critiques that have been lodged against "Racist Love," particularly about issues of gender representation and cultural nationalism, the kinds of dialogue that resulted from Chin and Chan's institutional activism led to changes in the way that NCTE administrators, and perhaps the public more generally, understood Asian American identity.

DWELLING, SLOW SCHOLARSHIP, AND RECURSIVE SPATIAL MOVEMENT

My work in the archives, and learning about the actions that Chan, Chin, Inada, and Lum had taken to impact the way NCTE would think of Asians and Asian Americans was meaningful to me on both a personal and professional level. Participation in Writing and Working for Change and the sessions arranged by Kirklighter, Blackmon, and Parks helped me to locate myself within a longer trajectory of activist contributions by Asians and Asian Americans, and to reconceptualize my own work as a form of scholarly and institutional activism. Looking back, I can say that the agency to situate my own scholarly identity in this way was empowering; despite being familiar with, and being influenced by, existing scholarship in composition studies that conceptualizes rhetoric and literacy as tools for social action and change, I never truly felt like I had the agency for political or institutional change until I was able to see, in detail, the ways in which other Asians have contributed to the organization for a very long time. Somehow, this mattered. I knew Min-Zhan Lu and Gail Okawa had made important contributions to the organization since at least the early 1990s, yet it felt to me like Asians were often cast as newcomers to institutional and political activism in the discipline. In this way, Writing and Working for Change set the groundwork for the caucus, and for me, to rewrite the history of the organization so that those entering the profession who identify as Asian would be able to see people who look like them reflected in the longer institutional history. It was meaningful to learn to see myself as standing on the shoulders of giants—and to reconceptualize whom I saw as giants.

In short, this work left me intellectually and spiritually fulfilled. As a PhD candidate at the time, it was more than I had ever really felt like I accomplished, and I was satisfied with the work I had done. Yet, as I spoke with Terese Guinsatao Monberg, feminist rhetorician, historiographer, and co-chair of the caucus at the time, I grew to see how I needed to dwell, further.

I had been influenced by Monberg's work, particularly what she articulated as a "culturally contingent model of feminist historiography" constituted by an emphasis on rhetorical listening, community memory, and reflexive historiography ("Listening for Legacies" 86). More specifically, Monberg says, to practice rhetorical listening means, "[t]o go beyond what is immediately visible and documented" ("Listening for Legacies" 87). That is, rhetorical listening consists of being attentive to what exists beyond what can be seen in more immediately visible contexts: in print, "at the podium," in the archives. Citing Gwendolyn Pough, Monberg explains how it is important to look not only for presence, but also the work that is being done "in *shaping* that sphere [...] to *enable that presence.*" ("Writing Home" 37–38, qtd. in Monberg; emphasis in the original). As an emerging scholar, I tried to apply this approach because I saw how Asian/Asian American participation in NCTE had not been well-documented in print, and because I understood that such an approach would be crucial for uncovering the wide range of contributions made by diverse members of the community. As I listened to AAAC founders, my mentors, my colleagues, and members of other CCCC identity-based caucuses, I came to see the importance of showing how a wide range of Asian/Asian American teacher-scholars have participated in diverse forms of political and institutional work in the larger discipline.

In retrospect, though, I seemed to enact this approach only in the context of the immediate present rather than the longer history of the institution. After all, I entered the archives aware of its limitations and institutional power. I was aware of gender and racial inequality in practically all spheres of public life. Ironically, this, combined with my fascination with Chin and Chan's legacy, and the embodied experience of being presented the four, small boxes meant to represent my caucus' history in that cold, air-conditioned room at the NCTE Archives, led me to expect and assume an invisibility of Asian participation in the organization in the earlier years. I assumed that larger social structures of racial inequality simply limited Asian participation in the organization. In this way, seeing a lack of participation by Asians in the organization only reaffirmed the expectation ingrained in me once I felt how light those boxes were, especially when compared to the many, full boxes that seemed to be identified for the other caucuses.

Monberg encouraged me to pause, dwell, and reflect more deeply on those invisible spaces, on the gaps that had not yet been filled. As a feminist historiographer, she raised important questions about the lack of women in my history, and she encouraged me to question if what seemed empty was really empty. In short, she helped me to engage in slow scholarship. In "For Slow Scholarship: A Feminist Politics of Resistance through Collective Action in the Neoliberal University," Mountz, Bonds, Mansfield, et al. critique the neoliberal temporal regimes of productivity and efficiency in the contemporary university, arguing that "slowing down represents both a commitment to good scholarship *and* a feminist politics of resistance to the accelerated timelines of the neoliberal university" (1238). The authors ask questions that resonate with this project: "What if we could re-valorize feelings of satisfaction for the dedication, persistence, and sustained energy devoted to creative works that may be years in the making?" (1244) "What if we accounted for planning and engagement, for following through rather than moving on?" (1245) Systemic elements of speed in current academia—including the pressures involved with completing the dissertation in a timely manner, the timelines of the academic job market and the tenure clock, and the varied turnaround times for publications in general—influenced my concern about getting this project done in an efficient manner. Several of these events were taking place in my professional life alongside this archival project, and the pressures of time, in conjunction with preconceptions about what defines a substantive academic contribution, ultimately shaped what I would allow myself to see.

But, I was haunted by the vague memory of a black and white photo, the face of a dark-haired Asian woman wearing cat-eye glasses, peering from the pages of an old NCTE convention program.

In "Writing Home or Writing *As* the Community," Monberg offers a methodology for engaging in slow scholarship. She centers the experiences of students of color to theorize the notion of recursive spatial movement as a way of encouraging writers to "move *within* their own borders or communities, so they might listen for the deeper textures present in the place(s) they might call 'home'" (22). For me, this recursive spatial movement would mean re-engaging my community of caucus members, having conversations about potential silences and erasures within the caucus, and looking for this woman, revisiting archival documents, the archival index, and the historical documents of the Black and Latinx Caucuses.

When I looked back at the archival documents on the Writing and Working for Change website with new questions in mind, I was astonished at what I had unseen all along.

LOOKING BACK: SEEING SAN-SU C. LIN, SHIZUKO OUCHI, AND DORIS C. CHING

Over the course of the decade leading up to the time Frank Chin and Jeffery Paul Chan were contacted by the NCTE Task Force on Racism and Bias in the Teaching of English, San-su C. Lin, Shizuko Ouchi, and Doris C. Ching, three women of Asian descent, were participating in and contributing to NCTE and CCCC. These women, who were based at post-secondary institutions across the United States, were three of the earliest contributors of Asian descent to these professional organizations: Lin, Ouchi, and Ching attended the NCTE Annual Convention, participated in the organization, and published scholarship on the teaching of English at the elementary, secondary, and post-secondary levels in NCTE journals since at least 1962. All three women's pedagogy-based research aimed to support students from multilingual, racialized, and systemically marginalized backgrounds. In addition, their scholarship reflected many of the values widely held within composition studies today—values like student-centered teaching and learning, and critical reflection of the positionings and biases of teachers. Below are profiles of these three women. While Lin, Ouchi, and Ching seem to have been largely forgotten within contemporary rhetoric and composition studies, the work they have left behind shows how women of Asian descent have been contributing to conversations within NCTE and CCCC, serving as leaders and organizers within these professional organizations, and supporting students of color since at least the 1960s.

San-su C. Lin (–2008)

The late San-su Chen Lin was one of the earliest individuals of Asian descent to participate in NCTE, present at the NCTE Annual Convention, and publish in *College Composition and Communication* and *College English* (see figure 1). A linguist who worked at two historically Black colleges, Claflin University in Orangeburg, South Carolina, and later, Southern University in Baton Rouge, Louisiana, Lin's work focused on teaching and learning strategies for working with systemically marginalized students. As evidenced by the publications she left behind, Lin often drew from her experiences teaching Black students at Claflin and Southern, and she often centered her students' feelings about their home languages and about learning "Standard American English." What's more, Lin articulated several perspectives that seem to be either reiterated or further developed by scholars down the road, and that have been attributed to esteemed essays within rhetoric and composition. She earned her doctorate in education from the Teachers College at Columbia University in 1953. Her dissertation was titled, "Practice Materials on the Use of the English Article: A Supplementary Textbook for Chinese Students Learning English," an early example of scholarship on teaching English for multilingual speakers. She served as the head of the English department at Claflin University, and began working at Southern University in Baton Rouge Louisiana in 1964.

Figure 1. Top left: Photograph of San-su C. Lin from the 1966 NCTE Convention Program.

In November 1962, Lin presented "An Experiment in Changing Dialect Patterns" at the NCTE Convention in Miami, Florida. She published this paper in *College English* a year later, as part of a roundtable assessing professional preparation. In this paper, Lin describes a national grant-funded, laboratory-based experiment at Claflin College that used "pattern practice techniques," which were "widely accepted in foreign language programs and in English-as-a-foreign-language programs," to test applicability for nonstandard dialect speakers learning "Standard American English" (645). By treating her students' home dialects as a second language, it can be argued that Lin implicitly validated Black language as its own distinct language. What's more, Lin was concerned with "not only [...] changing the student's dialect patterns, but also in changing the student's attitude toward his language and himself." For instance, she asked, "How does a student feel, when after twelve years of English instruction in elementary school and high school, his language is still considered 'substandard' or incorrect?" (644). This question signals similar kinds of concerns that resonate with Geneva Smitherman in her groundbreaking work on Students Right to Their Own Language. Lin goes on to explain that at this point in the program, she found student writings to be more purposeful and interesting when their home dialects were validated, "showing that the students really took pleasure in learning to express themselves" ("An Experiment" 647), rather than seeing "proper" English writing as an unattainable chore. Lin ends the essay with a reflection, saying, "I am not sure these students will break with their dialect patterns completely and forever. I suspect that they will not, and it is quite possible that they should not. On the other hand, the experiment has given them firm ground on which to build up their self-reliance and language resourcefulness. They will have something to fall back on when they find themselves in a situation vastly different from situations they encounter at home" ("An Experiment" 647). While Lin, at times, fell prey to describing Black students' backgrounds as a "shackle" disadvantaging them, she was also clearly ambivalent about the idea that they should completely break with their home dialect patterns ("Disadvantaged Student?" 752).

As one of the early researchers responsible for administering English education for black students, Lin was read and cited by scholars doing work on African American and Black language. For instance, her work is referenced in the notes of Geneva Smitherman's *Talkin and Testifyin: The Language of Black America* as an example of "difference" language programs (264), and Smitherman's "'God Don't Never Change': Black English from a Black Perspective" published in *College English* in 1973, footnotes Lin's *Pattern Practice in the Teaching of Standard English to Students with a Non-Standard Dialect* as an example program "for the 'disadvantaged'" Black student. Lin delivered a speech at Tougaloo College in 1966, as part of the sharply contested Brown-Tougaloo Language Project Lecture Series (Williams), in which she described the methodology of audiolingual pattern practice, complicated conceptions of "standard" English, and reflected on the limitations of teachers who sought to teach students the "standard" dialect ("College and School"). Lin was later awarded an Educational Professional Development Act grant from the U.S. Office of Education to develop an institute for Advanced Study in English, Grades 1–6, held at Southern University in 1970 ("Colleges").

As shown by Phuong Minh Tran's research on Asian/Asian American publications in *College Composition and Communication* (*CCC*) between 1950 and 2010 (included in this collection), Lin was the second Asian author to be published in *CCC*, and the first Asian writer to publish a *CCC* piece that explicitly addressed issues of social inequality pertaining to literacy. Her 1965 *CCC* essay was a Staffroom Interchange titled, "A Developmental English Program for the Culturally Disadvantaged." This publication, along with some of her later work, was concerned with not only student motivations, but also teacher attitudes and preparation, and the ways in which these attitudes were biased as a result of culture and class privilege. For example, Lin's 1967 "Disadvantaged Student? Or Disadvantaged Teacher?" published two years later in NCTE's *The English Journal*, discusses the kinds of biases that inevitably limit the perspectives of teachers working with populations that have been marginalized by the socially stratified infrastructures of education, arguing that:

> A teacher is disadvantaged in the same way that a student is disadvantaged. First, if the disadvantaged student is one who has a negative self-concept, the disadvantaged teacher is one who has a negative concept of the child he is supposed to help. Second, like the disadvantaged child, a disadvantaged teacher has a value scale very much limited by his own cultural or class orientation. Third, the disadvantaged teacher lacks adequate background to help him understand the nature of language and the functions of literature and their unique place in the education of the disadvantaged child. (752)

In so doing, Lin enacts a self-reflexivity that questions the positions of teachers and de-centers a hierarchy that positions teachers as simple authority figures. What's more, this excerpt in many ways is echoed by statements from Mina Shaughnessy's seminal "Diving In: An Introduction to Basic Writing," published nine years later in 1976: "But, as we come to know these students better, we begin to see that the greatest barrier to our work with them is our ignorance of them and of the very subject we have contracted to teach" (238). Lin goes on to explain that "[t]his tendency to repudiate anything different from one's own cherished values reflects an emphasis on strict conformity which is a narrowly conceived middle-class value. To enforce strict conformity, one is likely to lose sight of other values, to become inflexible, intolerant, self-righteous" ("Disadvantaged Student?" 753). She later reiterates, "[r]ich language experience can thus include the use of both standard English and the child's dialect; one need not be rejected in favor of the other" ("Disadvantaged Student?" 755).

Lin participated in NCTE in several programmatic capacities: she is listed as a consultant for a 1965 CCCC workshop on Teaching the Culturally Disadvantaged; she was part of the 1966 Committee on Dialect Recording, which worked to gain a sense of how dialects affect students' ability to learn "Standard American English"[10]; and she was elected to serve as a member of the College Section Committee in 1972.

Shizuko Ouchi (1911–88)

Shizuko Ouchi was a Program Specialist in Language Arts at the Secondary Level for the Hawai'i State Department of Education in Honolulu (see figure 2). Ouchi served as General Chairman of the Fifty-Seventh Annual Meeting of the National Council of Teachers of English with Richard S. Alm, Professor of Education at the University of Hawai'i (see figure 3). The 1967 convention took place at the Ilikai, Hilton Hawaiian Village, and Sheraton Hotels in Honolulu. Ouchi and Alm's organizational work is remarkable as the program reflects significantly more attention to Asian and Pacific Islander literacies than ever before. For example, the Arts and Cultures of the Pacific was one of five major strands included in the program. For the first time, the NCTE convention included panels on topics like "Significant Themes and Motifs in Polynesian Tradition," "Legends of Asia: Japan, China, Korea," and "Culture and Dance of the Philippines." The specificity of these panels to particular Asian and Pacific ethnic groups is notable, as it had been more common to see broader categories like World or Eastern Literatures in NCTE conven-

---

10   Elizabeth Carr, Mauna Richardson, and Barbara Kim's names are also listed for Pidgin.

tion programs up until this time. Among the twelve study groups included in the program were Folklore of the Pacific Basin; Teaching English as a Second Language with an emphasis on languages of the Pacific; and Literature of the Pacific and Asia (Marckwardt). These strands and study groups are significant as they likely opened up space for larger numbers of Asian and Pacific Islander conference participants. For example, Carlos P. Romulo, President of the University of the Philippines and Secretary of Education of the Republic of the Philippines, was an Opening General Session Speaker. Romulo spoke on "English and the Interpretation of the Asian Scene." Daniel Akaka, who later became the first U.S. senator of Native Hawaiian ancestry, participated as a panel Chairman.

Figure 2. Bottom center: Photograph of Shizuko Ouchi from the 1966 NCTE Convention Program.

While her work as General Chairman of the conference is significant, Ouchi's contribution to NCTE went well beyond this programmatic work. Her work in centering marginalized perspectives in the teaching of English goes back to at least 1962, when she was part of a team who planned and launched the journal *Educational Perspectives* at the University of Hawai'i at Mānoa. The journal was intended as "a place for local authors; a place to deal with local issues" (McEwan 25). At the 1963 NCTE Convention in San Francisco, Ouchi presented "Haiku Says Hi! to Tintern Abbey," on a panel titled

Figure 3. From the 1967 NCTE Convention program, Shizuko Ouchi and Richard Alm, General Chairmen.

"Interpreting the Literature of the East to Western Readers." At the 1965 convention in Boston, she presented "Toward Nongraded English Programs in the High School." Ouchi was nominated numerous times—though never elected—for various positions on NCTE committees, including the Secondary Section Committee and the Nominating Committee. In 1969, she was nominated for the position of Director-at-Large. In this same year, she spoke on a NCTE convention roundtable on *The Role of State Departments of Education in Shaping English Curricula*.

In October 1968, Ouchi published a short piece in *Hawaii Schools* describing a transitional elementary English program that was developed as a result of the 1966–67 legislative mandate ordering that the Hawai'i State Department of Education initiate a Programming-Planning-Budgeting System. In this essay, Ouchi describes the development of a transitional literature program, briefly touching on the decision to include Hawaiian literary texts, explaining, "no two teachers can agree wholly on titles to be included in a quality literature program, or even the grade level to which they should be assigned [...] [however,] appropriate Hawaiian literature [has been purchased]" (7). While it is unclear whether Ouchi was referring to what we now distinguish as literature about Hawai'i, local literature of Hawai'i, or indigenous Hawaiian literature, it is notable that Ouchi took explicit note of these issues regarding the selection of literary texts not long before the formation of the Task Force on Racism and Bias in the Teaching of English, and several years prior to the formation of the Textbook Review Committee.

In 1968 and 1969, Ouchi participated in a Special National Defense Education Act Institute for State Supervisors of English and Reading, which took place in five cities across the United States (Evertts, "Final Technical Report on the Institute"). Ouchi also attended the institutes on "New Content in English Programs" in Urbana, Illinois; "Composition, Rhetoric, and School Programs" in Seattle, Washington; and "Language and School Programs" in Sturbridge, Massachusetts. According to an NCTE follow-up report, the course instructor for the institute on "Composition, Rhetoric, and School Programs," Dr. Robert Gorrell, "invited participants to write a selection and bring [it] to the Institute" (Evertts, "Final Technical Report on the Institute" 146, 170). The report does not indicate a more specific prompt, but it does note that among three writings selected at random, "the group felt that Shizuko Ouchi's best expressed what [participants at the institute] felt about composition and its difficulties" (Evertts, "Final Technical Report on the Institute" 146). For this reason, the report included Ouchi's writing, and I quote it at length here:

> It's like this, see, my teacher she no understand I really like to learn how to write good, really good, but she no give me da chance.
>
> Like she tell da class, "On page 45, you will find a list of 10 topics. Choose one topic, think it over carefully, and write a two-page composition. Be sure to pay careful attention to organization, coherence, unity, and especially punctuation and spelling. And if your paper does not observe the standard form, I won't even read it. Be sure it's interesting."
>
> So da class, eager-beaver like, we all open da book, an' I read topic one: "A Meeting with a Skunk in the Woods." Now I tell you, dat's one stupid topic—da only skunk I ever know was da one what squealed on me when I stole four hubcaps. And it was in no woods. It was down by da beach.
>
> Da next one: "Camping in the Ozarks." What's dat? Or where's dat? But teacher says I no can write about da time us guys all camped at Makaha waiting for da big surf tournament. She must think you can only camp in da Ozarks, poor stupid thing. An' I could tell her a t'ing or two dat's real interesting that happen in da camp on da beach. Too bad for her.
>
> What's dis? "A Canoe Trip Down the Colorado." Dat's da square state. I got one Japanese friend. Da poor booger was born in Colorado so da grandfather named him Kakuro—square state boy. But da canoe— da only canoes I know stay in Waikiki where da rich fat tourists dat's too scared to go on da surfboard go—just pretending dey're getting big

thrills, only dey're really scared. An' dey pretend dey're oaring, but da beach boys doing all da work. How I goin' put da Waikiki canoe in Colorado anyway? Cost too much. Anyway, my ma only get enough kau kau for us because her soldier boyfriend bring us food from the PX.

"Our new car." Dat's a laugh. Ha, ha.

"My plans for college." I no plan for nothing, but I know I going land where I hear dere's a college of hard knocks, but it sure no be worse dan dis.

"Salmon Fishing in the Pacific Northwest."

At last, maybe I can write about da spear fishing down Maili, da time I run away from home and catch da squid and kill him by biting da eye (no faint, you guys), and da time I catch four lobsters in da coral hole. But was too good to eat, so I sell 'em to some rich looking guys—four for five bucks! Den we get the case of Primo and suck 'em up.

But da teacher tell me I no can choose dis topic, and I no talk about beer, gotta be salmon fishing without da beverage. Give up. Da only salmon I know is da lomi lomi salmon my ma make special when her guy come. And me, I no care who bring 'em, because it sure ono.

So dere's no more topics, only stupid kine. I think da teacher call them imaginative, and me, I call 'em no imagination.

If only she would let me write about da surf in Makaha, and my surfboards. See, I get five, one second-hand one I bought with my fish money, da other four, real good looking ones, I happen to find lying around da beach. But any board take me at least half mile out, and I wait, and I paddle little bit, and pretty soon I see dis big one come rolling in. No break, mind you, only roll, and I can see, she's going to give me some big thrill if only I can catch her right. Sometimes I just miss her, and I go under fast, and when I come up, dere's my board ready to konk me on da head, or a dumb surfer heading strayit for me. Auwe! When I catch her just right, the thrill, da smooth thrill—I balance, I pilot her, I push her to make the ride reach the beach. An' I no get tired or hungry or angry. It's only me an' my board.

But da teacher she tell me, "No, Moki."

An' anyway, I no give one damn for da comma or da colum or colon. She no try read my writing too. She tell me I no dot my eyes. How can I. I got good eyesight.

So you see, she really force me to play hookey. Da more worser part, when I start getting homesick for my friends an' go back to school she stil goin' tell me write about, if not canoes and skunks, going be something like training a cub, or going deer stalking or what I did when I no could go out to play because dere was too much snow.

Well, no can win 'em all, but I sure wish dey make teachers more smarter so I can write what I like. You think dis is big order? (Evertts, "Final Technical Report on the Institute" 170–71)

This piece, written in Hawai'i Creole English, vividly illustrates the perspective of a student who does not identify with the dominant, middle-class, European American culture, is from a geographical region that is not reflected in their textbooks or writing prompts, and speaks a dialect quite distinct from "Standard American English." Importantly, Ouchi shows how educational problems that might arise in such contexts may not be the result of a lack of creativity on the part of students, but instead a lack of creativity on the part of teachers, who might not tailor course materials for the specific, local population of students. In addition, Ouchi uses these writing prompts to illustrate the kinds of regional, cultural, class, and racial/ethnic misperceptions that pervade many English education programs, curricula, and teaching practices, including culturally-biased prompts, and a binary view of correct and incorrect writing.

In 1970, Ouchi served as a lecturer at an NCTE Education Program Development Act (EPDA) Fellowship Program at University of Illinois at Urbana-Champaign, which focused on the language learning of disadvantaged children for whom English is a second language or dialect. One participant responded, "Shizuko Ouchi presented an exciting view of inservice education that districts, regions, and even other states might look more deeply into" (Evertts, "Final Technical Report on the Special EPDA" 227). More specific documentation illustrating what, precisely, Ouchi presented has not been located, but one can only imagine that her presentation was as lively and creative as her own writing, above.

Doris C. Ching (c. 1931–)
Doris Camvone Ching spent much of her career at California State University in Los Angeles, researching curriculum and instruction for bilingual children at the elementary level. Ching earned her doctorate in education from Harvard University in 1960, her MA in education, from Harvard, and her BA in education from the University of Hawai'i in 1952 (Sinclair 88). Her doctoral research explored the English language learning of bilingual children attending elementary school in the Kalihi area of Honolulu, Hawai'i. Her dissertation was titled, *Evaluation of a Program for the Improvement of English Language Ability and Reading Achievement in Hawaiian Bilingual Children.* Ching taught at an elementary school in Kalihi for a short time, before taking leave without pay to accept a summer teaching position at Seattle University in 1961. That fall, she would begin a position as Assistant Professor of Education at Western Washington State College (now Western Washington University). One year later, in 1962, she moved on to take a position as a member of the faculty at Los Angeles State College (now California State University at Los Angeles). She remained at California State University, in the Division of Curriculum and Instruction, until her retirement from her position of Professor of Education in 1991 ("Emeriti Faculty").

Ching's "Effects of a Six Month Remedial English Program on Oral, Writing, and Reading Skills of Third Grade Hawaiian Bilingual Children," was published in *The Journal of Experimental Education* in 1963. In this essay, Ching presents lessons for dealing directly with "specific errors associated with pidgin English" (133), based on her study of a program for bilingual children. For this study, Ching tracked the progress of 246 third-grade children attending two public schools in Kalihi, Honolulu. What's more, she notes that the children were primarily from lower-middle socioeconomic backgrounds, with many of them coming from bilingual homes. She writes that the children spoke or understood Japanese, Chinese, Filipino, Hawaiian, Korean and Spanish. She also specified the backgrounds of the teachers: Chinese, Japanese, and Chinese-Hawaiian, all born in Hawai'i, and able to "speak English well and understand pidgin English" (133).

In "Methods for the Bilingual Child," published in 1965 in NCTE's *Elementary English,* Ching surveys existing methods in the literature on teaching English language to bilingual students, discussing studies in California, New Mexico, Puerto Rico, and Seattle, Washington. Ching contends that bilingualism can be used to describe even those English-speaking children for whom "Standard American English" is not the dominant language, "without qualification as to the degree of difference between the two languages or systems known; it is immaterial whether the two systems are 'languages,' 'dialects of the same language,' or 'varieties of the same dialect'" (22). Like Lin, Ching interrogated the lines between bilingualism and bidialectalism. The following year, Ching delivered a presentation at the 1966 NCTE Convention in Houston, Texas, titled, "Teaching Standard English Dialect—To Whom? When? How?" (see figure 4).

Figure 4. Top Right: Photograph of Doris C. Ching from the 1966 NCTE Convention Program.

Ching's 1976 *Reading and the Bilingual Child*, published with the International Reading Association, is where she elaborated on the "special needs of the bilingual child" (2), including awareness about differing cultural values and fostering a sense of the child's personal worth, in some ways echoing the attitudes of Lin's earlier work. For instance, she writes, "[i]f a child speaks a language, other than English or a nonstandard dialect of English at home, the teacher should be accepting of the language or dialect with which the child is most familiar. The teacher should help the child see that his language is accepted and that he may continue to use it with his family and friends" (10). While Ching did not appear to be particularly active in NCTE, her work on bilingual literacy education was widely cited by scholars in ELL, ESL, and bilingual education, and it was used to further research on English in Hawai'i,

American Indian literacy instruction, and literacy development in deaf students (Battle; Bockmiller; Evans; Tsuzaki and Reinecke).

CONCLUSION

I arrange this essay in two parts to make transparent my research process, and to draw attention to the contrasting narratives that emerged as I, in one moment, worked primarily from within the institutional archives at NCTE to tell a coherent caucus history, and in another, enacted a feminist approach of slow scholarship and recursive spatial movement. At the center of my former narrative were the voices of two men, Frank Chin and Jeffery Paul Chan, who made waves by exerting a compelling argument about the lack of Asian Americans within the literary canon in a way that was not only timely given the concurrent push for ethnic and Asian American studies in the United States, but also loud, forceful, and contentious. One might posit that Chin and Chan were more visible within the archives because their work was a kind of fast scholarship, and in many ways reflective of dominant perceptions of activism and institutional intervention. In the latter narrative were profiles of San-su C. Lin, Shizuko Ouchi, and Doris C. Ching—three Asian women who were active participants in NCTE and CCCC between 1962 and 1976. As women who spent their careers teaching, researching, and administering programs for multilingual and systemically marginalized students, they emerge as some of the earliest moments of Asian/Asian American institutional and scholarly activism in the discipline. Their interventions were no less significant, but they were, in some ways, slower, and what the introduction to this collection would refer to as important "sustaining threads." But San-su C. Lin, Shizuko Ouchi, and Doris C. Ching only became visible once I was forced to slow down, when I revisited documents from the archives, when I started looking more slowly and deeply, and when I stopped prioritizing getting the project done in an expedient manner.

My initial unseeing makes visible, for me, the ways in which the neoliberal ethic of expediency can work to render invisible particular bodies and their labor—especially those that tend to fall into a pattern of misrecognition in dominant U.S. academic culture. Indeed, the very visibility and embodiment of Ching, Lin, and Ouchi, is meaningful, particularly as Asian women's bodies are often rendered invisible in the discipline's tellings of its history. Their teaching, administrative, and scholarly work were early articulations of perspectives that are now commonly and widely held in our discipline, though largely attributed to those who came later—for instance, approaches that center the student, validate their cultural and linguistic perspectives, and take into account their emotionalized experience of literacy learning. In addition, slow labor—the kinds of work that are not typically met with immediate public response or institutionally-recognized, momentous results—tends to be rendered insignificant and is thus often invisible in disciplinary histories. A slow scholarship approach allowed me to better explore the "larger terrain of developed and undeveloped possibilities," as Royster puts it in the epigraph to this chapter. Through slow scholarship and recursive spatial movement, photographs and texts that initially seemed only marginally significant became increasingly important; in other words, there were traces of these women as they were included in NCTE convention programs, but it took more time to understand the impact of their work, and it required looking outside of the NCTE Archives.

We know relatively little about these women, in part because institutional interests have shaped the archives. Chin and Chan's legacy has been preserved through the NCTE Archives, perhaps in part because NCTE was concerned about potential legal outcomes that might result from "Racist Love." But we must also consider how the appeals of fast scholarship can make it difficult to see the value and significance of the stamina and patience required to engage in "slow" work, and to build "sustaining threads." On one hand, while fast approaches can be effective for appealing to administrators and enabling top-down change, and while the story of Chin and Chan indeed works to counter stereotypes about Asians as meek and compliant, the appeal of such approaches can render invisible equally important and needed approaches for systemic intervention that may be quieter, less outwardly antagonistic, and slower—for instance, teaching and research that supports systemically marginalized students and communities or that challenges the status quo in other ways, or local conversations that enable organizational and cultural shifts.

While fast scholarship may be exciting, we must also interrogate the ways in which such approaches are often tied to attachments to institutional and professional goals and anxieties over scholarly production. Mountz, Bonds, Mansfield, et al., suggest that "Care-full scholarship is also about engaging different publics (not least our own research subjects), refining or even rejecting earlier ideas, engaging in activism and advocacy, and generally amplifying the potential impact of our scholarship rather than moving on to the next product that 'counts' to administrators" (1245). What's more, by contrasting these sets of narratives based on a reflection of my research methods and concerns, I "not only emphasize women as an additional historical subject but also pose methodological challenges to predominant theoretical models" (Wu 85). Specifically, those methodological challenges include concerns about the unseeing that can result as a consequence of fast scholarship—of the kinds of work that are encouraged by the neoliberal temporal regimes of our current time. Thus, I argue for slowing down as a form of institutional and scholarly activism, particularly for those who have the agency and ability to slow down, whose livelihoods are not primarily contingent on their ability to successfully engage in fast scholarship. In calling attention to not only the works of Lin, Ouchi, and Ching, but also the structural circumstances that make telling a history that includes their work difficult, I aim to "[redirect] attention to patterns and traditions of rhetorical leadership" among Asian/Asian American teachers and scholars (Monberg, "Listening for Legacies" 87), and to call attention to the ways in which Asian/Asian American activism in NCTE and CCCC has often gone unnoticed. This institutional activism tends to take shape through everyday activities, sustaining threads that have collectively contributed to the function of these organizations and the workings of the discipline of rhetoric and composition.

Relatedly, questions must also be raised as to why these women have not been visible in more recent tellings of the organization's history, and why they have not been visible in relation to wider organizational efforts such as the Task Force on Racism and Bias in the Teaching of English, which was instituted while they were active members of NCTE and/or CCCC. Were Lin, Ouchi, and Ching asked to participate in the Task Force? Did they decline? Did their identities as Asian women play a role in this outcome? Was it because their professional identities were not primarily that of literary scholars? Were they overlooked, as they were by me, for two male Asian American literary writers whose affect also fit predominant conceptions of activist work? Given Ouchi's active role within the organization that went back several years prior to the 1969 Task Force on Racism and Bias in the Teaching of English, and given her interest in cultural bias within English education textbooks, one is left to wonder why she in particular was not a part of the Task Force.

Finally, I ask that we take a moment to consider these narratives not only in contrast to one another, but also as a complementary set of articulations about the nature of Asian/Asian American activism in institutional spaces. Monberg discusses recursive spatial movement as a way of (re)writing home and exploring "paths of becoming for community members"

("Writing Home" 28). I understand this to mean that moments that have been marked as key for one's becoming shape the path that can emerge as result. Through this project, I learned to "dwell differently with a community familiar to [me]: feeling deeper textures, hearing 'the different story under every rock,' seeing the complicated exigencies confronting [my community], and re/writing the histories of movement and social action that have taken place" in my life and my community (Monberg, "Writing Home" 42). Over the course of this project, my position within the caucus also shifted. I started the project as a newcomer who felt unsure about the goals or the purpose of the caucus. In the time that passed as the project unfolded, my relationships with caucus members and members of other caucuses deepened, and I began to see the caucus more and more as my "home" at CCCC. In this way, this project literally enabled my "civic and racial becoming" (Monberg, "Writing Home" 31).

More importantly, though, a story built around Chan, Chin, Ching, Inada, Lin, Lum, and Ouchi together can serve as an "alternative institutional memory" (Monberg, "Writing Home" 36) that rewrites the story of Asian/Asian American participation in NCTE and CCCC. As a collective, Chan, Chin, Ching, Inada, Lin, Lum, and Ouchi represent early and varied approaches to institutional and scholarly activism, and their stories remind us to recognize diverse forms of labor as necessary for meaningful change, especially in the midst of a neoliberal work ethic. Let us use these considerations to unpack what it means to be working toward that continual intervention.

WORKS CITED

Barnes, Clive. "Stage: 'Chickencoop Chinaman' Identity Problem." Rev. of *The Chickencoop Chinaman*, by Frank Chin. *New York Times* 14 June 1972: 46M. Print.

Battle, Edwina Larry. *A Comparison of Two Vocabulary Development Approaches on Intermediate Grade Menominee Indian Children*. Diss. The University of Wisconsin-Madison, 1975. Ann Arbor: UMI, 1975. Print.

Bockmiller, Patricia R. "Hearing-Impaired Children: Learning to Read a Second Language." *American Annals of the Deaf* 126.7 (1981): 810–13. Print.

Chan, Jeffery Paul, Frank Chin, Lawson Fusao Inada, and Shawn Wong. *The Big Aiiieeeee!: An Anthology of Chinese American and Japanese American Literature*. New York: Signet, 1991. Print.

Chin, Frank and Jeffery Chan. Letter to Robert Hogan. 9 July 1971. MS. NCTE Archives, Urbana, IL.

Chin, Frank and Jeffery Paul Chan. "Racist Love." *Seeing Through Shuck*. Ed. Richard Kastalanetz. New York: Ballantine Books. 65-79. Print.

Chin, Frank, Jeffery Paul Chan, Lawson Fusao Inada, and Shawn Hsu Wong. *Aiiieeeee!: An Anthology of Asian-American Writers*. Washington, D.C.: Howard UP, 1974. Print.

Chin, Frank, and Frank Ching. "Chin vs. Ching, Part II" *Bridge* 2.3, (February 1973): 34-37. Print.

Chin, Frank, and Frank Ching. "Who's Afraid of Frank Chin, or Is It Ching?" *Bridge* 2.2, (December 1972): 29-34. Print.

Ching, Doris Camvone. "Effects of a Six Month Remedial English Program on Oral, Writing, and Reading Skills of Third Grade Hawaiian Bilingual Children." *The Journal of Experimental Education* 32.2 (1963): 133–45. Print.

Ching, Doris C. *Evaluation of a Program for the Improvement of English Language Ability and Reading Achievement in Hawaiian Bilingual Children*. Diss. Harvard University, 1960. Print.

—. "Methods for the Bilingual Child." *Elementary English* (1965): 22–27. Print.

—. *Reading and the Bilingual Child*. International Reading Association, 1976.

"College and School Notes." *The Crisis: A Record of the Darker Races* November 1965: 598–99. Print.

"Colleges." *The Afro American* 29 March 1969: 12. Print.

Derrida, Jacques. *Archive Fever: A Freudian Impression*. Chicago: U of Chicago P, 1996.

Dwyer, Carlota Cardenas. "Early History of the Latino/Chicano Caucus." NCTE Centennial Writing and Working for Change Founders Panel, Part 1: 1960s-1970s. NCTE Convention. Chicago Hilton, Chicago, IL. 19 Nov 2011.

"Emeriti Faculty." *University Catalog 2012–2013.* California State University, Los Angeles. 2013.

Evans, Charlotte. "Literacy Development in Deaf Students: Case Studies in Bilingual Teaching and Learning." *American Annals of the Deaf* 149.1 (2004): 17–27. Print.

Evertts, Eldonna L. "Final Technical Report on the Institute for State Supervisors of English and Reading." National Council of Teachers of English; Office of Education. Department of Health, Education, and Welfare, 1969.

—. "Final Technical Report on the Special EPDA Institute and Fellowship Program in English for Speakers of Other Languages or Dialects for State Supervisors of English and Reading." National Council of Teachers of English; Office of Education. Department of Health, Education, and Welfare, 1970.

Fong, Katherine M. "FCC Oral Arguments of the Chinese Media Committee." Chinese for Affirmative Action. Chinese Media Committee. 8 Jan. 1973. Web. http://www.eric.ed.gov/PDFS/ED071442.pdf

Gibbs, Sandra E. Letter to Joe Huang. 3 August 1977. TS. NCTE Archives, Urbana, IL.

Gonzalez, Roseann Duenas, Rafael Castillo, John Gardenhire, Kris Gutierrez, Linda Hogan, Lawson Inada, Gwendolyn Alexander, and Sandra E. Gibbs. "Policy Expanding Opportunities: Academic Success for Culturally and Linguistically Diverse Students." NCTE 1986 Task Force on Racism and Bias in the Teaching of English. *College English* (1987): 550-552.

Hoang, Haivan V. *Writing against Racial Injury: The Politics of Asian American Student Rhetoric.* Pittsburgh: U of Pittsburgh P, 2015.

—. "Asian American Rhetorical Memory and A 'Memory that is only Sometimes Our Own." *Representations: Doing Asian American Rhetoric.* Ed. LuMing Mao and Morris Young. Logan: Utah State UP, 2008. 62–82. Print.

Hogan, Robert. Letter to Philip Zimmerly. 14 July 1971. TS. NCTE Archives, Urbana, IL.

Inada, Lawson Fusao. "A Selected Bibliography on Asian American Literature." NCTE Archives, Urbana, IL. 1975.

—. Letter to the author. 13 Dec. 2011. TS.

Kelly, Ernece B., ed. *Searching for America.* Urbana: NCTE, 1972. Print.

Leon, Kendall. "La Hermandad and Chicanas Organizing: The Community Rhetoric of the Comisión Femenil Mexicana Nacional." *Community Literacy Journal* 7.2 (Spring 2013): 1–20. Print.

Lin, San-su C. "A Developmental English Program for the Culturally Disadvantaged." *College Composition and Communication* (1965): 273–76. Print.

—. "An Experiment in Changing Dialect Patterns: The Claflin Project." *College English* (1963): 644–47. Print.

—. "Disadvantaged Student? Or Disadvantaged Teacher?" *English Journal* (1967): 751–56. Print.

—. *Pattern Practice in the Teaching of Standard English to Students with a Non-Standard Dialect.* New York: Teachers College, Columbia University, 1965.

—. *Practice Materials on the Use of the English Article: A Supplementary Textbook for Chinese Students Learning English.* Diss. New York: Teachers College, Columbia University, 1953. Print.

Lum, John. Memo to Sandra Gibbs. 25 May 1977. TS. NCTE Archives, Urbana, IL.

—. Letter to Task Force on Racism and Bias. 17 December 1971. TS. NCTE Archives, Urbana, IL.

Marckwardt, Albert H. "NCTE Counciletter: Plan Now for Hawaii." *English Journal* (1967): 759–60. Print.

Maxwell, John. Letter to Marjorie Farmer. 22 August, 1980. TS. NCTE Archives, Urbana, IL.

McEwan, Hunter. "*Educational Perspectives*: The First Ten Years." *Educational Perspectives* 33.2 (2000): 25–29. Print.

Mecenas, Jolivette. "A Career of Acting 'Ill-Mannered': An Interview with Jeffery Paul Chan on Reviewing Textbooks for NCTE and Teaching Ethnic Studies (Because it is Good for People)." *Listening to Our Elders: Working and Writing for Change.* Ed. Samantha Blackmon, Cristina Kirklighter, Steve Parks. Philadelphia: New City Community Press; Logan: Utah State UP, 2011. 28–44. Print.

—. "Beyond 'Asian American' and Back: Coalitional Rhetoric in Print and New Media." *Representations: Doing Asian American Rhetoric.* Ed. LuMing Mao and Morris Young. Logan: Utah State UP, 2008. 198–217. Print.

Monberg, Terese Guinsatao. "Listening for Legacies, or How I Began to Hear Dorothy Laigo Cordova, the Pinay Behind the Podium Known as FANHS." *Representations: Doing Asian American Rhetoric.* Ed. LuMing Mao and Morris Young. Logan: Utah State UP, 2008. 83–105. Print.

—. "Writing Home or Writing *As* the Community: Toward a Theory of Recursive Spatial Movement for Students of Color in Service-Learning Courses." *Reflections: Writing, Service-Learning, and Community Literacy* 8.3 (2009): 21–51. Print.

Mountz, Alison, Anne Bonds, Becky Mansfield, et al. "For Slow Scholarship: A Feminist Politics of Resistance through Collective Action in the Neoliberal University." *ACME: An International Journal for Critical Geographies* 14.4 (2015): 1235-59. Web.

"Nonwhite minorities are still not adequately represented in educational materials now being used in schools, according to the National Council of Teachers of English." NCTE Archives, Urbana, IL. 1971.

Novick, Julius. "No Cheers for The 'Chinaman.'" Rev. of *The Chickencoop Chinaman*, by Frank Chin. *New York Times* 18 June 1972: 3. Print.

Okawa, Gail Y. "Unbundling: Archival Research and Japanese American Communal Memory of US Justice Department Internment, 1941–45." *Beyond the Archives: Research as a Lived Process.* Ed. Gesa E. Kirsch and Liz Rohan. Southern Illinois UP, 2008. 93-106. Print.

Ouchi, Shizuko. "Elementary English Language Arts Program in Transition." *Hawaii Schools* 5.2 (1968): 6–9. Print.

Powell, Malea. "Dreaming Charles Eastman: Cultural Memory, Autobiography, and Geography in Indigenous Rhetorical Histories." *Beyond the Archives: Research as a Lived Process.* Ed. Gesa E. Kirsch and Liz Rohan. Carbondale: Southern Illinois UP, 2008. 115–27. Print.

"Proposed changes in the 'Criteria for Teaching Materials in Reading and Literature' to be presented to the Board of Directors, November 25, 1971." NCTE Archives, Urbana, IL. 1971.

Royster, Jacqueline Jones. "Disciplinary Landscaping, Or, Contemporary Challenges in the History of Rhetoric." *Philosophy and Rhetoric* 36.2 (2003): 148–67. Print.

Shaughnessy, Mina. "Diving In: An Introduction to Basic Writing." *College Composition and Communication* 27.3 (October 1976): 234–39. Print.

Shimabukuro, Mira. "'Me Inwardly, Before I Dared': Japanese Americans Writing-to-Gaman." *College English* (2011): 648–71. Print.

—. "Relocating Authority: Coauthor(iz)ing a Japanese American Ethos of Resistance under Mass Incarceration." *Representations: Doing Asian American Rhetoric.* Ed. LuMing Mao and Morris Young. Logan: Utah State UP, 2008. 127–49. Print.

Sinclair, Gregg M. *The University of Hawaii 1951–52: Report of Gregg M. Sinclair, President.* University of Hawai'i, Dec. 1952. Print.

Smitherman, Geneva. "African American Language and Education: History and Controversy in the Twentieth Century." *The Oxford Handbook of African American Language.* Ed. Sonja Lanehart. Oxford UP, 2015. 547-65. Print.

—. "'God Don't Never Change': Black English from a Black Perspective." *College English* (1973): 828–33. Print.

—. *Talkin and Testifyin: The Language of Black America.* Detroit: Wayne State UP, 1977. Print.

Tachiki, Amy, Eddie Wong, Franklin Odo, and Buck Wong, eds. *Roots: An Asian American Reader.* Los Angeles: U of California Los Angeles Asian American Studies Center, 1971. Print.

Task Force on Racism and Bias in the Teaching of English. "Criteria for Teaching Materials in Reading and Literature." National Council of Teachers of English. 1970. NCTE Archives, Urbana, IL. Print.

The Association of Chinese Teachers. *TACT/ESAA Newsletter: Project for Cross-Cultural Understanding.* 4.1 (Dec. 1977) NCTE Archives, Urbana, IL. Print.

Tsuzaki, Stanley M. and John E. Reinecke. "English in Hawaii: An Annotated Bibliography." *Oceanic Linguistics Special Publications* 1, (1966): 1–61. Print.

Wei, William. *The Asian American Movement.* Philadelphia: Temple UP, 1993. Print.

Williams, Niketa. "Brown-Tougaloo Language Project: A Controversial Experiment." Brown-Tougaloo Exchange. Freedom Now!: An Archival Project of Tougaloo College and Brown University. 2003. Web.

Wu, Hui. "Historical Studies of Rhetorical Women Here and There: Methodological Challenges to Dominant Interpretive Frameworks." *Rhetoric Society Quarterly* 32.1 (2002): 81–97. Print.

Zimmerly, Philip. Letter to Robert Hogan. 17 July 1971. TS. NCTE Archives, Urbana, IL.

CIRCULATION ESSAY

The Presence of Asian/ Asian American Scholars in College Composition and Communication (1950–2010)

Phuong Minh Tran

FOREWORD

Phuong Minh Tran presented the results of her study on the presence of Asian/Asian American scholars in the field as part of a co-presentation with K. Hyoejin Yoon in the 2015 CCCC panel, "Asian/Asian American Scholarship in Rhetoric and Composition: Risks and Rewards." As the title of the sponsored session suggests, the intention of the roundtable was to reflect on the status of the caucus and its desire to make the work of its members more visible. The session participants spoke to the work we have done since the 2014 CCCC: how the conversations at the caucus meeting have generated new studies, questions, and productive tensions. The papers explicitly name the caucus meetings as a place where presenters' work began, and we can see how the presenters pick up the work of other caucus members and carry it forward.

    Tran was among several graduate students who attended the 2014 caucus meeting, a part of which focused on our sense that Asian/Asian American scholars are not well represented in the field, despite the lack of "data" to prove our suspicions. In response, Tran initiated a project of digging into the scholarly archives, starting with the back issues of the discipline's flagship journal, *College Composition and Communication*, dating back to 1950. Her findings demonstrate that even in this one, admittedly narrow sample of scholarly outlets, Asian/Asian American scholars are and have been contributing to the field. As evinced in the number of articles by/about Asian/Asian Americans in the *CCC* journal over 60 years, much remains to be done to expand and extend the reach of the multifaceted developments in the scholarship of Asian/Asian American rhetoric.

We include Tran's piece as our first circulation essay. The historical, archival nature of the study dovetails nicely with Sano-Franchini's work, further fleshing out the contributions of Asians/Asian Americans in the field. In addition to the data she brings to our understanding of such contributions, Tran's work points to some of the methodological challenges of such a study and helps us to re/vision our understanding of these issues.

During the weeks of developing the paper, Tran grappled with issues of definition and categorization—struggles that come to all good researchers. We see productive tensions in this study that provide a glimpse into a work in progress, and capture the methodological difficulties in situ, as it were, as our study and understanding of Asian/Asian American rhetoric grows. Tran's work also foregrounds our living legacy and the present history of issues in our field.

Specifically, as Tran herself admits, it is difficult to systematically capture the work of Asian Americans without having to decide how to define "Asian American" in one's research framework. Initially Tran follows likely surnames, and diligently cross-references the names with biographical information that could be found on the Internet. Sometimes, she had to go by stated or written self-descriptions and self-identifications; other times she had to make judgments by pictures of the authors. However, as we might all agree, names and faces can be deceiving.

While some might quickly dismiss the study based on what could be seen as essentializing moves, doing so would risk overlooking important information about the prevalence of work which can be attributed to Asian American scholars. It makes me wonder if such methodological brambles have discouraged people from asking these questions or endeavoring such a study. In the spirit of Sano-Franchini's self-reflections, it would behoove us in the field to not be afraid to ask difficult questions; to risk being "improper" in our methods; to risk challenging methodological principles that might actually undermine our work, and our claims to our history.

Tran has provided us with a rich base of data from which, I hope, further studies will emerge, covering a broader swath of the field's publications and research venues. We have included in Appendix D the list of publications she compiled from her review of 60 years of *CCC*. She has also provided us with a starting point for a taxonomy of Asian/Asian American scholarship in the discipline by identifying three major trends. Tran's study provides us with something to work with, a heuristic; it provides us with landmarks on a yet uncharted map that I hope we will explore together, more, in the future.

While the pages of *CCC* may have not included Asian/Asian American scholars in the 1970s, for example, Sano-Franchini gives evidence to the fact that Asians/Asian Americans were busy in the organization and in the broader community and civic/public sphere. Read alongside Sano-Franchini's findings from the NCTE archives, Tran's overview helps us trace a legacy and a history in the field of rhetoric and composition. While their scholarship is not a pervasive presence, the kind of recovery work done by Tran and Sano-Franchini allows us to recognize and acknowledge the role that Asians/Asian Americans played and continue to play in the knowledge-making of the field. The restless efforts of these scholars in addressing Asian/Asian American literacy practices, second language writing, translingual writing, transnational culture, and racial legacies have carved out a significant area of Asian/Asian American rhetorics.

K. Hyoejin Yoon

RATIONALE

In the caucus meeting in 2014, new members expressed their concerns over the relatively low visibility of scholarship and paucity of Asian/Asian American scholars in rhetoric and composition literature when they did some preliminary research about Asian/Asian American rhetorics. I decided to explore this further by digging into the history of *College Composition and Communication*, the flagship journal of the discipline, and examining the publications by Asian/Asian American scholars and those about issues pertaining to Asian/Asian Americans over sixty years, from 1950 to 2010.

RESEARCH PROCESS

Research Questions

My research was guided by the following questions:

1. How visible was Asian/Asian American scholarship in *College Composition and Communication*, from 1950 to 2010? How many articles were published by Asian/Asian American scholars? What is the percentage of published work?

2. What were the specific issues/main concerns that Asian/Asian American scholars addressed through their presence in *College Composition and Communication*?

Research Methodology
I started my research with the following definitions:

- Asian/Asian American scholars in *College Composition and Communication* are those who have Asian/Asian American heritage, and had publications in the journal.

- Asian/Asian American publications are works which those Asian/Asian American scholars either authored or co-authored in *College Composition and Communication*.

To answer the first question, I measured the visibility of Asian/Asian American scholarship by the number of publications by and about Asian/Asian Americans in sixty years of *College Composition and Communication*. To avoid missing any Asian/Asian American publications, I reviewed each and every publication of *College Composition and Communication* in sixty years and filtered out Asian/Asian American publications. As such, supplementary materials including editor's notes, Staffroom Interchanges, book reviews, symposiums, and poems were also under my scrutiny.

With a publication, I identified two points: (i) whether the publication was written by an Asian/Asian American author, and (ii) whether the publication was about Asian/Asian American issues. First, with the search term of "(The author's name) composition/English," I sought to find the author's image, biography, profile, or curriculum vitae through Google. This search also allowed me to know more about the author's research interests, and determine if Asian/Asian American rhetoric and/or composition was among their research areas. With this search, I was also able to double-check the authorship of the *CCC* publication by seeing if the publication was listed among the author's publications. And lastly, if Google did not direct me to any page that had a picture of the author, I used Google Image to seek out the author's racial background and attempt to assess if they were Asian/Asian American.

For example, I came across a publication on feminism by Marian M. Sciachitano in *College Composition and Communication* Volume 43 Issue 3. Thanks to Google, I found her faculty page with her image on it at the Washington State University website. Thus, I could make a guess at her racial background, her professional profile with "Asian American women" as one of her research areas, and also her authorship of the *College Composition and Communication* article, since that article was presented in the publication section in her curriculum vitae.

However, not all authors could be traced for their profile through Google. For many authors, like Fan Shen in Volume 40, Issue 4, my search was made possible only by Google Image. In these cases, the author's image then linked me to their biographical pages.

During the research, however, I faced constraints that challenged my methodology and research feasibility. The biggest obstacle for me lay in the unavailability of online biographical information of many *College Composition and Communication* authors, especially those publishing between the 1950s and the 1980s. A high number of scholars in these decades did not have full nor sufficient profiling information on the Internet, which limited my Google searches. With these unsearchable authors, I decided to only examine whether their works were relevant to Asian/Asian American issues, which served the count of Asian/Asian American publications and the measurement of Asian/Asian American scholarship visibility, and I had to leave out the identification of their racial background, which was impossible with their names as the only biographical evidence I had.

Furthermore, for scholars who seem to have an Asian name, and limited background information, it was more difficult for me to trace their background when their research areas did not include Asian/Asian American rhetorics.

To explore the second research question about the specific issues/main concerns of Asian/Asian American scholars in *College Composition and Communication*, I coded the themes in the found Asian/Asian American publications under different keywords such as ESL writing, teaching pedagogy, multiculturalism, and comparative rhetorics. These keywords helped me keep track of (i) what Asian/Asian American topics were addressed in a publication, and (ii) whether the publication was related to Asian/Asian American rhetorics. Based on the keywords, my last and final step was to group the publications' themes under either "general rhetoric and composition issues" or "Asian/Asian American rhetorics" to record the relatedness to Asian/Asian American issues. For example, keywords such as teaching pedagogy, literacy practices, or ESL writing were categorized under "general rhetoric and composition issues," while Asian immigrants, Chinese rhetorics, or rhetorical strategies in Asian/Asian American discourse were categorized as "Asian/Asian American rhetorics." If a publication's content reflected both general rhetoric and composition issues and Asian/Asian American rhetorics, it was marked in both categories. Through the use of keywords and the final grouping task, I was able to chronicle what Asian/Asian American scholars have been discussing in their works within the sixty years of *College Composition and Communication*, which is the center of the second research question.

RESEARCH RESULTS

The Visibility of Asian/Asian American Scholarship in the History of College Composition and Communication from 1950 to 2010
From sixty volumes and 250 issues of *College Composition and Communication* over the course of sixty years, I identified a total of **twenty nine** publications by and about visible Asian/Asian Americans, including: (i) sixteen articles; (ii) four Staffroom Interchanges; (iii) six book reviews; (iv) one symposium; and (v) two other types of publication.

In particular, 16 articles were written by visible Asian/Asian American scholars. Half of them were explicitly focused on Asian/Asian American issues and the rest were not.

Asian/Asian American scholars authored four Staffroom Interchange publications, with only one being about Asians/Asian Americans.

Of six book reviews, five were composed by visible Asian/Asian American authors for non–Asian/Asian American books, and one by a non–Asian/Asian American scholar for an Asian/Asian American book, *Minor Re/Visions: Asian American Literacy Narratives as a Rhetoric of Citizenship* by Morris Young, an Asian/Asian American scholar. It should be noted that this was the first and only book about Asian/Asian American issues reviewed in the first sixty years of *College Composition and Communication*.

The symposium on East-West Comparative Rhetorical Studies consists of nine publications, all penned by Asian/Asian American authors. Nonetheless, I prefer to count these nine individual contributions as one substantive symposium publication, which serves to more accurately measure the combined presence and significance of Asian/Asian American issues in *College Composition and Communication*. I will return to this point later when the major trends in Asian/Asian American scholarship are analyzed.

Lastly, the two publications I listed as other types of publications include one symposium introduction by Marian M. Sciachitano, for a non–Asian/Asian American symposium entitled "Feminist Sophistics Pedagogy Group" in Volume 43 Issue 3, and one editor's note about cultural rhetorics but not directly addressing Asian/Asian American rhetorics in Volume 53,

Issue 3, which was co-penned by Gail Y. Okawa, an Asian/Asian American scholar, and Marilyn M. Cooper, a non-Asian scholar.

The distribution of Asian/Asian American publications that were visible to me over the decades is as follows:

- 1950s: 0 publications

- 1960s: 3

- 1970s: 0

- 1980s: 7

- 1990s: 5

- 2000s: 14

As can be seen from the distribution above, the number of publications in the 2000s doubled those in the 1980s and nearly tripled those in the 1990s. Also, half of the Asian/Asian American publications in *College Composition and Communication* came out in this decennium. With the aforementioned distribution, it can be concluded that Asian/Asian American rhetorics has become increasingly visible in the scholarship of *College Composition and Communication* in the past ten years.

From these 29 publications, three major trends can be observed in Asian/Asian American scholarship in *College Composition and Communication* from 1950 to 2010.

First, Asian/Asian American scholarship has moved from small-sized publications such as Staffroom Interchanges, book reviews, and short articles to larger publications, including longer articles and symposia. In particular, three out of four Staffroom Interchanges and four out of six book reviews were published between 1960 and 1990, while twelve of sixteen articles and the only symposium were published in the last twenty years.

Secondly, throughout sixty years, there have been shifts in terms of content in Asian/Asian American scholarship in *College Composition and Communication*. Specifically, Asian/Asian American publications have shifted from (a) general American composition issues to (b) Asian/Asian American concerns in the context of general American composition issues, and then to (c) identity-oriented issues about Asian/Asian American composition and presence in U.S. academia. Information about the content of the Asian/Asian

American articles, as well as which article addresses which content, can be found in Appendix D.

To illustrate, all articles and Staffroom Interchange works from 1962, when the first Asian/Asian American publication appeared in *College Composition and Communication* to 1987, shared topics of general writing issues such as semantics in freshman English, minority students, English teaching pedagogies, voice and style.

In Volume 40, Issue 4 in 1989, through a Staffroom Interchange, Fan Shen addressed issues of contrastive rhetorics between U.S. and Chinese composition and culture. This work, therefore, could be considered as weaving an Asian/Asian American issue into the context of U.S. composition. After Fan Shen, Min-Zhan Lu published three articles in 1994, 1999, and 2004, all of which situated Asian/Asian American issues like multiculturalism, Chinese ESL writing, World Englishes, racial legacies, and Asian immigrants in the U.S. composition environment.

The publication of LuMing Mao's "Rhetorical Borderlands: Chinese American Rhetoric in the Making" in 2005 is notable. It centers on comparative rhetorics between Chinese, European, and U.S. compositions, and delineates Chinese American rhetoric in the contact zone of those rhetorics. Since Mao's publication, more Asian/Asian American publications explicitly addressing issues of Asian/Asian American identity have appeared in *College Composition and Communication* scholarship. Xiaoye You's publication examines the rhetorics of "textbook production and existence in China"; Hui Wu investigates the teaching pedagogy and rhetorical strategies in discourse in a Japanese American Internment Camp; and Haivan V. Hoang challenges racial rhetorics by recounting the interracial conflicts and discourse strategies that occurred between students in a Vietnamese American organization and their college administration body. Lastly, in 2009, a symposium with publications by Asian/Asian American authors directly brought to the table a discussion of comparative rhetorics and Chinese rhetorics, juxtaposing Asian/Asian American rhetorics with other areas in composition.

The third and last trend to be noted about the development of Asian/Asian American rhetorics in *College Composition and Communication* is the divide in research areas among Asian/Asian American scholars. It is obvious that the tapestry of 29 publications by Asian/Asian American scholars was woven by different threads of research areas, and these areas have been coexisting over the decades despite the shifts of content in Asian/Asian American scholarship. In particular, research areas of Asian/Asian American scholars tended to fall into one of these two categories: (i) general rhetoric and composition issues, such as teaching pedagogies; ESL writing, World Englishes; feminism; disabilities, etc., or (ii) Asian/Asian American rhetorics. The second group, then, could be categorized into sub-groups: (a) those viewing Asian/Asian American issues in relation to the broad U.S. composition context and space (e.g.: Min-Zhan Lu, Haivan V. Hoang, Hui Wu); and (b) those focusing more on contrastive/comparative rhetorics in Asian/Asian American issues (e.g.: LuMing Mao, Xiaoye You, and the authors in the symposium).

Further Implications
Throughout sixty years of *College Composition and Communication,* Asian/Asian American publications have been growing in number and size. The evolution of Asian/Asian American rhetorics has reflected restless efforts of Asian/Asian American scholars in carving out a significant area by and about Asians/Asian Americans in *College Composition and Communication* scholarship. From my research experience, however, I would like to share Monberg and Yoon's argument, in their 2014 presentation on the AAAC-sponsored panel, that "scholarship by Asian and Asian American scholars often do[es] not carry the same kind of weight and extended relevance." Putting aside Asian/Asian American scholars whose research interests do not include Asian/Asian American rhetorics, those who do cultivate in this area, as a matter of fact, have investigated different, non-overlapping Asian/Asian American aspects. While this phenomenon is understandable regarding the personal research interests of Asian/Asian American rhetoricians, more synergic work on a shared set of Asian/Asian American issues should be taken into account by these scholars so as to ensure the development of Asian/Asian American research in both depth and breadth and to make room for Asian/Asian American rhetorics in composition studies.

WORKS CITED

"Asian/Asian American Scholarship in Rhetoric and Composition: Risks and Rewards." Conference on College Composition and Communication. Tampa Marriott Waterside, Tampa, FL, 19 March 2015. Sponsored by the Asian/Asian American Caucus.

Cooper, Marilyn M. and Gail Y. Okawa. "From the Editor." *College Composition and Communication* 53.3 (2002): 393–95. Print.

Hoang, Haivan V. "Campus Racial Politics and a 'Rhetoric of Injury.'" *College Composition and Communication* 61.1 (2009): W385–W408. Print.

Lu, Min-Zhan. "Professing Multiculturalism: The Politics of Style in the Contact Zone." *College Composition and Communication* 45.4 (1994): 442–58. Print.

—. "Redefining the Literate Self: The Politics of Critical Affirmation." *College Composition and Communication* 51.2 (1999): 172–94. Print.

—. "An Essay on the Work of Composition: Composing English Against the Order of Fast Capitalism." *College Composition and Communication* 56.1 (2004): 16–50. Print.

Lu, Min-Zhan and Elizabeth Robertson. "Review: Life Writing as Social Acts." *College Composition and Communication* 51.1 (1999):119–31. Print.

Mao, LuMing. "Rhetorical Borderlands: Chinese American Rhetoric in the Making." *College Composition and Communication* 56.3 (2005): 426–69. Print.

Monberg, Terese Guinsatao, and K. Hyoejin Yoon. "Ruptures, Wounds, Possibilities: Asian/Asian American Disciplinary History and Scholarship." Conference on College Composition and Communication. JW Marriott, Indianapolis, IN, 20 March 2014. Sponsored by the Asian/Asian American Caucus.

Sciachitano, Marian M. "Introduction: Feminist Sophistics Pedagogy Group." *College Composition and Communication* 43.3 (1992): 297-300. Print.

Shen, Fan. "The Classroom and the Wider Culture: Identity as a Key to Learning English Composition." *College Composition and Communication* 40.4 (December 1989): 459–66. Print.

Swearingen, C. Jan & LuMing Mao, eds. CCC Special Symposium on East–West Comparative Rhetorical Studies. *College Composition and Communication* 60.4 (June 2009): W99–W106. Web.

Wu, Hui. "Writing and Teaching behind Barbed Wire: An Exiled Composition Class in a Japanese–American Internment Camp." *College Composi-*

tion and Communication 59.2 (2007): 233–58. Print.

You, Xiaoye. "Ideology, Textbooks, and the Rhetoric of Production in China." *College Composition and Communication* 56.4: 632–53. Print.

Young, Morris. *Minor Re/Visions: Asian American Literacy Narratives as a Rhetoric of Citizenship*. Carbondale: Southern Illinois UP, 2004. Print.

CHAPTER TWO
"To Establish a Home within a Home": An Interview with LuMing Mao

Chanon Adsanatham

Since the early 1990s, LuMing Mao, professor and chair of the English department at Miami University of Ohio, has contributed to the field of rhetoric and writing studies through his research and active involvement in the Asian/Asian American Caucus. Mao's research focuses on the Chinese rhetorical tradition, Chinese American rhetoric, writing in multicultural spaces, comparative methodology, and critical discourse analysis. In 2009, he launched and became the first director of the Asian/Asian American studies program at Miami. With Morris Young, he edited *Representations: Doing Asian American Rhetoric,* the first anthology in our discipline on Asian American rhetoric—it won honorable mention for the Mina P. Shaughnessy Prize from the Modern Language Association in 2009.

Mao has developed many approaches for doing comparative rhetorical studies, approaches that foster contextualized dialogic engagement and heteroglossic reflection. His article on comparative framework in *College English,* "Studying the Chinese Rhetorical Tradition in the Present: Re-Presenting the Native's Point of View," won the Richard Ohmann award for outstanding essay in 2007. This publication along with other methodologies he advanced—reflective encounters, togetherness-in-difference, and the art of recontextualization—have provided invaluable approaches for scholars who seek to study minority discourses and non-Western rhetoric.

Besides his scholarship, Mao helped launch the Asian/Asian American Caucus at the Conference on College Composition and Communication in the late 1990s. "I was interested in getting something going at CCCC in order to establish a home within home, a community whereby Asian/Asian American scholars could find a voice, could have their voice listened to and heard... This is kind of a special setting," he explained.

CA: How did you become involved with the Asian/Asian American Caucus?

LM: I became involved mainly because I was asked. I am a Chinese American, and at the time, the caucus was an emergent organization within NCTE. There was not an AAAC entity within CCCC. I became involved in part because I was interested in getting something going at CCCC in order to establish a home within home, a community whereby Asian/Asian American scholars could find a voice, could have their voices listened to and heard. When you think of how big CCCC is, people get lost.

CA: You said you were asked to be involved. Who initially asked you?

LM: A woman named Nancy Lay, who was very much involved in NCTE's Asian Caucus. The focus then was more on teaching English as a second language. There was also a woman at NCTE who was in charge of the ethnic minority caucuses within NCTE. She has since left NCTE, but she was also a major figure in how I became involved in this organization within NCTE, and subsequently in CCCC.

CA: So the Asian/Asian American Caucus began as an NCTE initiative, and then it expanded to become a CCCC entity?

LM: Yes. CCCC gradually became an independent entity. So, as CCCC grew, so did the caucus.

CA: How did these people come to know you? Had you published a certain article that they came across?

LM: I think both by my work and also by my attendance at NCTE and CCCC. As you know, we would look at the index, look for names and projects that are similar to what we are doing, and we would go to those sessions. That's how we got to know each other. What we used to do—what we still do—is look at all the names at the end of the program book to identify people. Sometimes we were wrong, but oftentimes we got it right in terms of how many Asian/Asian Americans came to CCCC in a given year. Then we would make a list of these people and look at the program and try to go to their session to show support. We continue to do that. Last year Terese Guinsatao Monberg and Stuart Ching put together a program by Asian/Asian American presenters. That allowed people to get to know each other and this was how I gradually became connected.

CA: What got you interested in joining this group?

LM: First and foremost, as I indicated previously, I wanted to establish a community within the larger umbrella community we call CCCC. Doing so, I thought, would allow people like us and young scholars coming up to find a place where they can have direct, immediate support, mentoring and networking. As I said, CCCC is a huge organization. When you go there, you really feel lost if you don't know anybody. I thought it would be good for us to have a similar organization whereby Asian/Asian American scholars can find support, can have the resources they might find useful.

The second reason is I thought it would be fun for us to collaborate and work together, have a place where we can get to know each other's work. The caucus can put together a list from the program that deals with Asian/Asian American scholars' work that others might find interesting. Then we can go and find and show support and also begin to actually communicate with each other in ways that might not be immediately available without this kind of organization.

Thirdly, we can better ensure that our voice will be heard within the larger organization of CCCC, that voice that represents our interests, represents our needs and wants. Every year at CCCC, all of the caucus chairs meet on Saturday afternoon to report to the program chair and vice chair, the CCCC leadership team, what we have learned, what we think is good or bad, what we think should be improved upon, so now all caucus chairs gather together with the leadership team.

Also I wanted to ensure that each year's program would give space to represent Asian/Asian American studies issues. I find that to be highly important and I think we've been successful. In the early days, there were hardly any panels that featured Asian/Asian American issues. So we would sometimes ask the program chair to feature a particular panel to ensure that when people look at the totality of the program, there is a presence of Asian/Asian American scholars.

As our caucus grew, we began to feature people's work, to collaborate. *Representations: Doing Asian American Rhetoric* in part grew from the caucus' discussion and people's interests. We hope to do more of that in the days and weeks to come.

CA: What's your recollection of what the caucus was like when you first joined in 1998?

LM: It was a very small NCTE initiative called the Asian Caucus. I remember the first or second year we only had a couple people who showed up at our caucus at NCTE. The focus was narrowed more on ESL, second language writing. Early on, it was agreed that since I would normally go to CCCC, I would start the CCCC caucus. I was initially chair of the caucus in 1999, and then I got Morris Young involved. We became co-chairs.

CA: What issues or initiatives was the caucus tackling in 1999?

LM: One was to look after our needs and interests. Mainly it was to ensure that there would be an Asian/Asian American presence in the CCCC program. Prior to the caucus, it was a hit or miss; you would find a couple panels made up of Asian/Asian American scholars. Sometimes you found none. We wanted to ensure that there would be a presence.

We also wanted to feature some of the panels and to help people know that there is an Asian/Asian American Caucus, that we welcome scholars of Asian/Asian American ethnicity or descent, and we also welcome those who are not Asian/Asian American as long as they are interested in doing Asian/Asian American work or participating in our conversation. Initially, we had people who were Caucasian who came and participated, but now primarily, we have Asian/Asian American scholars who come to our caucus.

The second initiative we were involved in was to help networking, to provide support to young scholars who just joined the organization.

CA: You mentioned that you were the chair from 1999 to 2000. What roles did you play as chair of the caucus?

LM: As a chair, you plan for the annual meeting. Another thing I would do was create a program for the caucus, invite people to speak at the meeting. So if we were going to have four caucus members talk about issues of teaching in the classroom as an Asian/Asian American, pedagogical challenges, other challenges, we were able to put their names in the CCCC program and also the titles of their talks. That way if their other proposal was not accepted, or if they chose not to submit any other proposal, they could use that as their participation and go back to their home institution for reimbursement because they had a speaking role.

In the past, some members expressed to us that if their proposals were rejected, they would not be able to come because they wouldn't get institutional support. We used the caucus as a way to ensure that they would have a speaking role, which I thought was a very good way of ensuring participation from our members. So, for a number of years, we put together a program with a particular theme and then invited members to participate.

CA: Can you elaborate on what kind of work the Asian/Asian American Caucus did in conjunction with CCCC?

LM: The CCCC leadership would ask the caucus chairs to go back to our caucus to ask our members to tell us their concerns and their needs, what they think will be the highlights of the program, what they think needs to be fixed—problems, issues, concerns. The second thing as I recall is to encourage our members to submit proposals and panels for the following year's program. But I think the main thing is to ask our members to tell us what they want the organization to do and how it could help us.

CA: What were some of the things that the members wanted? Were there pressing issues?

LM: The pressing issue was really to have a visible presence in the program. Members often felt that they were not as supported as they would like to be. As I recall, the organization wanted to support us, but we needed to let them know how best they can support us because the organization is so huge.

This was in part why the organization began to have the Scholars for the Dream program, which helps minority scholars and encourages them to join by giving them the honor and travel support. Scholars for the Dream was one immediate response to the concerns expressed by our caucus, as well as by the other caucuses. There was an ongoing issue with diversity; that is, how the organization might encourage minority scholars to join but also make sure that they continue to attend because it is easier for the organization to attract newcomers, but retention is harder. People lost interest for a lot of reasons. They would stop coming back.

CA: What role or function has the caucus played to the larger field of rhetoric and writing studies?

LM: It has played a significant role in promoting and advancing studies on Asian/Asian American writing and rhetorical practices through our panel presentations, individual presentations, through our featured sessions, and through our individual work both in terms of our publications and work at our institution. Our edited collection, *Representations*, is an example of advancing, enriching, promoting our understanding of Asian American rhetorical practices.

With the caucus' work and all of the panel presentations at CCCC, Morris and I realized we have enough of a cohort within Asian/Asian American writing and rhetorical studies that we could put together a collection of essays focusing on Asian American rhetoric. Once we thought it was a good idea, that it was a good time historically to do something like that, we talked with the caucus, and through our individual communication, we sent our ideas to people. We encouraged folks to participate, and it grew and got a very good response. From there we wrote a proposal. We solicited a couple sample chapters and sent them to Michael Spooner, the editor at Utah State University Press. He was excited. He was quite supportive. His support was indispensable and made it successful. Then we got an award so that was quite satisfying.

CA: What's your most memorable moment as a caucus member?

LM: One memorable moment—there are quite a number—was when I heard and I shared the news with the caucus that Haivan V. Hoang's dissertation won the James Berlin dissertation award. We shared the news and celebrated with our caucus— that was a good moment. Another good moment was to see there was a noticeable increase in attendance at our Friday evening meeting. I felt quite good about that as well.

CA: Do you see any issue or change coming down the pipe that might impact the caucus and Asian/Asian American scholars?

LM: I feel quite positive about whatever changes might come down the pipe. I think there will be an increasing interest and demand for the kind of work our caucus members are doing, works that feature and focus on ethnic minorities, especially Asian/Asian American rhetorical practices and how these practices contribute to our understanding of writing and communication, but there are also challenges.

Challenges for me include continuing to make a case for our presence both in the organization, in the program, and the field at large, how to continue to resist essentializing tokenism, how to continue to resist binary construction, even if it's well intended. On the one hand, we always like to be featured, to be given presence, but the last thing I want to see is presence only for the sake of tokenism or simply as a very reductive representation without giving us an opportunity to talk about the complexity, the heterogeneous voices of our work.

CA: Any specific issues or initiatives you would like to see the caucus take on in the future?

LM: I really like what Terese and Stuart are doing for us, and also I really like Haivan and Nancy's work previously, especially how they work throughout the year to assure our caucus will play a more active role, rather than only right before the conference and at the conference. I certainly will continue to actively participate. I would like to see our caucus serve as a community, a home within a home to attract more members, Asian/Asian American scholars.

CA: Please fill in the blank: Ten years from now, you would like to see the caucus _____.

LM: I would like to see the caucus grow, and become a more visible place for us to congregate, for us to work to represent every single one of us.

CHAPTER THREE

"Developing Professional Relationships and Personal Friendships": An Interview with Morris Young

Robyn Tasaka

When I entered my master's program in English at the University of Hawai'i at Mānoa, I knew little about rhetoric and composition. I am grateful to my professors for introducing me to the work of Morris Young, Associate Professor of English at the University of Wisconsin-Madison. As an Asian American scholar from Hawai'i, his mere existence helped me feel that there was a place for me in the field. As I continued toward and through doctoral work in the Midwest, I felt that because of our similar backgrounds, I could turn to him for guidance. He and other more senior members of the Asian/Asian American Caucus have always taken a special interest in me and my work. This encouragement was invaluable through graduate school—in building my confidence in my scholarship and giving me practice in talking about my work.

    Morris' scholarship as well as the scholarship of other AAAC members has also been crucial as a foundation for my own research. My dissertation, for example, builds directly on Morris's scholarship, looking more closely at clubs formed by Hawaiian students attending college on the continent and the ways they construct their identities, which Morris touched on in a 2004 *College English* article, "Native Claims: Cultural Citizenship, Ethnic Expressions, and the Rhetorics of 'Hawaiianness.'" In the same project, I also draw on Haivan V. Hoang's discussion of the "memorial traces that index past uses" of words in "Asian American Rhetorical Memory and a 'Memory that Is Only Sometimes Our Own'" (72).

At CCCC, the AAAC helps me feel at home at such a huge conference; it is easy to get lost and overwhelmed by the sea of faces, but AAAC is one avenue through which I have had the opportunity to connect with other scholars, making CCCC a friendlier place—a place I feel I belong. The AAAC and its members have supported me both professionally and personally.

RT: I wanted to start by talking about some of the roles you have played in AAAC. I know you were co-chair for awhile . . .

MY: I've served as co-chair—whether that was official or unofficial I don't really know. Lu [Ming Mao] was asked formally in the mid-to-late '90s to take over the caucus. And since I had just started at Miami [University of Ohio] it made sense that we work together on the caucus.

I've always felt like it was important to participate in the caucus because there wasn't really one for Asian American members of CCCC when I was a grad student.

RT: Can you talk a little about when the caucus was started? Who was involved?

MY: When I was a grad student there was the "Asian Caucus" which was focused more on Asian rhetoric and English language learners of Asian background. It was more like a [Special Interest Group] focused on diversity issues of the membership. I never attended, but that's what I heard from Lu. When Lu was asked to restart the caucus we decided to set it up like the other caucuses—the Black Caucus, Latinx Caucus, etc.—as more of a political body to address membership issues within Cs.

Lu and I were involved and early on we attracted folks who had been involved with the Asian Caucus—so a lot of non-Asian faculty or people of Asian backgrounds who were interested in ESL or comparative rhetoric. We didn't want to exclude them, so we tried to make the caucus more about working with students of Asian backgrounds, research topics related to Asian and Asian American topics, and professional matters.

Eventually, we were able to identify grad students and faculty who are more in line with what the membership looks like today. It helped that Paul Kei Matsuda was Lu's former student, and then our colleague at Miami. Hui Wu started coming and then a whole generation of scholars, starting with Terese [Guinsatao] Monberg and then Haivan [V. Hoang], Stuart Ching, you, Jennifer Sano-Franchini, etc.

We asked Gail Okawa to come to the caucus but she had been attending the Latinx Caucus meetings because she didn't feel like she fit in the [former] Asian Caucus—she wanted something more political.

RT: So the AAAC is really recent then. What year was it started?

MY: [Based on past CCCC programs,] it looks like the Asian Caucus last met in 1997. It was absent in 1998. And Lu took over in 1999.

RT: You talked about how the caucus wasn't around when you were a grad student. Did you feel a need for it at the time? What would you have wanted out of it as a grad student?

MY: When I was a grad student [in the 1990s] there was no one doing Asian American rhetoric or literacy—even though that was my dissertation topic, I didn't imagine there would be a subfield that would develop. Even ethnic rhetoric or race and rhetoric was pretty new.

So I wanted a place where I could talk to people doing similar work. Also, I think professionally it would have been nice to see senior scholars who were Asian American and interact with them. I had great mentoring—Anne Gere and Steve Sumida—and a great friend in my grad program who is Latina, Renee Moreno. So I had senior scholars who were supportive and a friend who was facing similar kinds of questions about the profession. Renee really should get a lot of credit for raising my political consciousness in the profession and for looking out for me. She even invited me to the Latinx Caucus because she knew that Gail Okawa was a member.

I think seeing a whole series of CCCC chairs who were people of color also made a big impact on me: Bill Cook, Jacqueline Jones Royster, Victor Villanueva, Keith Gilyard, Shirley Wilson Logan—they were all chair when I was a grad student and junior faculty member, and with the exception of Bill Cook, I've gotten to know all of them.

RT: I've really enjoyed the support from the caucus and just having a way to meet other Asian American scholars. I think it is one of the highlights of CCCC for me. Would you say that is the primary purpose of the caucus—encouraging scholarship through support and mentoring?

MY: I think so. In those early years, we rarely had more than 8–10 people at the caucus meeting. And I think the representation of Asian Americans in CCCC is smaller than, say, African Americans. If there are a smaller number of us who attend CCCC, I think it's even more important that we have a place where we can get together.

I think scholarship is one aspect of it, and we used the caucus to help put together the [Asian American rhetoric] collection [*Representations*] as well as plan sessions not only at CCCC, but also RSA. I'd like to see more grad students attend because I think the networking aspect of it is important. It creates connections that can result in publication or even in supporting promotion and tenure.

RT: What are the other purposes of the caucus?

MY: You can't underestimate the value and importance of developing professional relationships and personal friendships. Grad school and the first part of an academic career can be really hard. I was lucky to get a job that was not only supportive of composition and rhetoric (I was one comp/rhet person in a group of 10 comp/rhet faculty), but also included Lu and many others who were committed to diversity issues of all sorts—disability, gender, social class, race and ethnicity, etc. I was lucky. A lot of people are in jobs where composition and rhetoric is not valued and where scholarship that addresses diversity issues might be on the margins as well. I know of at least one person in the caucus who has said that connecting to the caucus is what kept him in the profession.

RT: So that in turn influences CCCC and NCTE—in terms of the scholarship that is produced and the scholars that are present?

MY: I hope so. Interestingly enough we have seen at least two Asian Americans serve as president of NCTE but none for chair of Cs. We've had candidates but not elected anyone yet. We've had recognition in terms of scholarship. I won the book award. Xiaoye You also won the book award. Haivan won the Berlin award. Lu and Paul [Kei Matsuda] have won the Ohmann award. But I think it will be really important when we have that first CCCC chair.

I forgot to mention that I think studying at [the University of Hawai'i] was important. Even though the composition and rhetoric people at UH weren't local, I think they were really important early in helping me see that I could do important work. And look at the number of people from UH who have gone on to pursue composition and rhetoric PhDs.

RT: Important in terms of . . . ?

MY: When I was at UH, local literature as an area of study was emerging. Paying attention to pidgin as political and artistic language rather than as remedial was getting more attention. There were just a lot of faculty who were interested in supporting local students in pursuing PhDs. Candace Fujikane and Charlene Gima were my classmates. Candace went to Berkeley and Charlene went to Cornell. When I was at Michigan there were two other PhD students from Hawai'i. So it was important to see people from Hawai'i pursuing PhDs.

RT: I see. You're talking about what was important to you sort of in place of having an AAAC.

MY: Maybe. I don't think it was in place of AAAC because UH got me to grad school. But the AAAC really helped in terms of seeing my place in the profession.

RT: You've talked about this some already, but do you want to add anything else about how your background (professional and/or personal) influences your work in the AAAC?

MY: As I've said, I really benefited from excellent mentoring and seeing how a professional life can be—i.e., it doesn't have to be horrible, etc. That doesn't mean I don't understand or am unaware of the real difficulties that people do face. So I try to use the mentoring I've received as a model for working with students and junior faculty. I've been really fortunate.

I saw Anne Gere at the Penn State conference last month and remarked to her that this fall 20 years ago I started the PhD program at Michigan. She couldn't believe it, and I can't believe it.

RT: We should talk about the book that resulted from your dissertation. In *Minor Re/Visions* you talk about the unique role of literacy for people of color, in particular Asian Americans, in demonstrating citizenship or belonging in the U.S. Do you see a similar relationship in terms of a special role for the AAAC in CCCC?

MY: I'm not sure—in the brief "history" we've talked about, the disciplinary place for Asians or Asian Americans in CCCC was to address second language learning or comparative rhetorics. So maybe the role of AAAC now is to demonstrate belonging and political presence in CCCC. Victor Villanueva's keynote still resonates with me as he pointed out the demographics of CCCC and the way diversity and race are discussed in the organization. Is there going to be a point when Asian Americans in the organization have a presence that has some kind of impact on the organization? It won't be in terms of numbers. I'm not saying we need CCCC to recognize Asian American issues, but certainly concerns about diversity of students, of languages, or rhetorics, etc. should be more inclusive of the range of experiences rather than highlighting just the most obvious.

RT: I have heard critiques of scheduling all the caucuses at CCCC to meet at the same time, preventing participation in multiple caucuses. Do you think this has affected the members or mission of the AAAC?

MY: I don't think so. Maybe on occasion. I know Paul sometimes goes to the ESL SIG. And Gail Okawa always went to the Latinx Caucus. I think there have been efforts to try to create cross-caucus interaction recently. Really, I think the convention is overwhelming and people on a Friday evening are looking to decompress. I wonder if it would make a difference if the caucus meetings were held on Thursday or even during a mid-day session when we might all meet for lunch. What's the best way to get people connected to the caucuses?

The convention is just massive—so the idea of making significant structural changes can be daunting. But I think structural changes can make a big difference.

RT: Do you want to add anything more about what you envision as the future role of AAAC?

MY: I think the future of the AAAC depends on the future of the field. Will there be more people of Asian descent entering the profession? Will research that addresses race, ethnicity, culture continue to be taken up? I think the AAAC is important for the mentoring and professional support that it can provide. Even if research moves to other areas, I think it's still useful to talk to people who may have similar experiences.

WORKS CITED

Hoang, Haivan V. "Asian American Rhetorical Memory and a 'Memory That is Only Sometimes Our Own.'" *Representations: Doing Asian American Rhetoric.* Ed. LuMing Mao and Morris Young. Logan: Utah State UP, 2008. 62–82. Print.

Villanueva, Victor. "On the Rhetoric and Precedents of Racism." *College Composition and Communication* 50.4 (June 1999): 645–61. Print.

Young, Morris. "Native Claims: Cultural Citizenship, Ethnic Expressions, and the Rhetorics of 'Hawaiianness.'" *Rhetorics from/of Color.* Spec. issue of *College English* 67.1 (September 2004): 83–101. Print.

CHAPTER FOUR
Fostering Our Efforts to "Write in the Spaces Left": Stories of Emergence in Asian American Rhetoric

Terese Guinsatao Monberg and Haivan V. Hoang

> All of us, strangers and community members, need to find ways to sustain productivity in what Pratt calls contact zones (199), areas of engagement that in all likelihood will remain contentious.... As community members, we must learn to have new faith in the advantage of sharing. As strangers, we must learn to treat the loved people and places of Others with care and to understand that, when we do not act respectfully and responsibly, we leave ourselves open to wrath. The challenge is not to work with a fear of abuse or a fear of retaliation, however. The challenge is to teach, to engage in research, to write, and to speak with Others with the determination to operate not only with professional and personal integrity, but also with the specific knowledge that communities and their ancestors are watching.
>
> — Jacqueline Jones Royster, "When the First Voice You Hear Is Not Your Own" (33)

Fifteen years ago, we each found an intellectual home when we joined a small community of people with scholarly interests in Asian and Asian American rhetoric, literacy, and language practices, and with members who self-identified as Asian or Asian American. Formed only in 1999 at the Conference on College Composition and Communication (CCCC), the Asian/Asian

American Caucus (AAAC) was and still is quite young. Even so, we came to see the caucus as being deeply tied to long traditions of writers, rhetors, and educators of Asian ancestry. Put another way, we—as Jacqueline Jones Royster challenges—wrote, taught, and pursued research "with the specific knowledge that communities and [our] ancestors were watching." Back then, Terese was in the middle of her dissertation research on the rhetorical and pedagogical practices of the community-based Filipino American National Historical Society (FANHS), and Haivan was just starting her own dissertation research on a Vietnamese American student organization's extracurricular literacy practices in a California university. For both of us, the Asian/Asian American Caucus became a refuge when the first voice we heard was not our own; the caucus was a community that supported and critically fostered our efforts to "write in the spaces left."

"Writing in the Spaces Left" was the title of William W. Cook's 1992 CCCC Chair's Address[1] in which he privileges "those instances when the marginalized, by their very resistance to the texts of the national narrative, reconstruct such texts" (10). He explains that these "'erased' lives become the very center of new, resistant texts, texts which displace the univocal narrative of the nation with their multi-voiced musings on nation and identity" (10). In the 50th anniversary issue of the journal *College Composition and Communication (CCC)*, Jacqueline Jones Royster and Jean C. Williams' essay, "History in the Spaces Left," enacted and extended Cook's intervention by questioning the histories we tell about our discipline and by rearticulating African American contributions to composition history that have largely gone unnoticed. As emerging scholars in Asian American rhetoric, we too hoped to enact a more critical and inclusive inquiry into histories of writing, writers, and writing pedagogy. Indeed, we understood quite well that Asian Americans were scarcely recognized by the discipline, and even when recognized, Asian Americans were more often than not cast as second language learners and basic writers. The discipline had limited knowledge of how Asian Americans *use* language to disrupt racialized representations of themselves and their communities or "how they develop persuasive and other rhetorical strategies to create knowledge and to effect social, political, [rhetorical], and cultural transformations" (Mao and Young 3). "Writing in the spaces left" would require not only writing over spaces previously occupied but also writing

---

1 As CCCC Chair, William Cook instituted the Scholars for the Dream Travel Award Program, which, over the years, has been an important source of support and mentorship for both of us.

against the dominant forms of theory, evidence, and scholarly genealogies that either rendered Asian/Asian American writers invisible or conflated Asian/Asian American writers with second language learners. We found that "writing in the spaces left" was necessary and at times overwhelming, as this work required us to develop and draw from overlapping interdisciplinary conversations, most notably rhetoric and composition studies, education, Asian American studies, and American ethnic studies more broadly.

As we've learned through the Writing and Working for Change project, Asians and Asian Americans have been active in the National Council for Teachers of English (NCTE) and CCCC caucuses at least since the 1960s, long before an Asian or Asian American Caucus was founded. These Asian Americans formed alliances with other caucuses in their struggle to both "write in the spaces left" and "to push against the existing limits of our field and its organizations to insure that a broader sense of common responsibility and humanity was recognized" (Blackmon, Kirklighter, and Parks 1). Similar cross-caucus alliances were important for Terese who began attending CCCC in the mid-1990s. Because the Asian/Asian American Caucus did not exist in its current form when Terese first attended CCCC, she found support for her work among senior, junior, and emerging scholars through the Scholars for the Dream network. This network of support was invaluable not only for professional development and institutional support, but also for developing her ideas on writing, race, responsible research practices, and community-based collaborations.

> **Terese:** I first attended the CCCC in 1995 as a Scholar for the Dream Award recipient. I was a first-year master's student with developing interests in writing, race, ethnographic methodologies, and issues of representation. As a Dream Scholar, I was brought into a disciplinary network and system of support that has lasted through the years. Jacqueline Jones Royster and Victor Villanueva were supportive mentors for Dream Scholars in my early years at CCCC and their very presence in the discipline made it possible for me to imagine the kind of work that I now do, every day. It was also significant that Jacqueline Jones Royster was chair of CCCC that year. I met her at the Scholars for the Dream breakfast before the Opening Session, and I vividly remember sitting with other Dream Scholars at that Opening Session and listening to her Chair's Address, aptly titled "When the First Voice You Hear is Not Your Own." I had been through an interesting year of applying

to PhD programs, and that experience was the basis of the paper that was selected for the Dream Scholar Award that year. As a former high-school dropout, non-traditional and under-represented student, I was skeptical of certain approaches in cultural studies and other scholarship in the discipline that focused on "voices from the margins," especially after finding that many graduate programs weren't very willing to admit non-traditional students into the profession. Because I had already felt spoken about but rarely spoken to, Royster's address really resonated with me. To this day, her CCCC Chair's Address shapes a lot of what I do in the discipline: my research, teaching, and service, my work with graduate and undergraduate students, my collaborative work with Asian and Pacific American communities, and my work with the Asian/Asian American Caucus.

I recall that there was an "Asian Caucus" meeting listed in the 1995 program, but I remember being both confused and conflicted about whether to attend. At that time, I didn't fully understand what the caucuses were about, and I wasn't thinking specifically about situating my work as "Asian" or "Asian American." As a first-year master's student, I was just becoming aware of the importance of disciplinary conversations but I hadn't yet identified a specific research question or dissertation topic, and I didn't really understand what it would mean for me to "situate my work." The following year, the Asian Caucus meeting had listings for presentations on contrastive rhetoric and this was not a scholarly area of interest for me, so I didn't attend. What was important for me at that time was my work with a group of emerging scholars like Malea Powell, Janice Gould, Ellen Cushman, Scott Lyons, Mimi Wheatwind, and Joyce Rain Anderson, who were doing research on the rhetorical workings and legacies of empire. We called ourselves the "mixedblood collective." Members of this group—who were then specifically focused on rhetorics of decolonization, sovereignty, historical memory, and language revitalization—helped me develop a historical and methodological approach that recognized the complicated, layered history of colonization in the Philippines and how this history still situates Filipinx American community-based practices like those of FANHS.

As my work became increasingly focused on Filipinx American rhetoric, I began to see the importance of the caucuses. Cecilia Rodríguez Milanés, who I'd met through the Scholars for the Dream network, invited me to the Latinx Caucus meeting—and because of shared histories of Spanish colonization and U.S.-based coalitions between Chicanxs and Filipinxs, this felt like a good fit. But by that time, I was beginning to find essays on Asian rhetoric. Articles by LuMing Mao and Hui Wu, in particular, provided models for how Asian/Asian American rhetoric(s) challenge Western paradigms and the Western rhetorical tradition. Shortly after that, I met Morris Young in 1998 at Malea Powell's dissertation defense at Miami University, and I began to think more specifically about Asian American rhetoric. And it was probably Morris who encouraged me to come to a caucus meeting when he and LuMing began co-chairing the Asian/Asian American Caucus in 1999.

One precursor to the Asian/Asian American Caucus, as LuMing Mao and Morris Young explain in this collection, was actually the *Asian* Caucus—a caucus initially established by members of NCTE to serve those seeking to support English language learners of Asian ancestry. A similar caucus was later established at CCCC. Mao became chair of the CCCC caucus in 1999 and, with Young, gradually re-centered the caucus on Asian *and* Asian American representation within the professional organization and the larger scholarly conversation. From our perspective—and as Mao attests in his 2011 NCTE Centennial Writing and Working for Change Founders Panel presentation on the history of the caucus—it was fortuitous and important that both Mao and Young were at Miami University of Ohio in the late 1990s. Their scholarly interests came together to re-envision the earlier Asian Caucus in order to create additional space for those with Asian *American* research and teaching interests. Paul Kei Matsuda was also at Miami University with Mao and Young in the late 1990s, and because of their overlapping networks in the discipline, they were able to bring new members to the caucus including scholars doing work in second language writing, multilingual writing, Chinese rhetoric, Asian rhetoric, and Asian American rhetoric and literacy. Mao and Young co-chaired the caucus, and membership reflected this move to support a range of work that had affinity under the name of the "Asian/Asian American Caucus." This was particularly important for Haivan who was then a young scholar just being introduced to Asian American rhetoric.

Haivan: In 2001, I attended CCCC for the first time, though not as a presenter. Then a second-year graduate student at The Ohio State University, I had the opportunity to share and get feedback on an early idea for a dissertation in a roundtable at the Qualitative Research Network (QRN) workshop. I considered studying, through ethnographic inquiry, the ideologies circulating around English language education for college students at one of the Vietnam National University campuses. My idea presented many methodological difficulties (in retrospect, I see that there were too many difficulties for me then): my own lack of Vietnamese language fluency, the need to get assistance with translation, the challenges of a transnational project, and more. I hoped for suggestions on how to reconceptualize the proposed project in a way that would enable me to conduct a transnational study and address these challenges. The QRN facilitators had designed a productive workshop, but responses to my project from individuals at my roundtable were disheartening. These were responses that assumed ethnic and national authenticity: Why not study Vietnamese American college students' language education, one well-meaning respondent asked, instead of the language education of college students in Vietnam, in order to avoid travel expenses and translation problems?

Ironically, I did pursue a study of Vietnamese American college students' rhetorical practices on the West Coast; however, I did so in order to understand their rhetorical practices within the context of U.S. racial formation and post–Civil Rights movement struggles for ethnic studies in universities. What I found disheartening from the conversation was the sense that perhaps, even in 2001, there were assumptions about an authentic ethnic identity (i.e., studying Vietnamese American students in the U.S. would be essentially the same as studying Vietnamese students learning English in Vietnam), and about the bold line differentiating Vietnamese and Vietnamese American people from those who were truly American. We as a field still had so much work to do when it came to destabilizing notions of ethnic, racial, and national authenticity.

But this is not to say that the conference was uninviting. Quite the contrary. The following year, I was recognized as a Scholar for the Dream and welcomed by that community (particularly Amanda Espinosa Aguilar, Terese Guinsatao Monberg, and Malea Powell), I was invited to the Asian/Asian American Caucus by LuMing Mao, and I was inspired by presentations and had meaningful conversations with others who held shared interests. I am deeply appreciative of the several communities that I have found at CCCC; my entry into the conference provided me with support as well as an impetus to explore how we as a field understand ethnicity and race and their relation to writing and rhetoric.

It is not surprising that the profession's understanding of Asian/Asian American writers and their deeper rhetorical legacies was limited given that Asians/Asian Americans have historically been underrepresented in our professional organizations. According to the 2008 Report of the NCTE Task Force to Advance and Support Members of Color, only 27 of NCTE's approximately 57,000 members self-identified as Asian/Asian American. This is surely not news to those who study and teach writing. Underrepresentation of not only racial minority people, but also the writing, rhetorics, and language practices of racial minority people has been a visible concern since at least the civil rights movement era (see Jolivette Mecenas' interview with Jeffery Chan in *Listening to Our Elders*). CCCC as an organization has worked to address this underrepresentation (and misrepresentation) in important ways: the Scholars for the Dream Awards; "Students' Right to Their Own Language," the National Language Policy, and other position statements; and the Committees on Diversity, on Language Policy, and on Second Language Writing. The two of us are especially grateful to have been named Scholars for the Dream because we connected with generous friends, colleagues, and mentors in that network. The caucuses have also been spaces, in their own ways, used to address these issues in a manner that has been separate from but related to CCCC.

The Asian/Asian American Caucus became a space where Asian and Asian American scholars were looking to connect with colleagues who were doing similar work because we had difficulty situating ourselves in a discipline that did not reflect our ethnic and racial communities. We did not yet have a significant body of scholarship in Asian American rhetoric in which to set our work, and for those of us in graduate school, there weren't always faculty members in our respective departments who could help us examine and articulate the specificities of Asian American discursive practices and performances. Where would we find primary and secondary sources to write a literature review? How much time could we commit to digging up these sources, and what if we came across gaping silences in the histories of Asian American rhetorical traditions? How would we engage in interdisciplinary research in a rigorous manner? Would advisors, search committees, conference proposal reviewers, and journal editors be persuaded that scholarship on Asian American rhetoric was relevant to the wider field of rhetoric and composition studies, or would our work be ghettoized? In short, if the importance of research is to contribute to a scholarly conversation and the conversation had yet to be recognized as one worth having in the discipline, then we faced a daunting task.

With our colleagues in the Asian/Asian American Caucus, we were developing conversations about the rhetorical traditions, writing practices, and heritage languages of Asian and Asian American people at the same time that we searched for our own contributions to that conversation. Conversations in the caucus meetings and also during sessions at CCCC generated important and formative feedback for our scholarly production. The presence of Asian/Asian American scholars at CCCC in those years was sparse, but the caucus felt like a home to many of us and was a primary reason we continued to return to CCCC even when we felt invisible to the larger discipline. What the two of us have appreciated most in the caucus has been the critical mentorship and support that colleagues have generously given and the institutional strides senior members have made in creating greater representation for Asian/Asian American scholarship, concerns, and voices at CCCC.

> **Terese:** The first time I thought about explicitly naming myself an Asian American rhetorician was after I met Morris Young because he was one of the few scholars I'd met in the discipline who identified himself as an Asian Americanist. While I'd developed affinities and parallels with African American, American Indian, and Latinx studies in rhetoric and composition, I was finding it necessary to read more and more scholarship in Asian American and Filipinx American studies to give my work more grounding in the specific histories, immigration and transnational issues, cultural politics, decolonization strategies, and social movements in which individual and collective Asian American and Filipinx American rhetors locate themselves. Meeting Morris Young at this early stage of my work was significant because he really brought me into the Asian/Asian American Caucus, and it was through the caucus that I met LuMing Mao, Hui Wu, and a growing number of emerging scholars who were also conducting research on Asian

American writers. The collaborative spirit and support that I received from the caucus as I developed my work in this direction was extremely valuable, particularly since there were then very few published studies in Asian American literacy practices, rhetorical theory, rhetorical performance, or writing pedagogies. Lu and Morris were great mentors, role models, and sponsors. As co-chairs of the caucus, they encouraged and facilitated collaboration among members of the caucus. And their scholarly presence at CCCC not only served as a model, but also allowed them to utilize their professional networks to create a greater presence for our work at CCCC. As I began my dissertation work on the Filipino American National Historical Society, this support was vital to meeting the theoretical and methodological challenges of writing a dissertation in an underrepresented and emergent field of study.

Haivan: As a first-time presenter in 2002, I was surprised and grateful that LuMing Mao not only attended my presentation, but also asked thoughtful questions, gave encouraging feedback, and invited me to the caucus meeting that year. Around that time, I was about to begin dissertation research on the extracurricular literacy and rhetorical practices of a grassroots, political student organization called the Vietnamese American Coalition. And as I delved into a dissertation that was gradually becoming an interdisciplinary project drawing on literacy studies and Asian American studies, it became clear to me that I was treading new ground.

I again found support within the caucus, specifically from Morris Young, who offered to share his manuscript of *Minor Re/Visions* with me even before its publication and later from Terese whose dissertation on FANHS modeled for me the kind of critical weaving together of rhetorical analysis and Asian American history that my work required. I had no formal background in Asian American studies, and with little secondary literature on Asian American traditions in composition, literacy, and rhetorical scholarship, research by caucus members was and still is invaluable as I attempt to situate my own work.

Growing as teacher–scholars with the support of the caucus, we recognized that the Asian/Asian American Caucus was young in more ways than one. We had relatively few members who were tenured faculty, yet the two of us each recognized that we needed to become leaders in the caucus to sustain and give back to the community of support that had been so helpful to us. Haivan was the first of us to take on a leadership role in the caucus. In 2005, Haivan with Nancy Linh Karls began co-chairing the caucus, despite the fact that both were new junior faculty. Still exploring the purpose of the caucus themselves, they worked with the caucus to articulate a sense of who we were and what we believed and crafted the following mission statement:

> The mission of the Asian/Asian American Caucus is to **support composition scholarship by and/or about Asians and Asian Americans**. As a community that values research, pedagogy, and mentorship, we work to
>
> • increase the representation of Asian and Asian American scholars in composition studies; and
>
> • advance scholarship on Asian and Asian American rhetorics, literacy practices, and second language acquisition issues.
>
> The Asian/Asian American Caucus invites all to join this community of members who support one another on scholarship by and/or about Asian and Asian American language practices, rhetorics, and literacy education.

Haivan and Nancy believed that these two goals were interrelated, that the caucus could encourage Asian and Asian American scholars to join our field if rhetoric, composition, and literacy scholarship were to demonstrate deep engagement with Asian/Asian American discursive practices. Such scholarship would not only make research less overwhelming (where emerging scholars would not have to find their own way through Othered histories and cultures), but they also hoped that research on Asians/Asian Americans in our field would interpellate Asians/Asian Americans differently and would help the field see that we are part of an ethnic and racial heritage that is integral to U.S. culture.

During the five years that Haivan and Nancy were co-chairs, the caucus accordingly attempted to foster such research. They encouraged and sought out opportunities for panel presentations among caucus members. And they coordinated writing groups to encourage writing and to encourage caucus members to get to know one another. Though the writing groups only lasted one year—primarily because of the challenges of sharing work among scholars who only met face-to-face once per year and who had varied writing and other demands in their lives—we still learned about one another and also identified a major challenge for our caucus: many members were graduate students who were early in their research and who could not come to conferences and thus our annual meetings consistently. In essence, we listened to and had conversations with those who shared an interest in exploring Asian American writing and rhetorical traditions.

> **Haivan:** Nancy and I slipped into the co-chair seats uneasily; we believed that mentorship was invaluable and yet we were new faculty still finding our way. Early on, during my first year as Assistant Professor of English at the University of Massachusetts Amherst, I received an email from a graduate student in Louisiana who was seeking advice about a dissertation project on rhetorical practices of Vietnamese American Catholic priests and congregations in her area. We talked by phone, and as she asked questions about my own dissertation work, I described my meandering path from literacy and rhetorical studies to my research participants' perspectives to Asian American history and culture and, finally, to my own interpretive work. I hoped that, by describing my own process, I might help her find her way through what sounded like a compelling study. And talking with her, I started to realize the full impact of the work, as well as the time and the tolerance for uncertainty required to "write in the spaces left."

In the same year that Haivan and Nancy became co-chairs of the caucus, Terese began a tenure-stream position at the University of Kansas, working with graduate students in cultural rhetorics.

> **Terese:** When I began working with graduate students at the University of Kansas in 2005, none of the students I worked with were Asian American nor were any of them pursuing work in Asian American rhetoric; but I taught Asian American rhetoric along with cultural rhetorics in my graduate seminars to demonstrate the larger contributions this work makes to rhetorical theory and history, methodology, and notions of rhetorical memory, ethos, literacy, and gender studies. And many students, including some students of color, told me that they were beginning to think differently about the racialization of Asian Americans, their historical legacies, and their rhetorical capacities. Since moving to Michigan State University, I've worked with a handful of graduate

students, some more closely than others, who are Asian American or who are pursuing projects in Asian American rhetoric including Robyn Tasaka, Jennifer Sano-Franchini, Lehua Ledbetter, Lamiyah Bahrainwala, and Madhu Narayan. And there are also graduate students from other institutions who contact me or come up to me after a conference session, who are looking for connections, scholarly resources, or teaching strategies. As I continue to mentor graduate students, I emphasize the need to: see Asian Americans as having historical alliances with other communities, especially communities of color; ground this work in the specificities of Asian American history, racial identity, and past and present globalizing forces; recognize long legacies of community-based forms of knowledge; and situate Asian American rhetoric as relevant to broader disciplinary concepts and questions. I encourage them to draw upon scholarly material beyond rhetoric and composition and to look at work, for example, in Asian American Studies because this work is invaluable for delineating context but also for illuminating the specific values and assumptions that traditional notions of rhetoric may impose on Asian American practices. There are more scholarly studies available to graduate students doing work in Asian American rhetoric or literacy than there were when I was a graduate student, but it's also important to recognize that there will always be a gap for certain kinds of studies where young scholars are breaking new ground, exploring new intersections or transnational connections, or working with populations, like Burmese Americans and other South and Southeast Asian Americans, whose rhetorical and literate practices are only beginning to be studied and theorized in rhetoric and composition.

Perhaps one of the more important moments in the recent history of the caucus was the 2008 publication of LuMing Mao and Morris Young's edited collection, *Representations: Doing Asian American Rhetoric*. The collection reflects at least a decade of collaborative work in the caucus and, in many ways, illustrates the larger collaborative project—led by LuMing Mao and Morris Young—that emerged from the networks of support built through the caucus, not just among Asian/Asian American scholars but across the discipline and through interdisciplinary conversations. The edited collection was well received and, due to initiative on Morris Young's part, we had a featured panel on Asian American rhetoric at the 2011 CCCC. The panel was not only retrospective in examining how Asian American rhetoric has developed and evolved since the 2002 CCCC featured session but was also outward looking in framing the significance of Asian American rhetoric for the discipline. It was important for us as a caucus, but also for the larger discipline, to see how work in this area has grown larger and deeper over time. We have also reached a point in our history where we can see how our work has been shaped by these conversations. For many years, we shared works in progress and cited one another before our work was actually published. This way of collaborating was very important for Asian American rhetoric as an emerging field. LuMing Mao and Morris Young were particularly helpful to us as junior scholars. They attended our sessions, provided feedback, promoted our work, and shared their book proposals and other work in progress. By pulling together *Representations*, they also provided a forum for publishing work that was not always recognized by more mainstream venues as making a contribution to the discipline. So the collection's recognition as an honorable mention for the Modern Language Association's 2009 Mina P. Shaughnessy Prize was another important moment in our history.

In 2008, the caucus was again prompted to think about our purpose and, specifically, our role in the professional organization. NCTE's leadership—prompted by the findings of the Task Force to Advance and Support Members of Color—invited the chairs of our caucus and the chairs of the Black Caucus, Latinx Caucus, and American Indian Caucus to have a conversation about our place in the organization. Historically, the caucuses had been formed as independent communities that could examine and critique the ways in which NCTE was attending to racial minority people and their writing, rhetoric, language practices, and education. But we had no formal place in NCTE. Although we understood NCTE's argument that a formal place in its structure might make our perspectives more integral to the organization, our caucus agreed that we could build community without that formal place and perhaps, at least for now, the caucus could enact what Chandra Talpade Mohanty calls a "pedagogy of dissent," where we could challenge CCCC and NCTE to recognize marginalized writers and scholars in ways that would have been limited with a more formal relationship to the organizations. What mattered most to us was building our community so that the voices of both younger and more senior scholars could be heard within the field.

Fostering a culture of dissent is certainly not new to the Asian/Asian American Caucus in past or present forms. In fact, there is a long history of informal collaborations among members of our caucus and members of other caucuses. Through the Writing and Working for Change project, for example, we've learned more about the roots of the Asian/Asian American Caucus. Before this project, we weren't aware of Frank Chin and Jeffery Paul Chan's participation on the NCTE Task Force on Racism and Bias in the Teaching of English. We also learned that while there wasn't always an official Asian or Asian American Caucus, there were Asian Americans who worked in alliance with other NCTE/CCCC members of color and other race-based caucuses. Similar collaborations can also be found in our recent history. As one example, Terese collaborated with other caucuses to pull together a 2002 CCCC workshop on mentoring women of color in the discipline. The purpose of the workshop was to provide a space for women of color to feel some collectivity at CCCC; to focus on issues women of color face in the classroom, in departments, on committees, and within the profession at large; and to talk about the role of cross-disciplinary and inter-ethnic mentors. The workshop brought together women from the Asian/Asian American, Latinx, Black, and American Indian caucuses; presenters and participants included Terese, Gail Okawa, Jean Williams, Jane Hafen, K. Hyoejin Yoon, Dora Ramirez-Dhoore, Annette Harris Powell, Malea Powell, Drema Lipscomb, and Beverly Moss. Several years later, the AAAC collaborated with other caucuses on a day-long workshop on language diversity led by Geneva Smitherman. The 2008 meeting with NCTE inspired caucuses to recommend even more cross-caucus collaborations—a suggestion that we brought up at the standing concerns meeting. These have also been spaces for emergence for they bring us together "to understand and to theorize questions of knowledge, power, and experience in the academy so that [we can] effect both pedagogical empowerment and transformation" (Mohanty 216). And this history will be important for building future cross-caucus alliances and collaborations.

    Creating spaces that would continue to foster transformation and other stories of emergence continued to be a priority when Terese and Stuart Ching became co-chairs of the caucus in 2010. One of their first tasks was to initiate a discussion among caucus members about how to continue building the caucus over the next five years. Expanding the caucus' collaborative efforts, including work on this edited volume and the digital archive project related to the Writing and Working for Change project, was listed high among caucus members' priorities. Caucus members also prioritized collaborative panel presentations and publications as important methods for building and sustaining our networks of support and for making our work more visible to the discipline. Mao and Young began exploring the possibility of putting together an edited volume on primary texts in Asian/Asian American rhetoric, and caucus members began to think about ways to build on Nancy and Hai-van's writing group initiative by proposing a caucus-sponsored CCCC writing workshop. In addition to strengthening intellectual conversation among caucus members, Terese and Stuart thought a writing workshop might provide an institutional space at CCCC to support emerging scholars by bringing them into (and modeling) specific disciplinary conversations, providing feedback on their work, developing their disciplinary network, and building toward another edited volume of work by caucus members.

While the idea of a writing workshop was deemed unfeasible for our members, in the next few years we found other ways to foster stories of emergence and collaboration. At the 2012 CCCC, the caucus began pursuing the possibility of publishing a symposium or octalog on Asian/Asian American rhetoric, literacy, language learning, and pedagogy. K. Hyoejin Yoon, who joined Terese as co-chair in 2012, was instrumental in surveying caucus members about pursuing this possibility. At the same time, Jennifer Sano-Franchini's work on this edited volume prompted important conversations about our history as a caucus and how that history might inform our visions for the future. Organizing our first two AAAC sponsored sessions in 2014 and 2015 was central to these caucus conversations. Terese and Hyoejin, working with Jennifer, began to use the caucus meetings and sponsored sessions strategically to provide an infrastructure that might allow graduate students and early career faculty to "write in the spaces left." The meetings and sponsored sessions became spaces for interdisciplinary and intergenerational dialogue among members *and* spaces that made emergent work more visible at CCCC. These dialogues prompted by the Writing and Working for Change project also extended outward, strengthening coalitions and collaborations across the NCTE/CCCC caucuses.

Caucus members have also been thinking about ways to expand our reach beyond CCCC. We are particularly interested in finding ways to reach out to CCCC members who are interested in the caucus' work but are not able to attend the meetings (or the conference) regularly to bring them into the social network and support systems that are already in place (thanks to the great leadership of past co-chairs). We are also discussing the possibility of increasing the caucus' role within NCTE and exploring what kinds of support and leadership structure might best serve NCTE members interested in the Asian/Asian American Caucus. And, finally, caucus members have suggested we look for ways to advocate for issues impacting Asians and Asian Americans in higher education as well as opportunities to build coalitions with other caucus members to advocate on issues that impact across those populations represented by the caucuses. These are ambitious goals—and some will require more attention to sustainability in their design—but they illustrate the intellectual and public work our members envision for the caucus.

The caucus will continue to be important for scholars at every level. And while the caucus welcomes and encourages all scholars and teachers with interest in Asian/Asian American rhetoric, literacy, and language practices, young scholars who self-identify as Asian/Asian American—regardless of whether they are researching Asian/Asian American topics—will particularly benefit from being part of the caucus because it allows them to connect with senior and junior colleagues like them in terms of their cultural, racial, linguistic, and scholarly identities. It is important that there is a home for these emerging scholars at CCCC and that they see Asian/Asian American scholars represented at conferences and in scholarly journals. The caucus is a space where we can build strategies and support for facing shared struggles and where we can help demystify professional skills like networking, getting published, and becoming involved in the governing bodies of the organization and the profession. We have both written about the importance of rhetorical, collective, and alternative forms of institutional memory, and the caucus—within and outside of our annual meetings—is an important site for these forms of memory, which foster a sense of collective identity, community solidarity, and active participation in the wider discipline. There are forms of our collective history and memory that may only be accessible through conversations with trusted members, a form of gossip that, in the words of Lisa Lowe, serves as "a popular discourse that interrupts and displaces official representational regimes" (113). And it is important for young scholars to learn how this informal networking and knowledge-making happens not just in the caucus but also in the profession. But the caucus itself also benefits from young scholars because they keep us aware of the kind of challenges they're facing—challenges that are going to be different from the challenges we faced when we were emerging scholars. So the caucus, ideally, brings together members at different levels of the profession with different professional and scholarly interests and maintains open dialogue.

Because of the caucus, there is now a greater network of support for Asian American scholars who are engaging in theoretical and empirical research on Asian American rhetoric, who are exploring transnational rhetorics, and who are broadening our understandings of linguistic diversity. We now meet more graduate students and early career faculty who are doing work in these areas, and there is a sizable attendance at our caucus meetings now: we are building momentum. Not only are we starting to engage in cross-talk in our writing, but we are also more likely to hear about how we have influenced emergent work in the discipline. This is another accomplishment of the publication of *Representations: Doing Asian American Rhetoric*: it has formed a foundation for Asian/Asian American scholarship. We would like to see the discipline continue to recognize the contributions Asian/Asian American scholarship makes to the discipline, not just in practical terms but also in methodological and theoretical terms. To borrow from Gwendolyn Pough's 2011 CCCC Chair's Address, Asian/Asian American rhetoric "is bigger than me. It is bigger than you. Indeed it is bigger than [Asian/Asian American] comp/rhet" (302). And we would both like to see the work by caucus members impact disciplinary conversations beyond Asian/Asian American rhetoric.

Cultivating Asian/Asian American voices has been particularly important in light of recent moments, when attention to global economies have presented China and India as new "yellow perils"; when Asian American rhetorical and literacy traditions are not recognized as significant; and when, quite simply, the first voice we hear is not our own. The "model minority" myth—that Asian Americans are hardworking, are good at math and science, assimilate into U.S. society easily, and don't make waves—is one force that keeps Asian/Asian American rhetorical legacies hidden. These dominant myths work to displace other Asian/Asian American legacies—the atrocity of Japanese Internment, the Vietnam War, the Philippine–American War, and the Asian American movement, to name a few—in U.S. history and public memory. Familiar dominant narratives like "yellow peril" and "model minority" come together in more pronounced ways in contemporary discourses on globalization. Anxieties about globalization get mapped onto Asian bodies and languages on our college campuses, for example, as the number of Asian international students continues to grow.

Stories of emergence will always be necessary for members of our caucus as these racial contexts are always shifting, calling for new forms of rhetorical agency. In this way, Asian/Asian American rhetoric has affinity with Lisa Lowe's *Immigrant Acts* as it "names the agency of Asian immigrants and Asian Americans: the acts of labor, resistance, memory, and survival, as well as the politicized work that emerges from dislocation and disidentification" (9). Our colleagues in the caucus have been working hard to recognize and testify to these Asian and Asian American discursive acts in sites that include, to name a few, Japanese American internment camps, classrooms, sites of national and transnational citizenship, social media, and literary texts—sites that demonstrate "togetherness-in-difference."[2] Looking forward as a caucus, we seek to build on ongoing research and education that affirms the "traces of a stream" (Royster) left by Asian/Asian American writers, rhetors, activists, and educators and that reflects how these streams help constitute the deeper waters of our field.

---

2   Togetherness in difference" is a term used by Ien Ang to explain why hybridity, as a concept, holds particular importance for describing the cultural politics of Asia and the West in a globalized world (3). Because Mao has also made the term relevant to the makings of Chinese American rhetoric, we use it here to characterize the important spirit of "togetherness-in-difference" that characterizes the Asian/Asian American Caucus.

WORKS CITED

Ang, Ien. *On Not Speaking Chinese: Living Between Asia and the West.* London: Routledge, 2001. Print.

Blackmon, Samantha, Cristina Kirklighter, and Steve Parks. "Introduction: Listening to Our Elders." *Listening to Our Elders: Working and Writing for Change.* Ed. Samantha Blackmon, Cristina Kirklighter, and Steve Parks. Philadelphia and Logan: New City Community Press and Utah State UP, 2011. 1–5. Print.

Cook, William W. "Writing in the Spaces Left." *College Composition and Communication* 44.1 (February 1993): 9–25. Print.

Lowe, Lisa. *Immigrant Acts: On Asian American Cultural Politics.* Durham: Duke UP, 1996. Print.

Mao, LuMing. "Individualism or Personhood: A Battle of Locution or Rhetoric?" *Rhetoric, Cultural Studies, and Literacy: Selected Papers from the 1994 Conference of the RSA.* Ed. John Frederick Reynolds. Hillsdale: Lawrence Erlbaum, 1995. 127–35. Print.

—. NCTE Centennial Writing and Working for Change Founders Panel, Part 2: 1980s and 1990s. National Council of Teachers of English Convention. Chicago Hilton, Chicago, IL. 19 November 2011.

—. *Reading Chinese Fortune Cookie: The Making of Chinese American Rhetoric.* Logan: Utah State UP, 2006. Print.

Mao, LuMing, and Morris Young, eds. *Representations: Doing Asian American Rhetoric.* Logan: Utah State UP, 2008. Print.

Mecenas, Jolivette. "A Career of Acting 'Ill-Mannered': An Interview with Jeffery Paul Chan." *Listening to Our Elders: Working and Writing for Change.* Ed. Samantha Blackmon, Cristina Kirklighter, and Steve Parks. Philadelphia and Logan: New City Community Press and Utah State UP, 2011. 28–44. Print.

Mohanty, Chandra Talpade. "Race, Multiculturalism, and Pedagogies of Dissent." *Feminism Without Borders: Decolonizing Theory, Practicing Solidarity.* Durham: Duke UP, 2003. 190–219. Print.

Pough, Gwendolyn. "It's Bigger Than Comp/Rhet: Contested and Undisciplined." *College Composition and Communication* 63.2 (2011): 301–13. Print.

Royster, Jacqueline Jones. *Traces of a Stream: Literacy and Social Change Among African American Women.* Pittsburgh: U of Pittsburgh P, 2000. Print.

—. "When the First Voice You Hear Is Not Your Own." *College Composition and Communication* 47.1 (February 1996): 29–40. Print.

Royster, Jacqueline Jones, and Jean C. Williams. "History in the Spaces Left: African American Presence and Narratives of Composition Studies." *College Composition and Communication* 50.4 (1999): 563–84. Print.

Wu, Hui. "The Enthymeme Examined from the Chinese Value System." *Making and Unmaking the Prospects of Rhetoric: Selected Papers from the 1996 Rhetoric Society of America Conference.* Ed. Theresa Enos. Mahwah: Erlbaum, 1997. 115–22. Print.

Young, Morris. *Minor Re/Visions: Asian American Literacy Narratives as a Rhetoric of Citizenship.* Carbondale: Southern Illinois UP, 2004. Print.

CIRCULATION ESSAY

The Impact of Asian and Asian American Scholarship as a Productive, Contested Site

Linh Dich

The Asian/Asian American Caucus has been, itself, a contested site of identity, politics, and power. Its history, as others such as Morris Young have posited, points to internal fissure and conflict, but also provides us a rich understanding of collective formation and outcomes from within our very own organization. One such outcome are the networks and connections that have functioned to support and promote our individual and collective scholarship. Albeit too short to cover all of our collective labor, the past annual meetings at CCCC have been successful in helping junior faculty acquire speaking positions on panels with more established faculty. This sort of intentional supporting has spurned on other projects, helping all members create viable relationships for their scholarship.

To think about the question of impact, I turn to *Representations: Doing Asian American Rhetoric*: "we have seen few systematic studies that focus on how Asian Americans use language to perform discursive acts and on how they develop persuasive and other rhetorical strategies to create knowledge and to effect social, political, and cultural transformations. . . . In short, there is not much work done on the making of Asian American rhetoric" (Mao and Young 3). Since the first publication of *Representations* in 2008, how might we measure Mao and Young's call to action or the ways that Asian and Asian American scholars have made contributions to our field?

On one hand, we can point to hard data for understanding impact. Again, using *Representations* as an example, this collection has gone through three editions and is held by 694 WorldCat libraries worldwide. It has been translated into Chinese, underscoring its value on a global scale. Both LuMing Mao and Morris Young are key contributors in our field. Mao has published or contributed to 26 original works: one sole-authored book (*Reading Chinese Fortune Cookie*), two edited books, seven book chapters, eleven journal articles, one co-authored article, and he has made four contributions to journals as an editor or as author of an introduction. His book, *Reading Chinese Fortune Cookie: The Making of Chinese American Rhetoric*, has been translated into Chinese in 2013; collectively, Mao's works are held in 1,445 libraries worldwide. Young has published or contributed to 13 original works: one sole-authored book (*Minor Re/Visions*), one collection that he edited with Mao (*Representations*), four book chapters, two co-authored book chapters, four journal articles, and Young edited one journal edition. His works are held in 1,718 libraries worldwide (*MLA International Bibliography*; *WorldCat Identities*).

As traditional measures of impact, however, these numbers provide an incomplete picture of the significance of Mao and Young's collection. *Representations* also won honorable mention for the Modern Language Association's 2009 Mina P. Shaughnessy Prize. While impressive, such accolades and hard data do not account for the times that *Representations* has been assigned in graduate courses, cited informally at conferences, or used for subsequent projects due to its frameworks and approaches.

How might we think about Asian and Asian American scholarship as both productive and contested, especially when such scholarship can be seen as increasingly contributing to the field? On the one hand, the term, "Asian and Asian American scholarship" provides what Gayatri Chakravorty Spivak calls a "*strategic* use of positivist essentialism" (205; emphasis in the original) helping the field forge inroads into a rhetorical tradition dominated by Westernized perspectives. But on the other hand, it is still an essentializing term that has functioned to include and exclude people in our very own group.

I am reminded of our March 2014 AAAC meeting and how the term "Asian and Asian American" prompted discussion among members. Inevitably, we turned to excavating a historical narrative of how the AAAC has been shaped into what it is today by the very conflicts surrounding the politics of naming. Indeed, any name or label for a group is political work. We didn't end up resolving this issue during our meeting, but what I took away from this discussion wasn't failure but a deeper sense of community, shared goals for doing "good" scholarship. We were forwarding our own unique approaches and voices that ultimately came together as a collective desire to do better and be better teachers, scholars, and activists.

Maybe "positivist essentialism" or exclusion isn't the choice we have to make about naming our caucus. Can we maintain a "positivist essentialism" while opening this space and collective identity up to continuous, transformative possibilities? Perhaps, as Jolivette Mecenas argues, we can have "variation" (210) within broader, political labels, while continuously challenging the closure of possibility, whether individually or as a group by providing more time and space for interrogating what and who we are.

WORKS CITED

Mao, LuMing. *Reading Chinese Fortune Cookie: The Making of Chinese American Rhetoric.* Logan: Utah State UP, 2006. Print.

Mao, LuMing, and Morris Young. *Representations: Doing Asian American Rhetoric.* Logan: Utah State UP, 2008. Print.

Mecenas, Jolivette. "Beyond 'Asian American' and Back: Coalitional Rhetoric in Print and New Media." *Representations: Doing Asian American Rhetoric.* Ed. LuMing Mao and Morris Young. Logan: Utah State UP, 2008. 198–217. Print.

MLA International Bibliography. 2016. Web. 25. Aug. 2016.

Spivak, Chakravorty Gayatri. *In Other Worlds: Essays in Cultural Studies.* New York: Methuen, 1987. Print.

WorldCat Identities. 2010. Web. 25. Aug. 2016.

Young, Morris. *Minor Re/Visions: Asian American Literacy Narratives as a Rhetoric of Citizenship.* Carbondale: Southern Illinois UP, 2004. Print.

A Collection of Images and Archival Documents

The NCTE Archives at the University of Illinois Urbana-Champaign Archives Research Center, Urbana, Illinois, July 2010.

Samantha Blackmon and Cristina Kirklighter inside of the NCTE Archives at the University of Illinois Urbana-Champaign Archives Research Center, Urbana, Illinois, July 2010.

Issues of Bridge: The Asian-American Magazine at the NCTE Archives, University of Illinois Urbana-Champaign Archives Research Center, Urbana Illinois, July 2010.

July 9, 1971

Mr. Robert F. Hogan
Executive Secretary
National Council of Teachers of English
1111 Kenyon Road,
Urbana, Illinois 61801

Dear Bob:

Check with your attorney and I think you'll find your fears are unfounded. Virginia Lee was interviewed as the authoress of the novel, THE HOUSE THAT TAI MING BUILT, which featured Chinese and Chinese-American characters and a San Francisco Chinatown setting. She was interviewed on tape by a writer who announced himself as a writer, and photographed by a photrapher, with the understanding that the material would be made availible to scholars of Chinese-America and used. In fact, the material has been used, not only by us, who gathered it, but by Kai-yu Hsu in his introduction to the Asian-American anthology to be released this year by Houghton Mifflin Company.

The material quoted is about her writing and her subject matter and the Chinatown background used in her novel...not her character. Within the realm of literary criticism it is fair, in fact, it is the function of literary criticism, to question the intelligence and the competence of the author under discussion. And our paper is literary criticism.

As to the letter. Letters become the property of the addressee and are theirs to publish, file away, or destroy as they please. Ellen Whalen has nothing more to say about her letter, since it doesn't belong to her, but to Jeffery Chan. That's the law. So this letter is now yours. And I pooh pooh your worrying about that last satirical tag getting Ellen Whalen fired. If she does get the can it won't be because of anything in the paper. There's no case to get on. But if you're real uptight about it...that tag, you can substitute the word "bleep" for those words you feel are too charged and offensive.

Jeffery and I had a good time that week.

Sincerely,

Frank Chin
    and
Jeffery Chan

Letter from Frank Chin and Jeffery Chan to Robert F. Hogan, Executive Secretary at NCTE, dated July 9, 1971.

July 14, 1971

Mr. Philip C. Zimmerly
Attorney at Law
302 West Hill
Champaign, Illinois 61820

Dear Phil:

Another muddy one.

We had a Task Force of people meeting here two or three weeks ago concerned with the treatment of minority groups in conventional textbooks, particularly American literature textbooks at the college level.

Two of the participants were representing Asian-Americans. During their time here they drafted an ''Asian-American'' position paper. They left a copy behind.

I was troubled by parts of it and wrote to them in that connection. The first attachment is a copy of my letter of June 15.

The second attachment is a photocopy of those pages in question. I won't trouble you or burden you with the whole thirty odd pages. One passage begins on page 8 and concludes in about the middle of page 11. The other begins in the middle of page 29 and concludes on the next page.

I've got lots of concerns about their work, but two issues of the moment are those two that I touched on in my letter of June 15. Their response to those concerns is the final attachment. Am I right in thinking that if something were to happen to the lady in that publishing company not long after the Council published and widely distributed the statement, we might be vulnerable?

I'm leaving for England on July 15 and won't get back until the night of the 27th. But I'll be in the office then for the rest of that week and much of the following week. At your convenience, after you've had a chance to read the stuff, would you give me a call and let me know what you think?

Sincerely,

Robert F. Hogan

Letter from Robert F. Hogan to Philip C. Zimmerly, Attorney at Law, dated July 14, 1971.

LAW OFFICES OF

PHILIP C. ZIMMERLY

302 WEST HILL STREET · CHAMPAIGN, ILLINOIS 61820 (217) 352-7676

PHILIP C. ZIMMERLY
JAMES M. LANGAN

July 17, 1971

Mr. Robert F. Hogan
National Council of Teachers of English
1111 Kenyon Road
Urbana, Illinois 61801

Dear Bob,

    With reference to your letter of July 14, which arrived this morning, I agree thoroughly with the advice you gave Msrs. Chan and Chin. I am dropping you this note because I now have scheduled a medical malpractice jury trial in Danville the week of the 26th, which may well take the entire week. Thereupon, I have reservations to fly to Portland the night of the 30th for a trial lawyers convention there, followed by a week of vacation in San Francisco (where I will be a stereotype tourist).

    I have marked my calendar to try to call you on the 28th. But if I do not reach you, stick to your guns and refuse to print the materials you sent me.

Sincerely,

Philip C. Zimmerly

PCZ/jae

Letter from Philip C. Zimmerly, Attorney at Law to Robert F. Hogan, dated July 17, 1971.

Program photo of Frank Chin, who was featured as a convention luncheon featured speaker for the CCCC at the Sixty Fifth Annual NCTE Convention in 1975.

The NCTE Headquarters in Urbana, Illinois, July 2010.

SAN FRANCISCO UNIFIED SCHOOL DISTRICT
135 VAN NESS AVENUE, Rm. #203
SAN FRANCISCO, CALIFORNIA 94102
Telephone: (415) 863-4680

DEC 17 1971

Task Force on Racism and Bias
National Council of Teachers of English
1111 Kenyon Road
Urbana, Illinois, 61801

Dear Sir:

I have just finished reading a copy of your "Criteria for teaching materials in reading and literature." I would appreciate very much a copy of the paragraph revision concerning Asian-Americans, if and when it ever comes out.

I would like to point out that racism in the urban areas was perfected by racist elements on Asian-Americans. Urban racism, as we now know it, was first perfected on the Asians, and is now, in turn, being used on other out-groups. I think that I have enough evidence to back up what I have just said with a great amount of authority. The point is, then, that one of the Asian-Americans' "contributions" to America is their being victims of marginal racism, a type of racism that sometimes is so covert that it is impossible to combat.

If there is anything I can do to help in your task force, especially as it pertains to Asian-Americans, I would be most happy to serve.

Sincerely,

John B. Lum, Ph.D.
Evaluator, Multi-ethnic Curriculum (ESAP Project)
Consultant, Title VII Chinese Bilingual Project

p.s. Please thank Mrs. Betty Kuykendall for sending me all the information and materials that I requested.

Letter from John B. Lum, Evaluator of Multi-ethnic Curriculum and Consultant for the Title VII Chinese Bilingual Project, to the NCTE Task Force on Racism and Bias, date stamped December 17, 1971, regarding the Criteria for Teaching Materials in Reading and Literature.

Jennifer Sano-Franchini, Cristina Kirklighter, and Samantha Blackmon at NCTE Headquarters, Urbana, Illinois, July 2010.

The room where past convention programs are stored. NCTE Headquarters, Urbana, Illinois, July 2010.

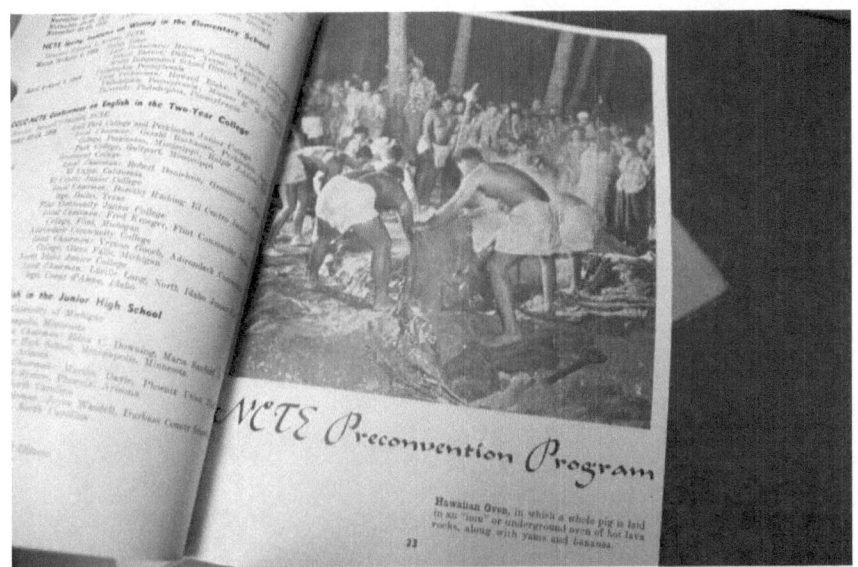

The NCTE Preconvention Program for the Fifty-Seventh Annual Meeting in Honolulu, Hawai'i, 1967.

Morris Young and LuMing Mao receive honorable mention for the Mina P. Shaughnessy Prize, 2009.

Representations: Doing Asian American Rhetoric, *edited by LuMing Mao and Morris Young.*

The first caucus website, developed by Haivan V. Hoang and Mark Koyama.

LuMing Mao delivers his presentation at the 2011 CCCC Featured Session "Contesting and Constructing Asian American Rhetorics: Reflections and Possibilities," with Mira Shimabukuro, Morris Young, and Terese Guinsatao Monberg (not pictured). From "Writing and Working for Change Video Project" by Alexandra Hidalgo.

Terese Guinsatao Monberg delivers her presentation at the 2011 CCCC Featured Session "Contesting and Constructing Asian American Rhetorics: Reflections and Possibilities," with Mira Shimabukuro, Morris Young, and LuMing Mao. From "Writing and Working for Change Video Project" by Alexandra Hidalgo.

Haivan V. Hoang and LuMing Mao meet at CCCC 2012. From "Writing and Working for Change Video Project," by Alexandra Hidalgo.

Stuart Ching and Terese Guinsatao Monberg at the AAAC business meeting at CCCC 2012. From "Writing and Working for Change Video Project" by Alexandra Hidalgo.

Morris Young, Terese Guinsatao Monberg, and Haivan V. Hoang at the AAAC business meeting at CCCC 2012. From "Writing and Working for Change Video Project" by Alexandra Hidalgo.

Anam Govardhan at the AAAC business meeting at CCCC 2012. From "Writing and Working for Change Video Project" by Alexandra Hidalgo.

Ilene Crawford and K. Hyoejin Yoon at the AAAC business meeting at CCCC 2012. From "Writing and Working for Change Video Project" by Alexandra Hidalgo.

Chanon Adsanatham and Haivan V. Hoang at the AAAC business meeting at CCCC 2012. From "Writing and Working for Change Video Project" by Alexandra Hidalgo.

Terese Guinsatao Monberg is interviewed for the Writing and Working for Change project. From "Writing and Working for Change Video Project" by Alexandra Hidalgo.

Terese Guinsatao Monberg, K. Hyoejin Yoon, Jennifer Sano-Franchini, Linh Dich, and Asao Inoue (Respondent) at the AAAC sponsored session at CCCC 2014. Photograph by Jerry Lee.

Storify of tweets during the AAAC sponsored session at CCCC 2014, "Voices from the Asian/Asian American Caucus: Opening Up Our Disciplinary History and Scholarship." Curated by Patti Poblete (@voleuseCK).

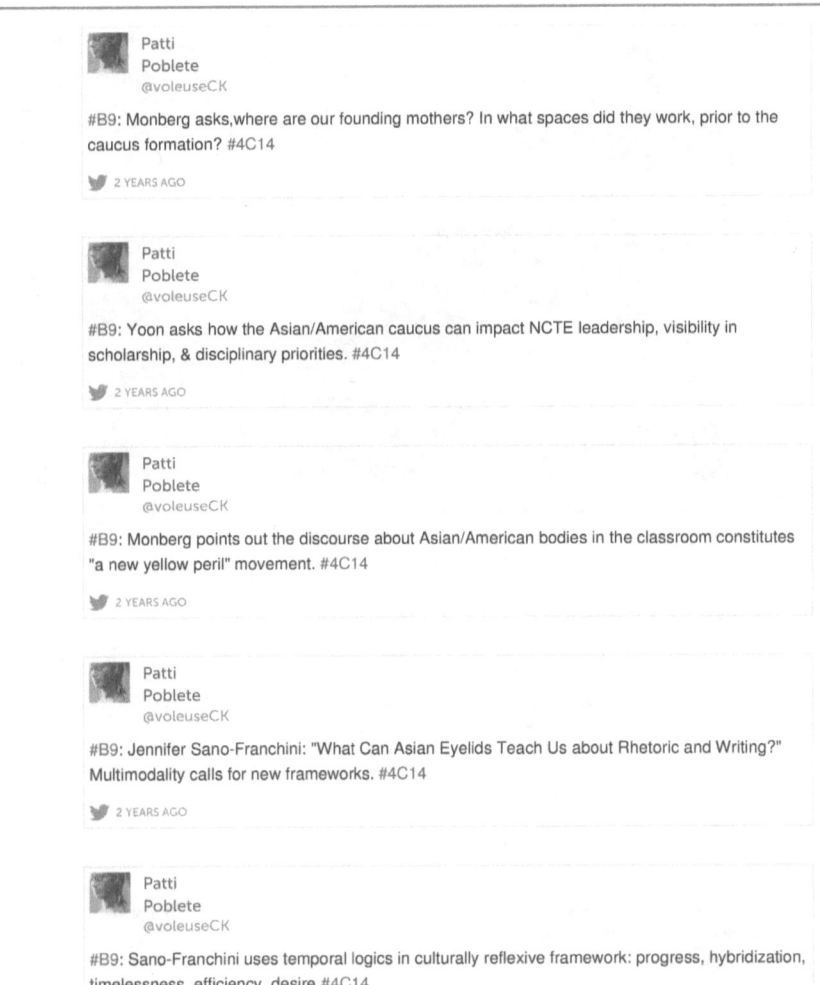

Storify of tweets during the AAAC sponsored session at CCCC 2014, "Voices from the Asian/Asian American Caucus: Opening Up Our Disciplinary History and Scholarship." Curated by Patti Poblete (@voleuseCK).

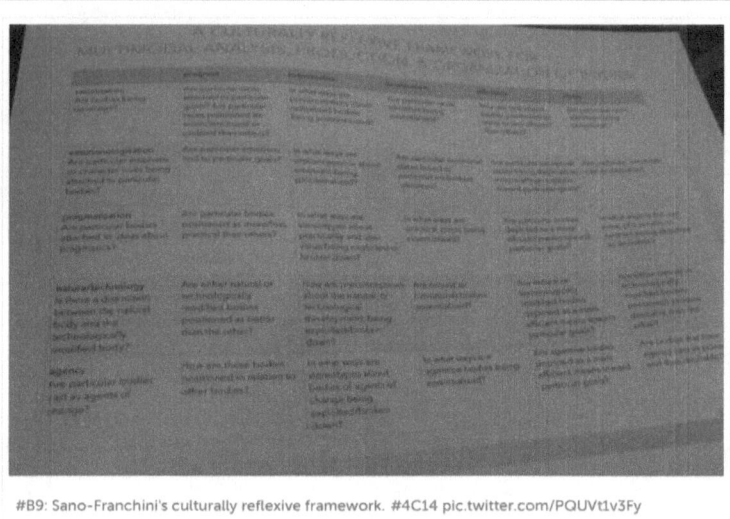

#B9: Sano-Franchini's culturally reflexive framework. #4C14 pic.twitter.com/PQUVt1v3Fy

 PATTI POBLETE @VOLEUSECK 2 YEARS AGO

Patti Poblete
@voleuseCK

#B9: Linh Dich addresses the way international students are recruited to and then discriminated against on college campuses. #4C14

 2 YEARS AGO

Patti Poblete
@voleuseCK

#B9: Dich asks is to consider how increased international recruitment requires more mindful consideration of campus dynamics. #4C14

 2 YEARS AGO

Storify of tweets during the AAAC sponsored session at CCCC 2014, "Voices from the Asian/Asian American Caucus: Opening Up Our Disciplinary History and Scholarship." Curated by Patti Poblete (@voleuseCK).

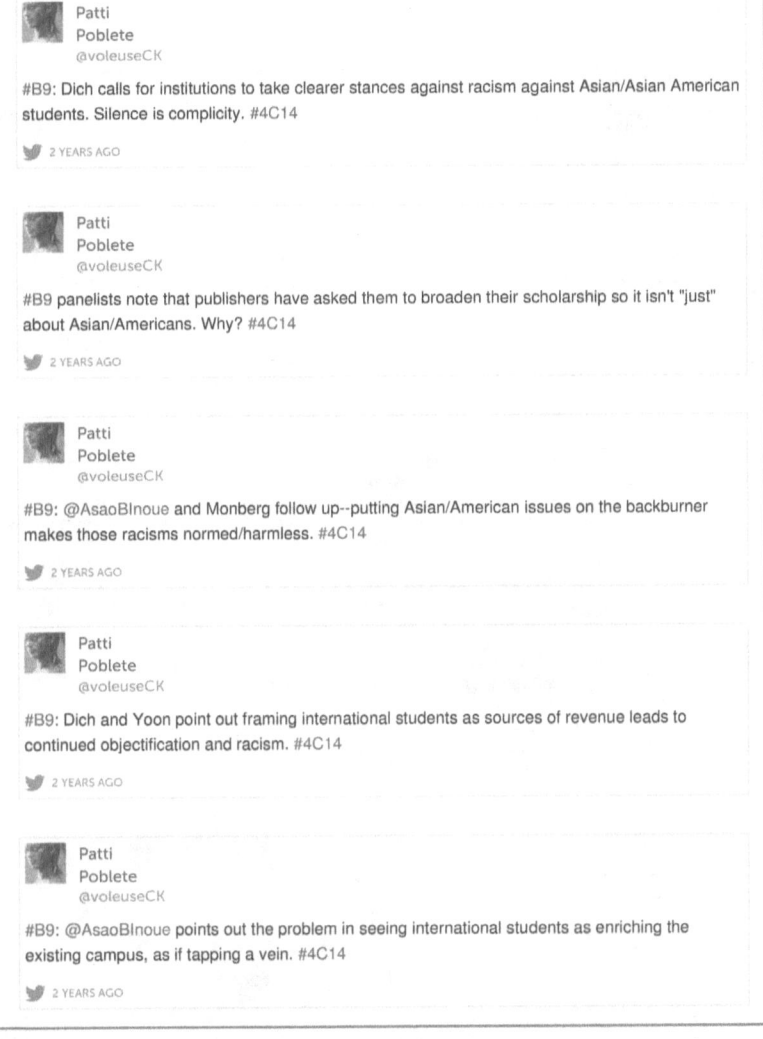

Storify of tweets during the AAAC sponsored session at CCCC 2014, "Voices from the Asian/Asian American Caucus: Opening Up Our Disciplinary History and Scholarship." Curated by Patti Poblete (@voleuseCK).

> **Storify** by voleuseCK a year ago
>
> ## #4c15 #B06: Asian/Asian American Scholarship in Rhetoric and Composition: Risks and Rewards
>
> Terese Guinsatao Monberg, chair; K. Jyoejin Yoon; Phuong Tran, Edward Lee, Michael Pak, Scott Kaalele; Jo Mecenas; Linh Dich; Lehua Ledbetter; Hui Wu, respondent
>
> I volunteered to livetweet this session, since I'm a member of the A/AAC and curator of its Twitter account. taking pictures of most of the speakers, but my cameraphone + lighting + distance weren't quite ideal.
>
> > **B.06 Asian/Asian American Scholarship in Rhetoric and Composition: Risks and Rewards (Sponsored by the Asian/Asian American Caucus)**
> > Discusses historical and emergent work in Asian/Asian American studies in rhetoric/composition to explore its risks and rewards.
> > **Chair:** Terese Monberg, Michigan State University, East Lansing, MI
> > **Speakers:**
> > - K. Hyoejin Yoon & Phuong Tran, "The Presence of Asian/Asian American Scholars in College Composition and Communication (1950-2010)"
> > - Edward Lee, Michael Pak, and Scott Kaalele, "Racial Identities, Visual Representations, and Performative Capacities: Rhetorical Production(s) of/by Asian/Asian Americans in Hawai'i"
> > - Jolivette Mecenas, "Racial Formations of Second Language International Students and the Responsibility of the WPA"
> > - Linh Dich, Miami University, Oxford, OH, "The Impact of Asian/Asian American Scholarship as a Productive, Contested Site"
> > - Lehua Ledbetter, University of Rhode Island, Haslett, MI, "Risks and Affordances: Naming the Asian/Asian American Caucus"
> >
> > **Respondent:** Hui Wu, University of Texas at Tyler
> >
> > Come join #B06, the Asian/Asian-American Caucus sponsored panel in Marriott, Florida Salon VI on the 2nd floor! #4c15 pic.twitter.com/hYukIFpoCP
> >
> > CCCC A/AAC   @CCCCAAAC   @voleuseCK · A YEAR AGO

Storify of tweets during the AAAC sponsored session at CCCC 2015, "Asian/Asian American Scholarship in Rhetoric and Composition: Risks and Rewards." Curated by Patti Poblete (@voleuseCK).

B.06 Asian/Asian American Scholarship in Rhetoric and Composition: Risks and Rewards (Sponsored by the Asian/Asian American Caucus)
Discusses historical and emergent work in Asian/Asian American studies in rhetoric/composition to explore its risks and rewards.
Chair: Terese Monberg, Michigan State University, East Lansing, MI
Speakers:
- K. Hyoejin Yoon & Phuong Tran, "The Presence of Asian/Asian American Scholars in College Composition and Communication (1950-2010)"
- Edward Lee, Michael Pak, and Scott Kaalele, "Racial Identities, Visual Representations, and Performative Capacities: Rhetorical Production(s) of/by Asian/Asian Americans in Hawai'i"
- Jolivette Mecenas, "Racial Formations of Second Language International Students and the Responsibility of the WPA"
- Linh Dich, Miami University, Oxford, OH, "The Impact of Asian/Asian American Scholarship as a Productive, Contested Site"
- Lehua Ledbetter, University of Rhode Island, Haslett, MI, "Risks and Affordances: Naming the Asian/Asian American Caucus"

Respondent: Hui Wu, University of Texas at Tyler

Seriously, this @CCCCAAAC panel is going to be INTENSE and fun. Look at this roster of presenters! #B06 #4c15 pic.twitter.com/naBdQiiaPu

 PATTI POBLETE @VOLEUSECK · A YEAR AGO

Patti Poblete
@voleuseCK

Terese Guinsatao Monberg introduces the session, framing the @CCCCAAAC's work in histories, identities, and educational research. #B06 #4c15

A YEAR AGO

Patti Poblete
@voleuseCK

Terese Guinsatao Monberg asks us to draft action items for @CCCCAAAC, ways that we can be participant in @NCTE_CCCC's agenda. #B06 #4c15

A YEAR AGO

Patti Poblete
@voleuseCK

Hyoejin Yoon invokes David Palumbo-Lui's "Asian/American" work as a work that explores and digs into the conventions of naming. #B06 #4c15

A YEAR AGO

Storify of tweets during the AAAC sponsored session at CCCC 2015, "Asian/Asian American Scholarship in Rhetoric and Composition: Risks and Rewards." Curated by Patti Poblete (@voleuseCK).

Storify of tweets during the AAAC sponsored session at CCCC 2015, "Asian/Asian American Scholarship in Rhetoric and Composition: Risks and Rewards." Curated by Patti Poblete (@voleuseCK).

Phuong Tran, detailing her findings of 3Cs pubs w/ A/AA scholarship--less than 10%. #B06 #4c15
pic.twitter.com/des4kNGSyS

PATTI POBLETE @VOLEUSECK · A YEAR AGO

Patti Poblete
@voleuseCK

Tran invokes Swearingen--not A/AA by racial background, but does research in Chinese rhetoric. Does she count as an A/AA scholar? #B06 #4c15

A YEAR AGO

Patti Poblete
@voleuseCK

Next, @lehualedbetter presents, "Risks and Afordances: Naming the AAAC." #B06 #4c15

A YEAR AGO

Storify of tweets during the AAAC sponsored session at CCCC 2015, "Asian/Asian American Scholarship in Rhetoric and Composition: Risks and Rewards." Curated by Patti Poblete (@voleuseCK).

Storify of tweets during the AAAC sponsored session at CCCC 2015, "Asian/Asian American Scholarship in Rhetoric and Composition: Risks and Rewards." Curated by Patti Poblete (@voleuseCK).

Storify of tweets during the AAAC sponsored session at CCCC 2015, "Asian/Asian American Scholarship in Rhetoric and Composition: Risks and Rewards." Curated by Patti Poblete (@voleuseCK).

Storify of tweets during the AAAC sponsored session at CCCC 2015, "Asian/Asian American Scholarship in Rhetoric and Composition: Risks and Rewards." Curated by Patti Poblete (@voleuseCK).

Storify of tweets during the AAAC sponsored session at CCCC 2015, "Asian/Asian American Scholarship in Rhetoric and Composition: Risks and Rewards." Curated by Patti Poblete (@voleuseCK).

Storify of tweets during the AAAC sponsored session at CCCC 2015, "Asian/Asian American Scholarship in Rhetoric and Composition: Risks and Rewards." Curated by Patti Poblete (@voleuseCK).

Patti Poblete
@voleuseCK

The intensity of 3-minute presentations for each speaker in #B06 is cool--big, complicated ideas, distilled into major questions. #4c15

 A YEAR AGO

Patti Poblete
@voleuseCK

Mecenas invokes Inoue and Poe's "Race and Writing Assessment." eric.ed.gov/?id=ED533148 #B06 #4c15

 A YEAR AGO

Mecenas asks what WPAs' responsibilities toward multilingual writers are. #B06 #4c15
pic.twitter.com/STgPZtk3wF

 PATTI POBLETE @VOLEUSECK · A YEAR AGO

Patti Poblete
@voleuseCK

Mecenas invokes Matsuda, thinking about doing research that will "generate more descriptions" rather than obsess over RAD. #B06 #4c15

A YEAR AGO

Storify of tweets during the AAAC sponsored session at CCCC 2015, "Asian/Asian American Scholarship in Rhetoric and Composition: Risks and Rewards." Curated by Patti Poblete (@voleuseCK).

Patti Poblete
@voleuseCK

Linh Dich starts by invoking LuMing Mao, in "The Impact of Asian/Asian American Scholarship as a Productive, Contested Site." #B06 #4c15

 A YEAR AGO

Patti Poblete
@voleuseCK

Dich considers the terminology "Asian/Asian American," invoking Spivak, re: strategic essentialism. It includes, and excludes. #B06 #4c15

 A YEAR AGO

Dich calls back to last year's @CCCCAAAC caucus, & how we struggled w/ the generative/restrictive labels. #B06 #4c15 pic.twitter.com/vFXtJJjjEy

PATTI POBLETE @VOLEUSECK · A YEAR AGO

Storify of tweets during the AAAC sponsored session at CCCC 2015, "Asian/Asian American Scholarship in Rhetoric and Composition: Risks and Rewards." Curated by Patti Poblete (@voleuseCK).

Storify of tweets during the AAAC sponsored session at CCCC 2015, "Asian/Asian American Scholarship in Rhetoric and Composition: Risks and Rewards." Curated by Patti Poblete (@voleuseCK).

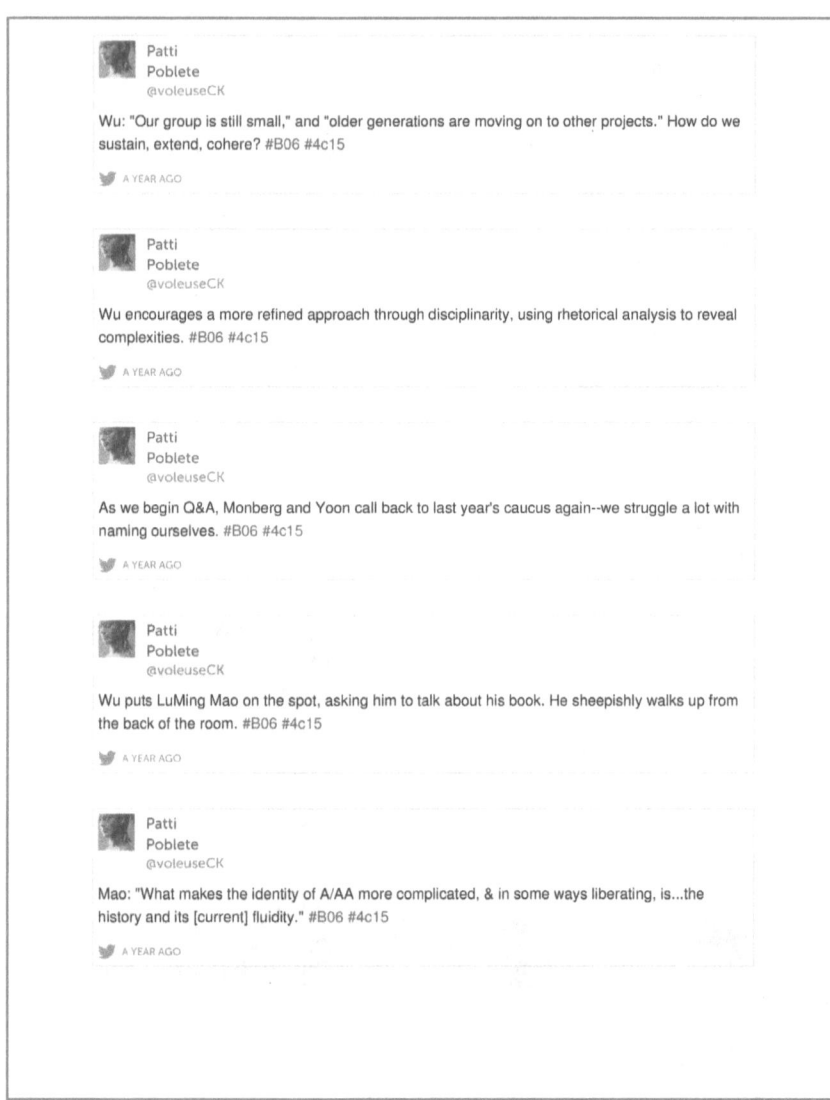

Storify of tweets during the AAAC sponsored session at CCCC 2015, "Asian/Asian American Scholarship in Rhetoric and Composition: Risks and Rewards." Curated by Patti Poblete (@voleuseCK).

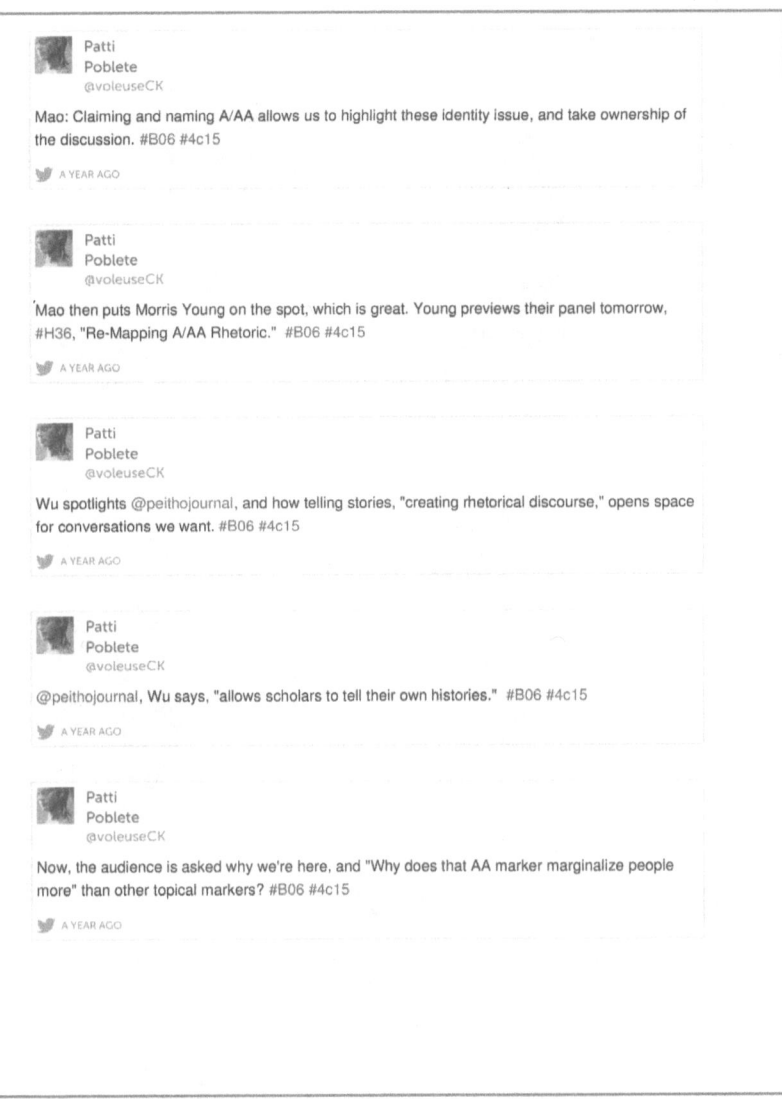

Storify of tweets during the AAAC sponsored session at CCCC 2015, "Asian/Asian American Scholarship in Rhetoric and Composition: Risks and Rewards." Curated by Patti Poblete (@voleuseCK).

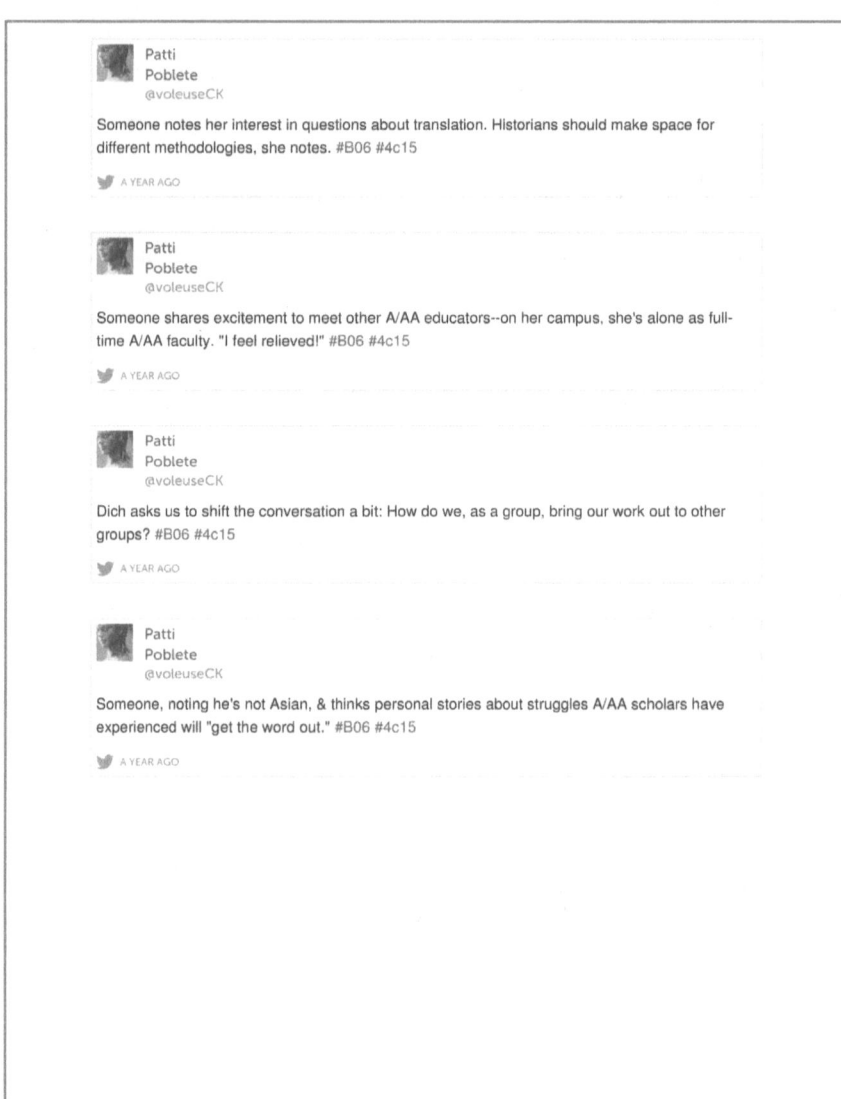

Storify of tweets during the AAAC sponsored session at CCCC 2015, "Asian/Asian American Scholarship in Rhetoric and Composition: Risks and Rewards." Curated by Patti Poblete (@voleuseCK).

CCCC A/AAC @CCCCAAAC · 19 Mar 2015
Come join #B06, the Asian/Asian-American Caucus sponsored panel in Marriott, Florida Salon VI on the 2nd floor! #4c15

> **B.06 Asian/Asian American Scholarship in Rhetoric and Composition: Risks and Rewards (Sponsored by the Asian/Asian American Caucus)**
> Discusses historical and emergent work in Asian/Asian American studies in rhetoric/composition to explore its risks and rewards.
> *Chair:* Terese Monberg, Michigan State University, East Lansing, MI
> *Speakers:*
> - K. Hyoejin Yoon & Phuong Tran, "The Presence of Asian/Asian American Scholars in College Composition and Communication (1950-2010)"
> - Edward Lee, Michael Pak, and Scott Kaalele, "Racial Identities, Visual Representations, and Performative Capacities: Rhetorical Production(s) of/by Asian/Asian Americans in Hawai'i"
> - Jolivette Mecenas, "Racial Formations of Second Language International Students and the Responsibility of the WPA"
> - Linh Dich, Miami University, Oxford, OH, "The Impact of Asian/Asian American Scholarship as a Productive, Contested Site"
> - Lehua Ledbetter, University of Rhode Island, Haslett, MI, "Risks and Affordances: Naming the Asian/Asian American Caucus"
>
> *Respondent:* Hui Wu, University of Texas at Tyler

The AAAC (@CCCCAAAC) twitter account announces the sponsored session at CCCC 2015, March 19, 2015: "Asian/Asian American Scholarship in Rhetoric and Composition: Risks and Rewards. Presentations by K. Hyoejin Yoon, Phuong Minh Tran, Edward Lee, Michael Pak, Scott Ka'alele, Jolivette Mecenas, Linh Dich, and Lehua Ledbetter, with Terese Guinsatao Monberg as chair and Hui Wu as respondent.

Belle Xiaobo Wang and Hui Wu at the AAAC sponsored session at CCCC 2015.

Belle Xiaobo Wang, LuMing Mao, and Shui-Yin Sharon Yam at the AAAC sponsored session at CCCC 2015.

5-History

D.07 New Directions in Transnational Asian/Asian American Rhetoric and Composition: Issues for Historiography, Digital Rhetoric, Racial Justice, and Writing Center Research

This Asian/Asian American Caucus–sponsored roundtable highlights new directions in transnational Asian/Asian American rhetoric and writing.

Hilton Ballroom of the Americas Salon F, Level Two

Chair: Jolivette Mecenas, University of La Verne
Speakers: Chanon Adsanatham, University of Maryland, "Re-Placing Archival Studies in the Global Turn: Critical Methods for Researching Asian Rhetorics"
Priya Sirohi, Purdue University, "Rhetorics of South/Asian American Identity: Mapping Context, Purpose, and Use"
Patricia Poblete, Iowa State University, "Taking Action on Campus: Re-Examining 'Asian' Identities of Writers in the Writing Center"
Morris Young, University of Wisconsin-Madison, "Historicizing Transnational Asian American Rhetoric"
Vani Kannan, Syracuse University, "#ModelMinorityMutiny: Defining"
Xiaobo Wang, Georgia State University, "Convergence and Situatedness of Free Speech: WeChat as Site of Activism"
Respondent: Jennifer Sano-Franchini, Virginia Polytechnic Institute and State University

Listed in the CCCC 2016 convention program, the AAAC sponsored session at CCCC 2016: "New Directions in Transnational Asian/Asian American Rhetoric and Composition: Issues for Historiography, Digital Rhetoric, Racial Justice, and Writing Center Research." Presentations by Chanon Adsanatham, Priya Sirohi, Patti Poblete, Morris Young, Vani Kannan, and Belle Xiaobo Wang, with Jolivette Mecenas as chair, and Jennifer Sano-Franchini as respondent.

Chanon Adsanatham (@chanson_2013) tweets about New books by AAAC members: Anti-Racist Writing Assessment Ecologies by Asao B. Inoue, Writing Against Racial Injury by Haivan V. Hoang, Relocating Authority by Mira Shimabukuro, and South Asian in the Mid-South by Iswari Pandey.

> **Storify** by **voleuseCK** 5 months ago
>
> ## 4c16 #D07: New Directions in Transnational Asian/Asian American Rhetoric & Composition
>
> Jolivette Mecenas, Morris Young, Priya Sirohi, Vani Kannan, Xiaobo Wang, Patricia Poblete, Chanon Adsanatham, Jennifer Sano-Franchini (@CCCCAAAC)
>
> **New Directions in Transnational Asian/Asian American Rhetoric and Composition: Issues for Historiography, Digital Rhetoric, Racial Justice, and Writing Center Research**
> This Asian/Asian American Caucus–sponsored roundtable highlights newdirections in transnational Asian/Asian American rhetoric and writing.
>
>> 5•History
>>
>> **D.07 New Directions in Transnational Asian/Asian American Rhetoric and Composition: Issues for Historiography, Digital Rhetoric, Racial Justice, and Writing Center Research**
>> This Asian/Asian American Caucus–sponsored roundtable highlights new directions in transnational Asian/Asian American rhetoric and writing.
>> Hilton Ballroom of the Americas Salon F, Level Two
>>
>> *Chair:* Jolivette Mecenas, University of La Verne
>> *Speakers:* Chanon Adsanatham, University of Maryland, "Re-Placing Archival Studies in the Global Turn: Critical Methods for Researching Asian Rhetorics"
>> Priya Sirohi, Purdue University, "Rhetorics of South/Asian American Identity: Mapping Context, Purpose, and Use"
>> Patricia Poblete, Iowa State University, "Taking Action on Campus: Re-Examining 'Asian' Identities of Writers in the Writing Center"
>> Morris Young, University of Wisconsin-Madison, "Historicizing Transnational Asian American Rhetoric"
>> Vani Kannan, Syracuse University, "#ModelMinorityMutiny: Defining"
>> Xiaobo Wang, Georgia State University, "Convergence and Situatedness of Free Speech: WeChat as Site of Activism"
>> *Respondent:* Jennifer Sano-Franchini, Virginia Polytechnic Institute and State University
>
> About to go present in #D07, a roundtable sponsored by @CCCCAAAC! Come join us at 3:15 PM! #4c16 #aaacaucus pic.twitter.com/OXvEulgBCh
>
> 🐦 PATTI POBLETE @VOLEUSECK · 5 MONTHS AGO
>
> https://storify.com/voleuseCK/4c16-d07

Storify of tweets during the AAAC sponsored session at CCCC 2016, "New Directions in Transnational Asian/Asian American Rhetoric and Composition." Curated by Patti Poblete (@voleuseCK).

Storify of tweets during the AAAC sponsored session at CCCC 2016, "New Directions in Transnational Asian/Asian American Rhetoric and Composition." Curated by Patti Poblete (@voleuseCK).

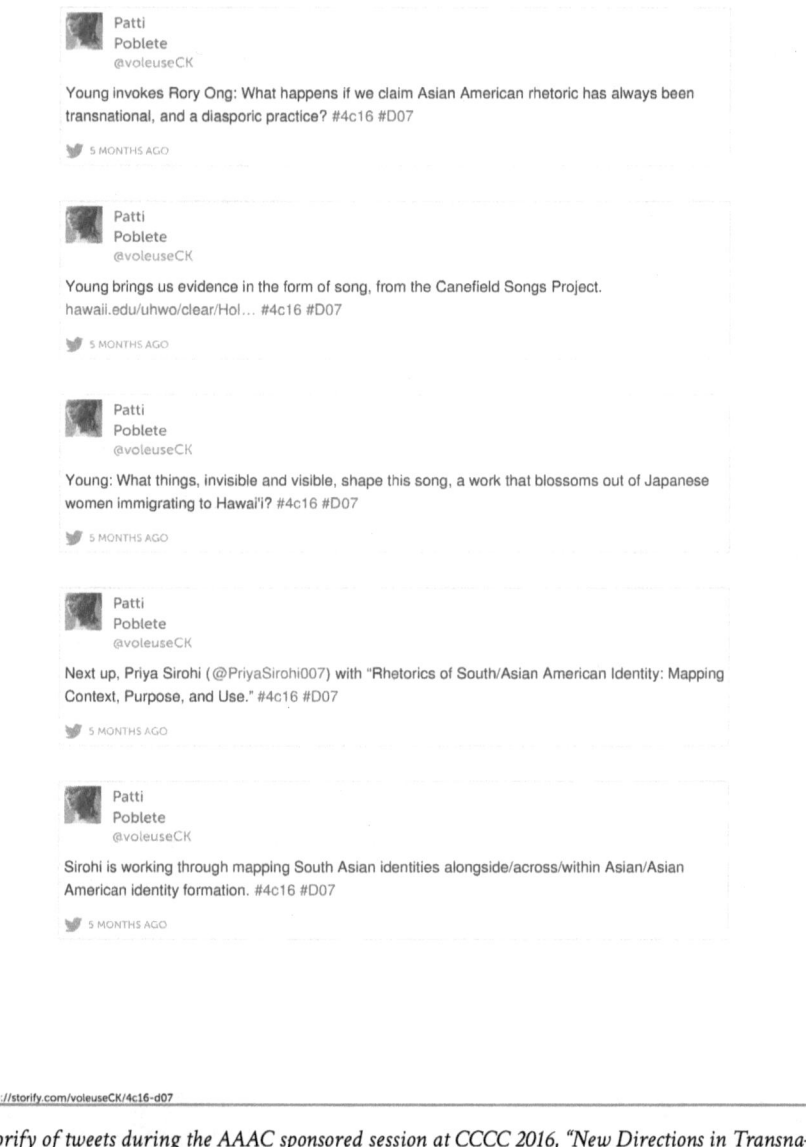

Storify of tweets during the AAAC sponsored session at CCCC 2016, "New Directions in Transnational Asian/Asian American Rhetoric and Composition." Curated by Patti Poblete (@voleuseCK).

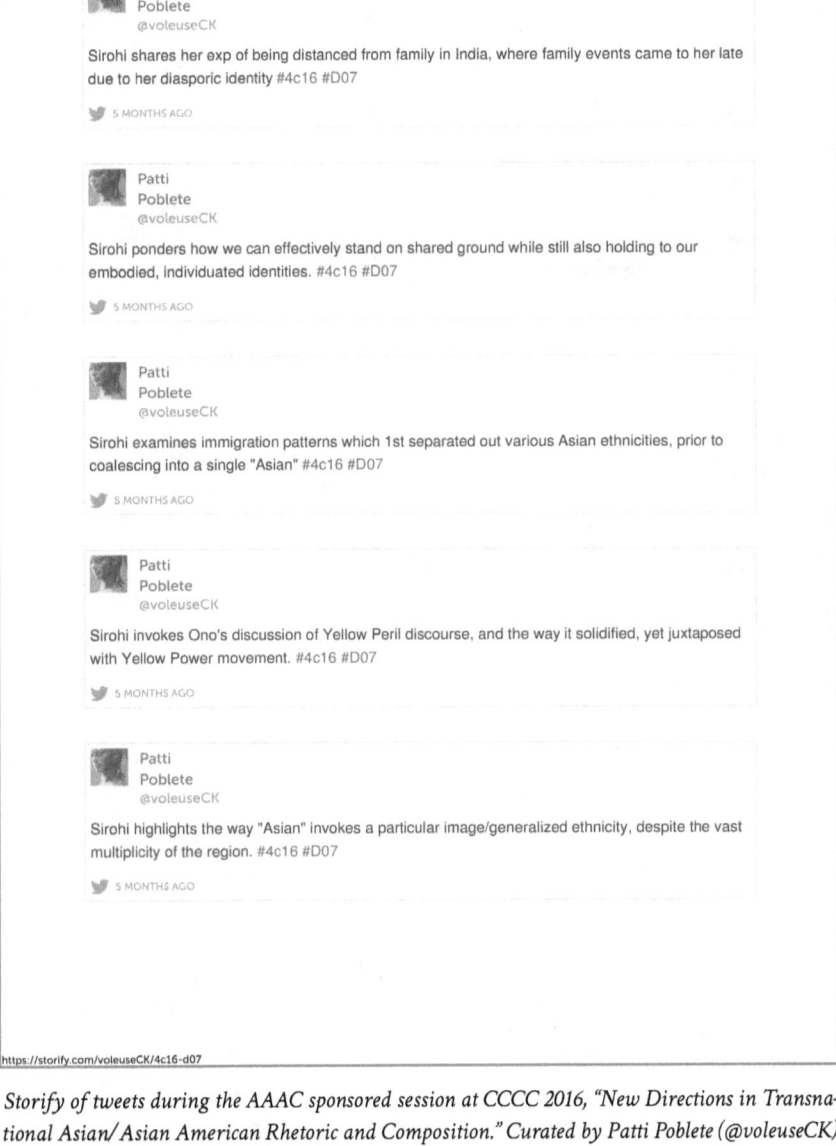

Storify of tweets during the AAAC sponsored session at CCCC 2016, "New Directions in Transnational Asian/Asian American Rhetoric and Composition." Curated by Patti Poblete (@voleuseCK).

Storify of tweets during the AAAC sponsored session at CCCC 2016, "New Directions in Transnational Asian/Asian American Rhetoric and Composition." Curated by Patti Poblete (@voleuseCK).

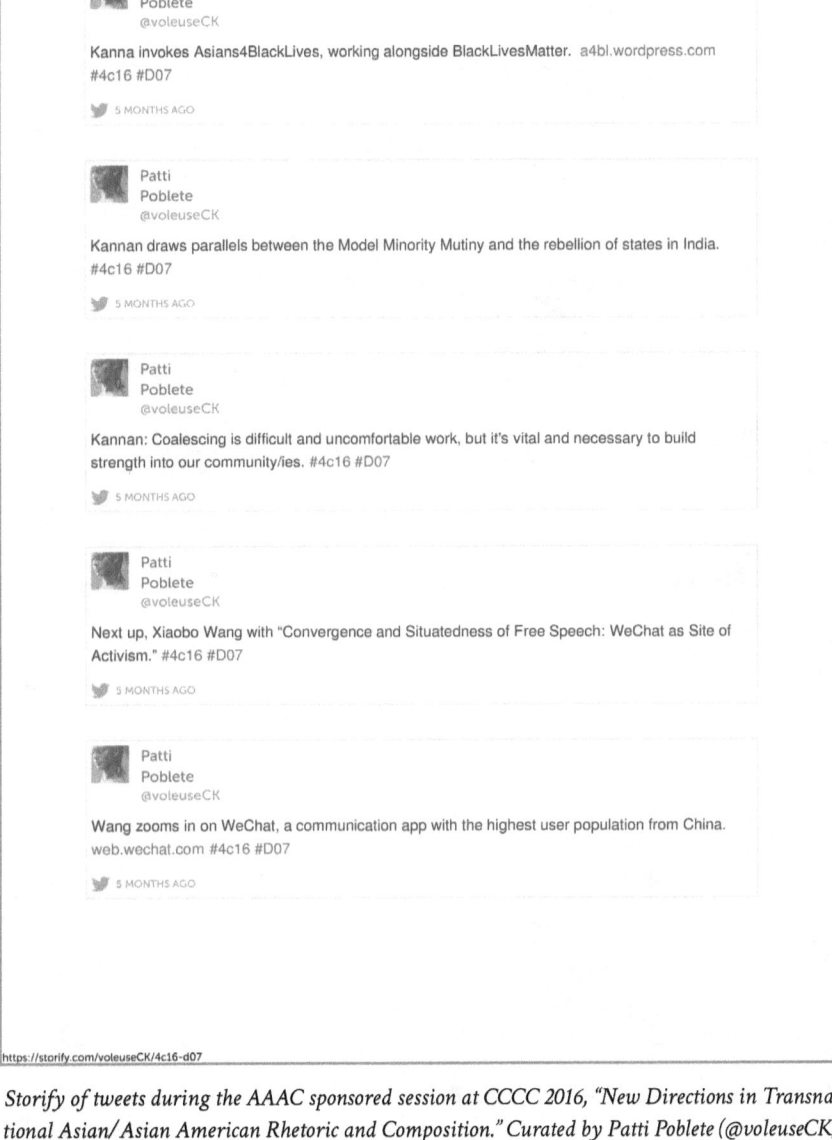

Storify of tweets during the AAAC sponsored session at CCCC 2016, "New Directions in Transnational Asian/Asian American Rhetoric and Composition." Curated by Patti Poblete (@voleuseCK).

Storify of tweets during the AAAC sponsored session at CCCC 2016, "New Directions in Transnational Asian/Asian American Rhetoric and Composition." Curated by Patti Poblete (@voleuseCK).

Storify of tweets during the AAAC sponsored session at CCCC 2016, "New Directions in Transnational Asian/Asian American Rhetoric and Composition." Curated by Patti Poblete (@voleuseCK).

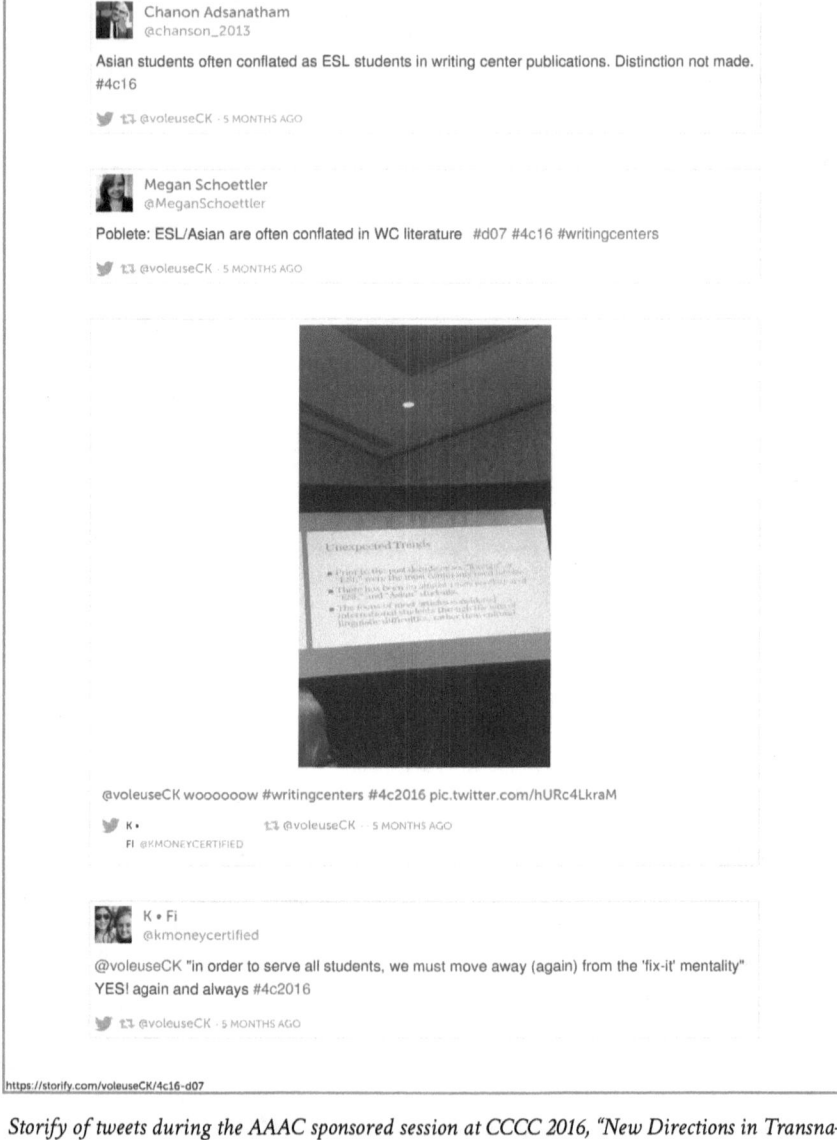

Storify of tweets during the AAAC sponsored session at CCCC 2016, "New Directions in Transnational Asian/Asian American Rhetoric and Composition." Curated by Patti Poblete (@voleuseCK).

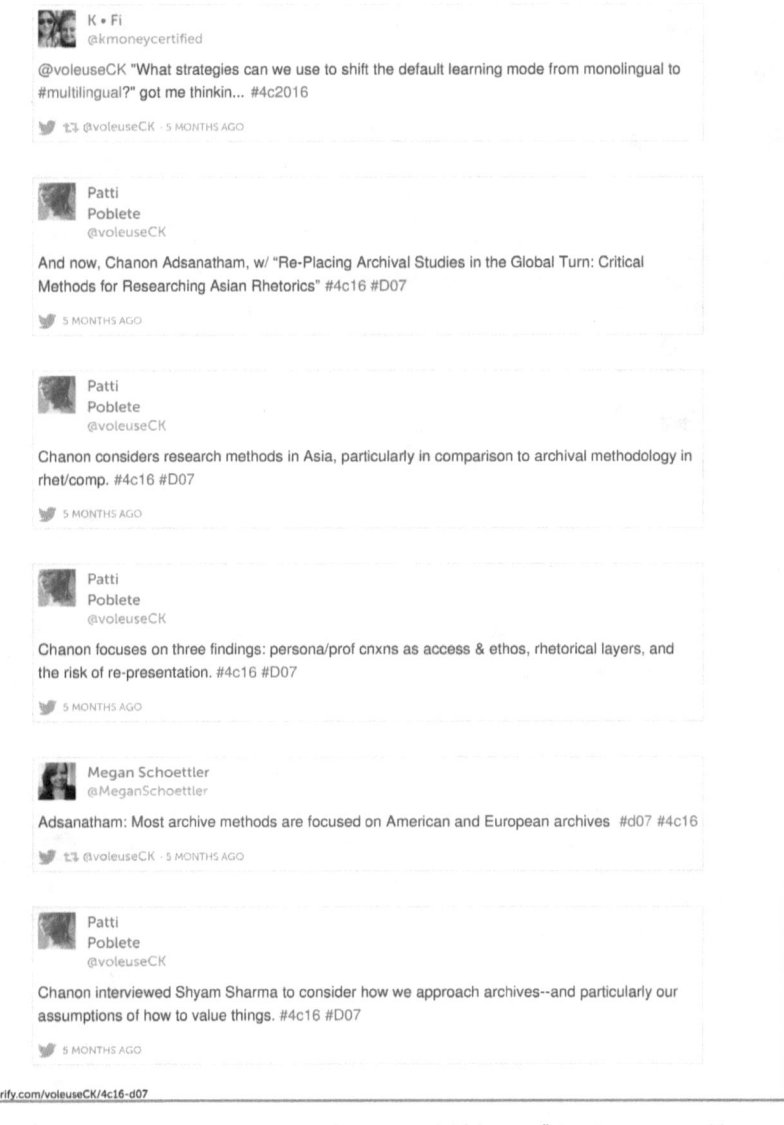

Storify of tweets during the AAAC sponsored session at CCCC 2016, "New Directions in Transnational Asian/Asian American Rhetoric and Composition." Curated by Patti Poblete (@voleuseCK).

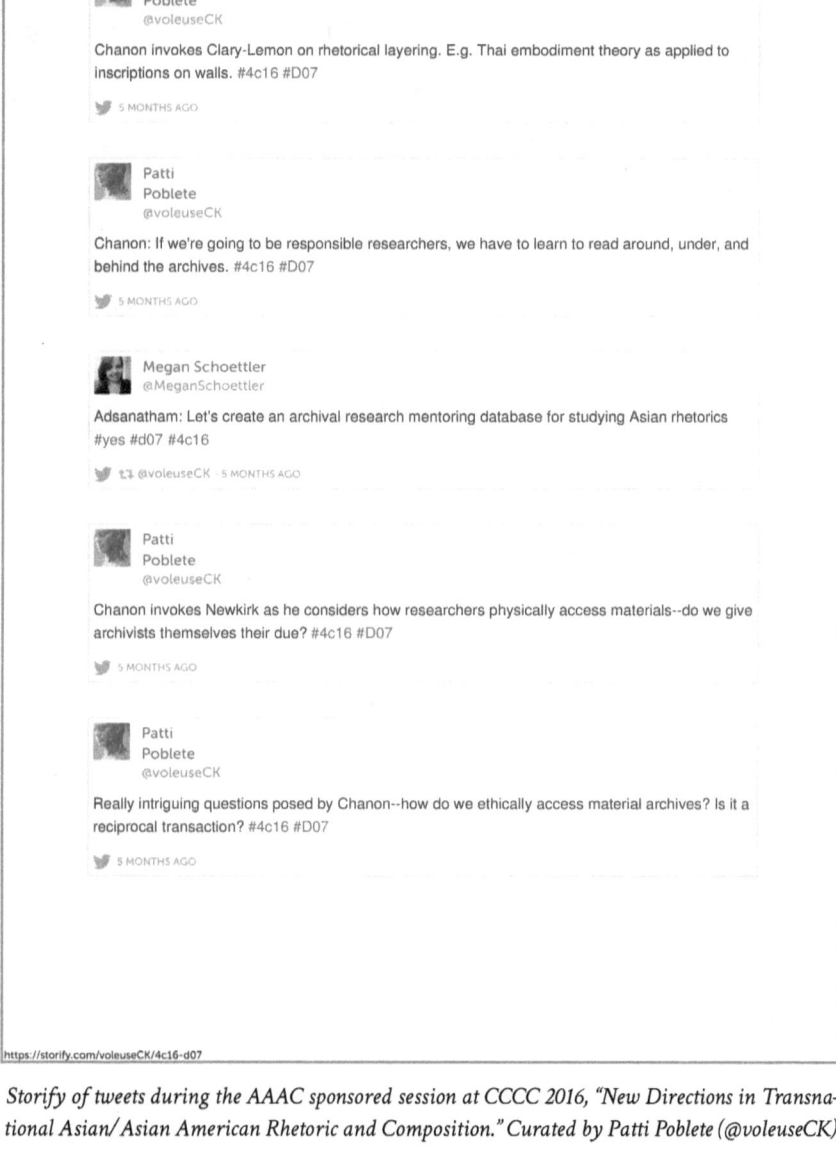

Storify of tweets during the AAAC sponsored session at CCCC 2016, "New Directions in Transnational Asian/Asian American Rhetoric and Composition." Curated by Patti Poblete (@voleuseCK).

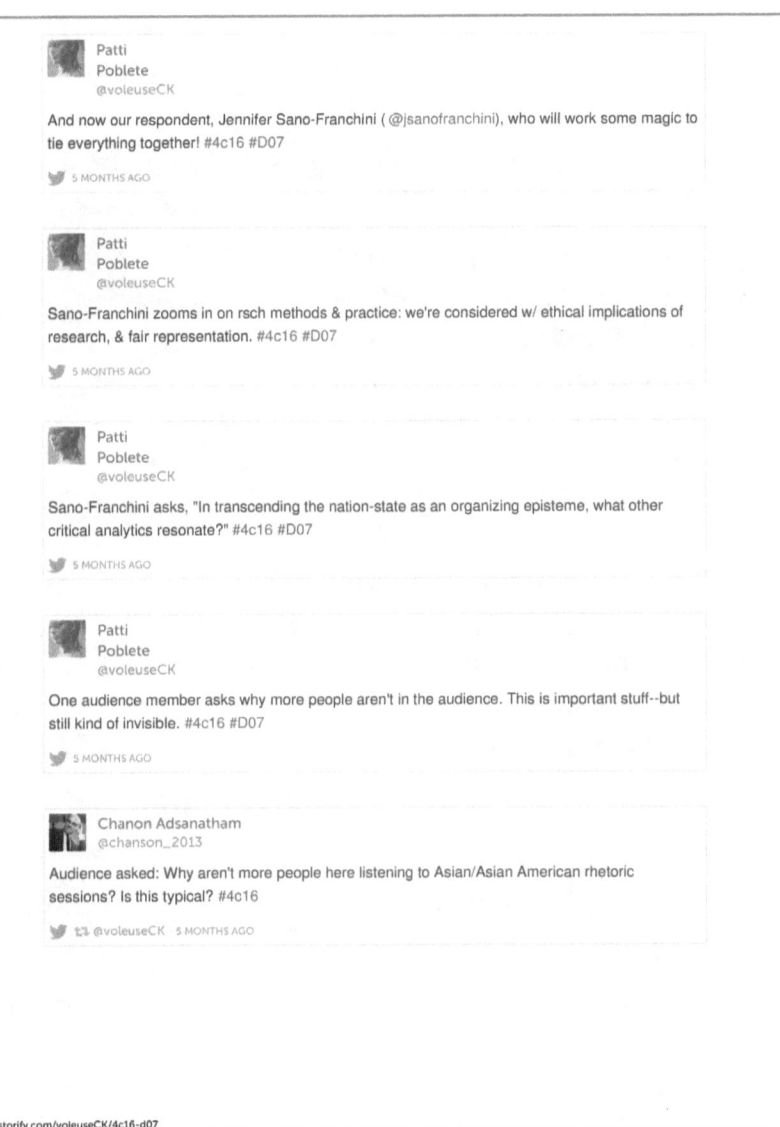

Storify of tweets during the AAAC sponsored session at CCCC 2016, "New Directions in Transnational Asian/Asian American Rhetoric and Composition." Curated by Patti Poblete (@voleuseCK).

"Across the 24 years that I have taught writing at the middle school, high school, and college levels, I have returned innumerable times, vicariously now through the writing of my students, to that initial transformational encounter with language—through language, that process of assembling fragmented traces and broken pieces of identity and, within the whole of memory, composing oneself and one's world anew."

- Stuart Ching

Stuart Ching is featured on NCTE Vice President Jocelyn Chadwick's blog, as part of her Legacy of Pride series.

CHAPTER FIVE
A Survey of Research in Asian Rhetoric*

Bo Wang

REFLECTIONS ON "A SURVEY OF RESEARCH IN ASIAN RHETORIC"

As I prepared to draft some comments to contextualize "A Survey of Research in Asian Rhetoric" (the "Survey" for short), I thought of how I took up the task of conducting the "Survey": it was written as part of a project I pursued as an intern with *Rhetoric Review*, an initial attempt on my part to understand an emerging field in Rhetoric and Composition and Communication I would enter as a student of rhetoric. The theoretical and methodological issues discussed in the "Survey" provided heuristics for my own research then, and, unexpectedly, continue to solicit conversations about the study of non-Western rhetorics across the disciplines today.

When I reread the piece now, I marvel at what we have accomplished collectively in the last decade to make Asian rhetoric a legitimate and vigorous field of study. The scholars I interviewed assumed authority to speak of their concerns about and hopes for Asian rhetoric, a young discipline facing existential challenges. When I was recruiting survey participants, I couldn't find or get in touch with those whose scholarship covered Asian traditions beyond Chinese rhetoric. The only senior scholar who had published a book on comparative studies of Western classical rhetoric and non-Western rhetorics declined my invitation because he was no longer doing research in comparative rhetoric. In the 2004 "Survey," the scholarship of all participants was in Chinese rhetoric and writing. In fact, I had to include a footnote to

---

* This piece first appeared in *Rhetoric Review*, 23.2 (2004): 171–81. Thanks to Taylor and Francis for granting permission to republish this piece.

emphasize that "Asian rhetoric includes Chinese, Indian, Japanese, Korean, and many other Asian rhetorical traditions."

In the past few years, the key issues raised in the "Survey"—from discovering new modes of inquiry to developing appropriate terminologies, to theorizing a particular rhetorical tradition in its own cultural context—have been further explored and advanced by specialists in our field. Moving away from a Eurocentric paradigm, scholars have identified and used indigenous concepts to study Asian rhetorics in their own historical and cultural contexts or to read Western rhetoric through the lens of non-Western discourse. These endeavors have shown for the first time various practices and conceptions of speaking and writing in China, India, Japan, Korea, and other areas in the East. Rhetoric and Communication scholars, such as Steven Combs, Mary Garrett, Andy Kirkpatrick, Xing Lu, Arabella Lyon, LuMing Mao, Hui Wu, Xiaoye You, and myself, have contributed to a growing body of work on classical, modern, and contemporary Chinese rhetoric, leading to a more nuanced understanding of a particular rhetorical tradition, in this case, Chinese rhetoric.

In retrospect, my article did perhaps two things: it called attention to research in Asian rhetoric, then a largely marginalized field; and generated heuristic questions, however limited, about the disciplinary work of Asian rhetoric. Published at a time when research in other non-Western and indigenous rhetorics was beginning to gain momentum, the voices represented in the "Survey" articulated clearly the necessity of granting both scholarly and institutional support for Asian rhetoric. The survey participants seized a kairotic moment to reflect on and advocate the development of Asian rhetoric as a field of study. Reprinted here, it might well be read as a professional and rhetorical artifact in the context of the recent advances of non-Western rhetorics and other marginalized rhetorics in Rhetoric and Composition and Communication. Together with scholarship in Asian rhetoric and writing, the "Survey," I hope, provides another opportunity for reflection and for dialogue about the past, present, and future of Asian rhetoric.

Abstract: *This survey offers a forum for scholars who have been studying Asian rhetoric to express their views about some important issues in the discipline. Covering a variety of topics from the existing state of research in Asian rhetoric to the modes of inquiries and the development of scholarship in this area, the survey reveals that* *researchers must challenge the fundamental assumptions about rhetoric embedded in classical Western rhetorical theories to start a conversation between East and West. By representing different voices, the survey also invites deeper discussion of related issues among researchers in the field.*

Asian rhetoric is a young discipline of rhetoric studies, its history traced back to the 1960s.[1] Starting with the seminal work by Robert Oliver in 1961 with the publication of "The Rhetorical Implications of Taoism," research in Asian rhetoric has progressed through four decades and has yielded noticeable fruits. Gradually departing from the influence of various modes of inquiry that favor the Greco-Roman rhetorical tradition and bias against non-Western rhetorical traditions, practitioners in this field recently have started to study Asian rhetorical practices in their own social, historical, and cultural contexts (Kaplan "Cultural Thought Patterns Revisited"; Jensen, "Rhetorical Emphases"; Jensen, "Rhetoric of East Asia"; Jensen, "Teaching"; Jensen, "Values" Garrett,, "Chinese Buddhist"; Garrett, "Classical"; Garrett, "Pathos"; Garrett, "Some Elementary"; Garrett, "The 'Three Doctrines'"; Li; Liu; Kennedy; Lu; Mao "What's in a Name?"). Closely related to the development of the field of rhetoric, which gives more and more attention to the way people communicate, research in Asian rhetoric, in light of its recognition of the existence of other rhetorical traditions alongside the Western rhetorical tradition, has broadened our vision of rhetoric. To get a clear picture of this area, I surveyed several scholars who have done or have been doing research in Asian rhetoric.[2] The purpose of this survey is to encourage research and scholarship in an emerging but very important area in the field.

The five scholars I surveyed have been doing historical, theoretical, and empirical studies in different disciplines such as rhetoric and composition, linguistics, and communication studies, and all have made significant contributions to the developing field of Asian rhetoric. For example, Professor Vernon Jensen is one of the pioneers who opened up this new area. His study of East Asian rhetoric has led the field to a new and more appropriate mode of inquiry—studying Asian rhetoric by examining its own concepts and con-

---

1 I thank Theresa Enos for giving me the idea to conduct this survey and for her encouragement and support. I also thank Ed White and Roxanne Mountford for their assistance and suggestions regarding an earlier draft of the survey questions.
2 As the title indicates, this survey is about research in Asian rhetoric. Although the scholars who participated in the project have primarily done studies on Chinese rhetoric, I would like to make it clear that Asian rhetoric includes Chinese, Indian, Japanese, Korean, and many other Asian rhetorical traditions.

texts ("Rhetorical Emphases"; "Rhetoric of East Asia"; "Teaching"; "Values"). Professor Mary Garrett, in a series of essays published in the 1990s, studied the rhetorical practices in classical China by unpacking the implications of various argumentative speech activities in Chinese philosophical, historical, and cultural contexts. Her study of pathos in the rhetorical practices in early China provides a good example of reexamining Western rhetorical tradition through the lens of a non-Western rhetorical tradition ("Chinese Buddhist"; "Classical"; "Pathos"; "Some Elementary"; "The 'Three Doctrines'").

Professor XiaoMing Li has devoted herself to empirical studies of Asian rhetoric. In *"Good Writing" in Cross-Cultural Context*, an ethnographic study of Chinese and American teachers of composition, she compared the standards of good writing in two different cultures. This study has broken the stereotype of Chinese rhetoric formed by some misinterpretations and overgeneralization in previous scholarship and has provided a new research method to studies in contrastive rhetoric. Professor Xing Lu studied classical Chinese rhetoric by using its own terms and examining its own philosophical, political, and cultural contexts. Her daring and original scholarship represented by *Rhetoric in Ancient China, Fifth to Third Century B.C.E.: A Comparison with Classical Greek Rhetoric* (1998) provides a systematic and convincing account of classical Chinese rhetoric. Professor LuMing Mao, a linguist and rhetorician, has published extensively in Asian rhetoric. In his recent research, he has explored the conflict in ideology between the conception of Western rhetoric and the implication of Confucian discourse ("What's in a Name?"). His new article, "Reflective Encounters: Illustrating Comparative Rhetoric," presents important scholarship in the field, applying linguistic and postmodern rhetorical theory to the research of Asian rhetoric.

The survey was composed of questions about several subtopics. Some questions were designed to get general information about the research in this field. The scholars' responses to these questions tell us in which journals their research has been published, for whom they wrote, and what kind of research is considered as important contributions to this area. Such information will be helpful to those who want to know about the evolution of this area and publish their work on Asian rhetoric. According to their responses, most of the scholars I surveyed have published in journals such as *Argumentation and Advocacy, Journal of Asian Pacific Communication, Philosophy and Rhetoric, Quarterly Journal of Speech, Rhetorica, Rhetoric Review, Rhetoric Society Quarterly, Style, Western Journal of Communication*, and *World Communication*. Their audience is primarily rhetoricians and communication scholars who are interested in intercultural communications. The important research being done in Asian rhetoric includes research that is mindful of the logic of Orientalism, that studies Asian rhetoric in its own cultural and political contexts, that appropriates Asian rhetoric for Western contexts, and that applies Asian rhetorical traditions to the study of pedagogical issues.

Other questions in the survey were set up for the scholars to give voice to their own opinions about more specific issues in Asian rhetoric. Their responses to these questions not only express their concern with the development of research in Asian rhetoric but also invite deep thought about some important issues in rhetoric. Two topics received the most attention from these scholars and solicited thought-provoking comments.

One is the approaches scholars have been using in researching Asian rhetoric. Their discussions about this issue indicate that, just as in any other new or marginalized area in the field of rhetoric, researchers in Asian rhetoric must challenge the fundamental assumptions about rhetoric embedded in classical Western rhetorical theories to start a conversation between East and West. For example, when asked about what approaches and terminologies should be used in the study of Asian rhetorics, these scholars pointed out that we need to be cautious not to impose the Western conception of rhetoric upon the description of Asian rhetorics despite the fact that they did not fully agree with each other on every aspect of this issue. Ultimately we need to answer an unavoidable question: How do we define rhetoric? There is no denying that we have to start from somewhere, but relying too heavily on classical Western rhetorical theory without transforming it from the perspectives of non-Western rhetorical traditions might perpetuate the idea that the Greco-Roman rhetorical tradition is the only rhetorical tradition. Therefore, it is essential that we rewrite rhetorical theory and explore new research methodologies as these and many other scholars are trying to do.

The other topic is the development of research in Asian rhetoric. The scholars I surveyed provided valuable comments from both scholastic and administrative perspectives. Their responses show that we need more scholars who have the tools and expertise to study Asian rhetorics in their original texts and cultures. We should explore a broader scope of genres from the rhetorical perspective and encourage more interdisciplinary research in this area. Moreover, they suggest that more financial assistance and support should be provided for the study of Asian rhetoric.

Asian rhetoric is still a young and immature enterprise in the field of rhetoric. Although there are many difficulties along the road, it has the potential of growing into a strong discipline, considering the depth and significance of the subject matter itself and the achievements researchers have made in a relatively short period of time. But its development needs more attention and support from the academy. I hope that this survey will not only provide a forum for the scholars to voice their opinions and concerns but also leave space for further and deeper discussions on Asian rhetoric among practitioners in the discipline. I hope that what this survey offers is a continuation of the dialogue between the Western rhetorical tradition and non-Western rhetorical traditions.

THE SURVEY
The Existing State of Research in Asian Rhetoric

Question: How do you feel about the present state of the research in this field? Is it vigorous or lackadaisical? Why do you think so?

Mary Garrett: I would say it is desultory. There is not yet a critical mass of scholars devoting themselves to this field. Many people turn out something occasionally, sometimes as a digression from their main line of research.

Vernon Jensen: I think the present state of research in Asian rhetoric is promising (avoiding the extremes of "vigorous" and "lackadaisical"!). I am glad to see the great variety of subjects being explored, the variety of modes of inquiry, and the increasing appearance of scholars who can work in Asian languages in their own research.

Xing Lu: There is still a lack of research on Asian rhetoric. We need research on other Asian rhetorical traditions; we need more comparative works between Asian rhetoric and non-Asian rhetoric.

LuMing Mao: The present state of the research in this field is still quite young or nascent, and a lot needs to be done in order to avoid simplicity, to move away from Orientalism.

The Modes of Inquiry Used in Asian Rhetoric Research
Question: What modes of inquiry should be applied to the study of rhetorical traditions in Asian cultures? Why?

> **Xing Lu:** Scholars in general agree that analytical and definitional modes of thinking tend to create obstacles in rendering a more nuanced and authentic understanding in the study of rhetoric and communication of non-Western cultures. It is important to be sensitive to the implicit, multifaceted, and sometimes paradoxical nature of rhetoric embedded in Chinese philosophical, literary, and religious texts. An effort to search for a single definition of Chinese rhetoric or to try to find an equivalence from the Western terminology may fail to uncover the richness of Chinese rhetorical tradition (or any other rhetorical traditions for that matter) and run the risk of imposing meanings of Western rhetoric onto the Chinese context.

> **LuMing Mao:** We've heard those catch-words like analytical, contextual, critical, etc., to characterize various kinds of modes of inquiry. I am more interested in studies that are historicized and that are leery of making claims or generalizations with little or flimsy evidence. [S]uch [comparative] studies should be more mindful of local textual and contextual forces and of their concomitant assumptions—both of which can be uncommon and unexpected in relation to the dominant, to the expected. Of course, such work calls for careful, immersed study rather than some superficial comparisons that can be easily guilty of creating a forced fit or distinction. I am also nervous about those that advocate some kind of evolutionary trajectory and that transfer Western terminologies uncritically.

Question: In *Rhetoric in Ancient China, Fifth to Third Century B.C.E.: A Comparison with Classical Greek Rhetoric*, Xing Lu suggests that the Chinese term *bian* (argumentation and disputation) be used to describe the ancient Chinese rhetoric. If you are familiar with this work, what do you think of this approach? Why?

> **Mary Garrett:** Well, this is a definitional issue: How is rhetoric being conceived? As argumentation and disputation? As including epideictic? As symbolic inducement? The definition applied will determine, to what extent, what is seen and brought forward. I myself think that see-

ing rhetoric as argumentation and disputation is too narrow for both the Western and the Chinese situations; too many important and interesting phenomena are missed.

XiaoMing Li: I have read her work only once and was much impressed by the breadth and depth of her knowledge of ancient Chinese rhetoric. [B]*ian*, I think, is closer to the Western rhetorical tradition than the dictionary translation of rhetoric, *xiuci*. Using *bian* as the focal point of Chinese rhetoric helps build conceptual links between the two otherwise little-related traditions. At the same time, though, her strategy to realign Chinese tradition in accordance with the Western tradition inevitably leaves out things that don't fit in that conceptual frame yet are essential to the tradition. One obvious result of such an approach is that her study is largely confined to China's ancient political and philosophical treatise, giving only tangential attention to China's rich literary tradition. In my own research on present-day Chinese students' writing, I have found that the impact of China's literary tradition is far more palpable on their writing than the entire enterprise of philosophical treatise. For example, *sanwen*, one of the more popular genres in Chinese schools, a prose that resembles to some extent English free verse, is a direct offshoot of a tradition that regarded poetry as the supreme genre.

Xing Lu: I actually proposed "*Ming Bian*" as the close appropriation to English "rhetoric." Another appropriation could be "*Shui Bian*." Whatever terms are being used, it should be generated from the original Chinese context, not the imposition of Western meanings. This would allow a discovery and reconstruction of Chinese rhetoric with respect to Chinese contexts.

LuMing Mao: I am aware of her argument. I think it is quite productive because of its emphasis on local contexts, on diachronic (I think she uses evolutionary, which I am somewhat less excited about) history, and on what she calls "a language of ambiguous similarity" (Lu 91). On the last point, in general I agree with this kind of move, though I sense there is at least an implicit effort on her part to move Chinese terms closer to the Western counterparts—rather than, say, vice versa. I wonder why.

Question: What terminology should be used to describe rhetorical practices in Asian cultures in ancient times? Why?

> **Mary Garrett:** I would not want to dictate what terms people use. There will be pluses and minuses in every case. What is more important, I think, is their awareness of the implications of their choices, and how they communicate this to the reader.
>
> **LuMing Mao:** I don't think you can get away from studying those key terms used by the practitioners in their times—just like what Lu did—quite ably I might add. To build on her work, we may want to further explore how those terms in turn influenced and affected the rhetorical behaviors of their users and how they interacted with each other at different historical moments.

The Impact of Asian Rhetoric Research

Question: What impact do you think the research in this field has exerted on the study of Western rhetoric?

> **Mary Garrett:** I don't think it's had much effect at all. There is an awareness, perhaps, that another rhetorical tradition besides the Greco–Roman exists, but so little is known about it, outside of this awareness. There has been no significant impact.
>
> **Vernon Jensen:** Direct cause-and-effect relationship may be difficult to establish, but surely a strong correlation seems to be present as scholarship roams more freely between East and West, bringing greater mutual understanding and respect.
>
> **XiaoMing Li:** I think those who are outside this small circle of Asian rhetoric scholars are in a better position to answer this question. As far as I see, all the studies on non-Western rhetoric have barely made a dent on Western rhetoric. The reasons are hard to pin down. One would think in the current multicultural environment there would be strong interest in non-Western rhetoric, yet the fact of the matter is that Eurocentrism still dominates. The vogue to do postmodern theory in the last decade may have contributed to the slighting of cultures that are perceived "ancient" rather than "modern," that tend to express their thinking in literary tropes instead of syllogism, that write in a sincere

and plain manner rather than with "indirectness, elusiveness, ambiguity" and irony (Swearingen 7). New theories with a French accent, therefore, are adopted with great gusto, while non-Western rhetoric is accepted with polite tolerance. Of course, there are important exceptions.

Xing Lu: It has helped rhetorical scholars to recognize that Western rhetoric is not the only rhetorical tradition in the course of human history; there are other rhetorical traditions out there to be explored and studied. An increased knowledge of non-Western rhetorical traditions may help expand and illuminate Western rhetorical practices such as the studies done by Mary Garrett on Pathos and Steven Combs on Sunzi, both published in the *Quarterly Journal of Speech*.

LuMing Mao: I hope the values are obvious: Not only does it help us better understand Western rhetoric, but it also illustrates the multifaceted significances of what it means to communicate and to speak "rhetorically."

Question: How has the research being done in Asian rhetoric changed the Western perspective of argument?

Mary Garrett: As far as I can tell, there has been no integration, or even fruitful comparison.

Vernon Jensen: Again, a definite cause-and-effect relationship may be difficult to establish, but it seems apparent that Western perspectives of argumentation have been broadened as a result of research in Asian rhetoric.

Xing Lu: I am not sure if it has changed anything in real argumentative practices. The works are mainly read by a limited group of rhetorical scholars. Unless this body of knowledge is incorporated in the curriculum of rhetorical education, no major change will take place in the West.

The Future of Asian Rhetoric Research
Question: Where is the research in Asian rhetoric taking us in the future?

Xing Lu: It will help Westerners understand Asian culture and communication behavior. It will help facilitate the effective and appropriate communication between Asians and non-Asians at different levels of interaction. It will help extend our knowledge and practice in human rhetoric and communication in general.

LuMing Mao: I imagine there will be more local studies of non-Western rhetorical traditions.

Question: How does your own research reflect the future in this field?

Xing Lu: By introducing various modes of communication and rhetorical practices, I am hoping to achieve those goals mentioned above.

LuMing Mao: My own research intends to focus precisely on local matters, on illustrating Chinese rhetorical traditions with a comparative lens.

Question: Is there any research you would like to see done in this field in the future?

Mary Garrett: I think there has been an understandable but unfortunate concentration on the so-called classical period, at the expense of the next twenty-some centuries. There was tremendous development of rhetorical practices and theories in China after 200 BCE, but very little of it has been researched and written about.

Vernon Jensen: More focus on similarities between East and West to move on from earlier work that tended to highlight differences. Don't overlook Southeast Asia. More research on conflict resolution not only between East and West, but between groups within particular Asian nations. Continue exploration of the importance of the ethical dimension in Asian communication within nations and between Asian nations and between East and West. Analysis of the impact of mass media, both Western and Asian, on individual Asian nations. Continue to explore the impact of Asian ancient religion and history on contemporary Asian rhetoric and communication.

XiaoMing Li: I'd like major works of Western rhetoric and our works on Chinese rhetoric to be read and criticized by local scholars in China, most of whom are far more knowledgeable of their own rhetorical tradition than us, but lack a comparative perspective because Western rhetoric, unlike other disciplines, has not found its way into Chinese universities. I want their perspectives, presumably diverse and even contradictory to one another, to be heard. In addition, I believe that Chinese rhetoric, never a disciplinary study in China, should not be drawn according to the Western template, and the new one should include, among others, Chinese literary theories and works. I prefer Kenneth Burke's notion of rhetoric, which does not place inordinate emphasis on persuasion or style, but views rhetoric as including all of the "symbolic means of inducing cooperation" (43).

Xing Lu: Yes, more studies on the history of Asian rhetoric in different time periods; more studies on rhetorical texts (ancient and contemporary); and more comparative studies of rhetoric.

Question: What do you think should be done to improve the development of research in Asian rhetoric in the future?

Mary Garrett: There needs to be a core group of specialists, just as there is for Greek and Roman rhetoric, specialists who have the tools to deal with the texts and their cultures and who develop a conversation amongst themselves about these texts. In other words, there needs to be a group of authoritative voices, authoritative in the sense that the reader can go to their scholarship with some confidence.

Vernon Jensen: Encourage more Asian offerings in university departments of rhetoric and communication. Increase interdisciplinary collaboration (for example, with political science, sociology, history, journalism, psychology, Asian languages), resulting in publications reaching broader audiences and expanding our horizons. Encourage universities to provide financial assistance for research travel and study in Asia.

Xing Lu: Plant interest in the area among students; organize conferences devoted to this area of research; encourage the publication of such work in scholarly journals.

Question: Is there anything else you think I should know in order to get a broader picture of this subject?

Mary Garrett: The published work on Chinese rhetoric is of wildly uneven quality. Some is based on careful analysis; some is highly impressionistic. Some researchers have studied classical Chinese and can read the texts in their original language; others rely on modern Chinese translations, or entirely on English translations. In some cases individuals generalize from their own experience as native Chinese to all of Chinese history. In other cases Orientalism (from both Westerners and Chinese) runs wild. It is very difficult for the naive reader to discern these shortcomings, and as a result, inaccurate and bizarre impressions of Chinese rhetoric are reproduced.

WORKS CITED

Burke, Kenneth. *A Rhetoric of Motives*. Berkeley: U of California P, 1969.

Combs, Steven C. "Sun-zi and the Art of War: The Rhetoric of Parsimony." *Quarterly Journal of Speech* 86.3 (2000): 276-294. Print.

Garrett, Mary. "Chinese Buddhist Religious Disputation." *Argumentation* 11.2 (1995): 195–209. Print.

—. "Classical Chinese Conceptions of Argumentation and Persuasion." *Argumentation and Advocacy* 29 (Winter 1993): 105–15. Print.

—. "Pathos Reconsidered from the Perspective of Classical Chinese Rhetorical Theories." *Quarterly Journal of Speech* 79 (1993): 19–39. Print.

—. "Some Elementary Methodological Reflections on the Study of the Chinese Rhetorical Tradition." *International and Intercultural Communication Annual* 22 (1999): 53–63. Print.

—. "The 'Three Doctrines Discussions' of Tang China: Religious Debate as a Rhetorical Strategy." *Argumentation and Advocacy* 30 (Winter 1994): 156–61. Print.

Jensen, J. Vernon. "Rhetorical Emphases of Taoism." *Rhetorica* 5 (Summer 1987): 219–29. Print.

—. "Rhetoric of East Asia—A Bibliography." *Rhetoric Society Quarterly* 17 (1987): 213–30. Print.

—. "Teaching East Asian Rhetoric." *Rhetoric Society Quarterly* 17 (1987): 135–49. Print.

—. "Values and Practices in Asian Argumentation." *Argumentation and Advocacy* 28 (Spring 1992): 153–66. Print.

Kaplan, Robert. "Cultural Thought Patterns in Inter-cultural Education." *Language Learning* 16 (1966): 1–20. Print.

—. "Cultural Thought Patterns Revisited." *Writing across Languages: Analysis of L2 Text*. Ed. Robert Kaplan and Ulla Connor. Reading, MA: Addison-Wesley, 1987. 9–22. Print.

—. "Foreword: What in the World Is Contrastive Rhetoric?" *Contrastive Rhetoric Revisited and Redefined*. Ed. Clayann Gilliam Panetta. Mahwah, NJ: Erlbaum, 2001. vii–xx. Print.

Kennedy, George A. *Comparative Rhetoric. An Historical and Cross-cultural Introduction*. New York: Oxford UP, 1998. Print.

Li, Xiao-Ming. *"Good Writing" in Cross-Cultural Context*. Albany: State U of New York P, 1996. Print.

Liu, Yameng. "To Capture the Essence of Chinese Rhetoric: An Anatomy of a Paradigm in Comparative Rhetoric." *Rhetoric Review* 14.2 (1996): 318–35. Print.

Lu, Xing. *Rhetoric in Ancient China, Fifth to Third Century B.C.E.: A Comparison with Classical Greek Rhetoric.* Columbia: U of South Carolina P, 1998. Print.

Mao, LuMing. "Reflective Encounters: Illustrating Comparative Rhetoric." *Style* 37 (Winter 2003): 401–425. Print.

—. "What's in a Name?: That Which Is Called 'Rhetoric' Would in the Analects Mean 'Participatory Discourse.'" *De Consolatione Philologiae.* Ed. Anna Grotans, Heinrich Beck, and Anton Schwob. Gopingen: Verlag, 2000. 507–22. Print.

Oliver, Robert T. "The Rhetorical Implications of Taoism." *Quarterly Journal of Speech* 47 (1961): 27–35. Print.

Swearingen, C. Jan. *Rhetoric and Irony: Western Literacy and Western Lies.* New York: Oxford University Press, 1991. Print.

CIRCULATION ESSAY

Racial Identities, Visual Representations, and Performative Capacities: Rhetorical Production(s) of/by Asians/Asian Americans in Hawaiʻi

Scott Kaʻalele, Edward Lee, and Michael Pak, with K. Hyoejin Yoon

FOREWORD BY K. HYOEJIN YOON

This "circulation" chapter includes excerpts of presentations given by Edward Lee, Scott Kaʻalele, and Michael Pak in the 2015 Asian/Asian American Caucus sponsored session "Asian/Asian American Scholarship in Rhetoric and Composition: Risks and Rewards" at the Conference on College Composition and Communication. As the larger caucus manuscript evolved, we wanted to include more emerging voices to help us to capture a genealogy, if you will, of Asian/Asian American rhetoric. This particular sponsored session itself was developed based on conversations during the 2014 AAAC meeting. One of the exigencies the caucus members tried to address was the issue of mentorship: how we support the next generations of scholars in Asian/Asian American rhetoric; how and who we credit for our ideas; and how and with whom we share research and publication opportunities.

    Lee, Kaʻalele, and Pak were first-time presenters at CCCC at the sponsored session, and we wanted to give their voices a space in our collection. They each presented a brief paper in their co-presentation, which is excerpted below. We wanted their words to stand by themselves, while at the same time providing the reader a scaffold, a productive frame for engaging with early work of graduate students as they first enter the professional and scholarly conversation in Asian/Asian American scholarship on a national and international scale. As editors, we wanted to share our perspective on the value they bring to the profession, and to the collection. For example, we found it instructive to grapple with how the writers name the problematics of race and identity, and to examine how they claim rhetorical ground and establish the ethos to describe and theorize what they observe in their day-to-day lives.

The excerpts provide a snapshot of the evolving thinking and writing of the next generation of Asian/Asian American scholars. We are fortunate to have their contributions here to engage with, to challenge us, and to help us see what kind of response and impact our work has elicited so far and how we might continue to build on that. We are grateful for their courage and boldness in allowing their work to be made public and to be analyzed at these early stages of writing and of their careers.

The papers are based in the context of Hawai'i, exploring the tensions and contradictions embedded in the history, rhetoric, and performances of Asian and Native language and identity. The influence of Morris Young's work extends across the presentations, as does the collection *Representations: Doing Asian American Rhetoric* edited by LuMing Mao and Morris Young. Young's work on Hawai'i as a site of cultural rhetorics in his article "Native Claims: Cultural Citizenship, Ethnic Expressions and the Rhetorics of 'Hawaiianness'" is especially salient. And Jolivette Mecenas's "Beyond [Asian American 'and Back: Coalitional Rhetoric in Print and New Media" is influential in and resonates with all three papers.

To provide a little bit of demographic context for Hawai'i, in the 2010 census, those identifying as "Asian alone" made up almost 40% of Hawai'i's population, followed by 24% identifying as "two or more races," and only 10% as "Native Hawaiian and Other Pacific Islander alone." The Native Hawaiian population, however, has increased almost 20% since the 2000 census. Asians increased by 4% and the mixed-race population increased 24% (US Census Bureau, 2010).

It is not surprising that, in this context, specific questions emerge about what "Hawaiian" or "American" identity means. Unlike the prevailing staging of race in terms of Black and White in the continental U.S., the history, population, and socioeconomic dynamics of Hawai'i shed light on the ways in which Asian settlers have, in many ways, benefitted from the colonization and ongoing political and economic struggles of Native Hawaiians (Young, "Native" 95; see also Fujikane and Okamura; Trask; Yamamoto). Asians/

Asian Americans who have lived and worked in Hawai'i since as early as the late 18th century are called Locals, "a category of identity used in Hawai'i to describe those born and raised in Hawai'i or long-time residents who see themselves as distinctly different from the mainland" ("Native" 92). Pak and Lee explore the nuances of Local identity in Hawai'i, elaborated in popular representations and in cultural interactions, respectively. Ka'alele argues that the view of Hawaiian identity through the lens of mainstream popular culture show *Hawaii-Five-O* suggests a conflation of Asian and native Hawaiian and suggests the power of the rhetorical context of Hawai'i to challenge fixed notions of identity.

PERFORMING AS AN ASIAN AMERICAN: IDENTITY, PLACE, AND CLASS, BY MICHAEL PAK

In the past few years, Asian Americans have become increasingly visible in U.S. popular culture. Ken Jeong has found success on both television and film, starring in the sitcom *Community* and the film series *The Hangover*. Jeremy Lin was the NBA story in 2012, sparking the cultural phenomenon of "Linsanity." In 2014, ABC debuted *Fresh Off the Boat*, a TV series based on Eddie Huang's life and memoir of the same name. This resurgence of representations of Asian Americans provides the public sphere with what LuMing Mao and Morris Young call "a rhetoric of becoming" (5). For the two cultural critics, such representations bring forth "a rhetoric that participates in [a] generative process, yielding an identity that is Asian American and producing a transformative effect that is always occasioned by use" (5). However, the examples of Jeong, Lin, and Huang can be seen to essentialize a particular formation of Asian American identity. I offer Hawai'i as an example that produces nuanced conceptions of identity that are inseparable from issues of race, class, and place.

In the cases of Jeong, Lin, and Huang, their mass media articulations reproduce similar constructions of middle-class suburban East Asian male Americans. For Richard Schechner, these reproducible articulated acts become what he deems "restored behavior":

> Restored behavior is symbolic and reflexive: not empty but loaded behavior multivocally broadcasting significances. These difficult terms express a single principle: The self can act in/as another; the social or

transindividual self is a role or set of roles . . . Performance means: never for the first time. It means: for the second to the nth time. Performance is "twice-behaved behavior." (36)

As representations of Asian Americans become more and more prevalent in mass media, these representations serve to cement, rather than contest, a restored behavior that is Asian American. And for Asian Americans themselves, the responsibility to add important identity signifiers can lead to what Mecenas calls "identity fatigue," or "a weariness brought about from prolonged exposure to others 'non-imaginative representations of their cultural and/or ethnic identity" (199).

Hawaiʻi has a large Asian American population, yet—or perhaps as a result—seems to resist a unifying Asian American identity. As a former monarchy and sovereign country and as a historically important economic crossroad in the Pacific, it is home to an indigenous ethnic group and multigenerational settled multicultural population that has created its own unique culture. As a result, Hawaiʻi is a place simultaneously American, *kānaka maoli* (Native Hawaiian), and local in identity. Some *kānaka maoli* scholars like Haunani-Kay Trask argue that a "local" identity is "the latest elaboration of foreign hegemony" in Hawaiʻi and position it as a settler identity collaborating with an American colonialist identity (2). For Trask:

"locals" don't want any reminder of their daily benefit from the subjugation of Hawaiians. For them, history begins with their arrival in Hawaiʻi and culminates with the endless re-telling of their allegedly well-deserved rise to power. Simply said, "locals" want to be "Americans." (20)

Stuart Hall maintains that "identities are the names we give to the different ways we are positioned by, and position ourselves within, the narratives of the past" (225). Local culture is a mosaic of many Asian, Pacific, European, and American threads, all situated within the history of Hawaiʻi.

One immediate consequence of this racial hybridity is that race itself does not work as it does on the continental United States. In Hawaiʻi, the differences between local Japanese and a Japanese tourist or immigrant matter in different ways than they do on the continent. As such, in Hawaiʻi, the identity-constructing "What are you?" is oftentimes replaced with the more informative "What school you went?" The latter, spoken in Hawaiʻi Creole English, or pidgin, is more than a question of place; it also articulates notions of class. The sentiment in the inquiry "What school you went?" reflects community rather than isolation. For Fijian writer Epeli Hauʻofa, the sensibilities of the Pacific see "a sea of islands" rather than "islands in a far sea" (7). The former "is a more holistic perspective in which things are seen in the totality of their relationships," unlike the latter, which stresses "the smallness and remoteness of the islands" (Hauʻofa 7). In this way, formations of identity in Hawaiʻi tend to connect people with particular communities rather than differentiate people into separate categories. While the continental United States and Hawaiʻi are different places and thus construct identity in different manners, Hawaiʻi can offer the rest of the country, and world, a particular understanding beyond "Asian American" that prompts us to question restored behaviors of our cultural assumptions.

LOCAL ASIAN AMERICAN IDENTITIES IN HAWAIʻI, BY EDWARD LEE

Although scholarly discussions in minority rhetorics often address the complexities and tensions that exist when a minority discourse works within and/or against a dominant culture, challenges arise when one considers the issues surrounding Asian American identity and acceptance in the state of Hawaiʻi. According to Morris Young,

> Hawaiʻi's history as a sovereign nation, its existence as a nonwhite-majority community, its social movements for Asian Americans and Pacific Islanders, and its strong maintenance and adaptations of Asian American and Pacific Islander cultural practices create a site for rhetorics of/from color. ("Native" 84)

Asian Americans are a majority in the state of Hawaiʻi. But in terms of societal acceptance, race seems to allow some phenotypical ethnic Asians to gain entry or status as Hawaiʻi "locals"[1] while at the same time allowing some phenotypical ethnic Asians to be "othered" due to their multilingual and/or multicultural mores, demonstrating how the term "local" can become more dynamic and variable when considering the realities of life in Hawaiʻi.

In "Native Claims: Cultural Citizenship, Ethnic Expressions, and Rhetorics of Hawaiianness," Morris Young defines the term "Local" and examines

---

1   I use the term "locals" as distinct from "Local" (with the capital L) to refer to "new locals."

the relationship (and the tensions and complications that accompany it) between "Local" and Native Hawaiians (92). But I want to take one step back to examine the relationship between new "locals" and presumably older "Locals" within Hawai'i as "a site for rhetorics of/from color" (Young "Native," 84).

As an Asian American born in Pennsylvania and raised on "Standard English" in Catholic grade and high schools in northeastern Pennsylvania, my "schooled literacy" has served as cultural capital in Hawai'i. Native Hawaiians, "Locals," and tourists assume that I am "Local," and that I attended private K–12 schools due to the way I speak. I am treated with the familiarity afforded to Locals even after I disclose my North American origins. However, when I am speaking Korean with my wife, a Korean native who moved to Hawai'i with me five years ago, we are both treated with indifference or hostility by Locals. Once, as I was conversing with my wife in Korean while waiting in line at a cash register, an Asian American male in front of us looked at us for a bit and then turned to his Local partner and said loudly enough for all to hear that "the problem is that these Koreans come to visit, but they don't leave."

The recurrence of such incidents makes it clear how the "new local," namely, the recent Asian immigrant to Hawai'i—or in my case, the Asian American who can code switch and competently express himself in an Asian language and/or culture—is positioned by the "older Local." It is actually no surprise that the diversity of the Asian diaspora in Hawai'i yields a less-than-uniform standard for the different nationalities, classes, and genders, which means that, more often than not, different segments of or individuals in the Asian American diaspora are privileged or marginalized, depending on the situation. In fact, Asian American scholars routinely refer to such tensions; for example, Tomo Hattori and Stuart Ching's essay, "Reexamining the Between-Worlds Trope in Cross-Cultural Composition Studies," challenges the "binary representations of race and literacy" by calling for "fluid and multiple articulations of culture, ethnic identity, and citizenship within the nation" (47). But what surprises me is the Asian-on-Asian (or Pacific Islander-on-Pacific Islander) "othering" and how such rhetoric demonstrates how the term "local" and its definition can become more contested and variable when considering the realities of the multicultural milieu that is Hawai'i.

Young's definition of the term "Local" becomes more selective than one might think. Asians who identify as Locals in Hawai'i may not be considered Locals by the established Local gatekeepers. In his monograph, *Ethnicity and Inequality in Hawai'i*, John Okamura asserts that "ethnic and racial groups, and certainly not individuals, are not free to create any identity of their own choosing for themselves and, in fact, can be severely limited by the ethnic or racial identities ascribed to them by other groups through denigrating stereotypes" (94). For Asians in Hawai'i, the racial marker of Asianness becomes a liability when accompanied by a lack of English language fluency and U.S. cultural competency.

HAWAII FIVE-O AND ASIAN AMERICAN REPRESENTATION: A UNIQUELY HAWAIIAN DYNAMIC, BY SCOTT KA'ALELE

One of the great popular culture representations of Hawai'i took place on national television between 1968 and 1972. The original version of the television show *Hawaii Five-O* ran for twelve years, but it was the first four years that featured actor Gilbert Francis (Zulu) Lani Damian Kauhi, playing Detective Kono Kalakaua. Kauhi was the first Native Hawaiian man with a recurring role on a national television show, and his presence resonated with Hawaiian and Local working-class viewers. Starting off slowly the first year, the television show has become a popular culture icon, and inspired a remake that went on air in 2010, which is still in production today. To update the show for a modern audience, changes were made to the roles of the main characters; Kono Kalakaua, once a large, dark, burly Hawaiian man, became a petite, sexy, markedly Asian woman.

Barry Brummett asserts, "people need to see their engagement with popular culture as participation in rhetorical struggles over who they are," which is a dynamic that is "inherently subversive," yet hinges on "the creation of awareness in people of how culture rhetorically influences them" (xxi). This interactivity with popular culture also serves as a recombining factor of identity, as Buckley and Ott explain that individuals are primarily consumers that articulate self through consumer choice (210). While consumerism would suggest a blind voracity, "in performing their personas, 'individuals' simultaneously reproduce the codes of dominant culture through adoption and assimilation, as well as undermine those codes through creative recombination and bricolage" (Buckley and Ott 210). In the case of *Hawaii Five-O*, the codes of dominant culture seem to have been reapplied to the role of Kalakaua, perhaps speaking to the conflation of Asian American and Hawaiian identity. If we look back through a rhetorical lens, we are able to see the unique placement of Kalakaua as anathema to the subjectivity of lingering colonial residue, while also subverting dominant perceptions of Hawaiians in mass media. I contend that as sites of inquiry, popular culture interpretations of Hawai'i present a unique opportunity to examine the conflation of race, identity, and culture, intermingling within the perfect storm that is the mixed-race context of Hawai'i.

Through Jolivette Mecenas' "Beyond 'Asian American' and Back: Coalitional Rhetoric in Print and New Media," we can see one of the ways that Asian American identity is refashioned rhetorically through the unique cultural dynamic in Hawai'i. Focusing on the ways that media can build "coalitional readerships . . . or publics" through rhetorical strategies organized around identity, Mecenas is concerned with how these coalitions build and maintain agency "through shared practices of popular culture" (201). In her analysis of bloggers, Mecenas observes a vigorous debate concerning identity politics in Hawai'i, including what it means to be *kama āina* (native born), "Hawaiian," and "local." She argues that

> identity politics is used as an empowering rhetoric to articulate the nuances of race and race relations as lived in the geopolitical and neocolonial context of Hawai'i. The bloggers from Hawai'i actively resist being subsumed under a unitary and homogenizing Asian American identity, successfully employing identity politics as a political rhetoric to voice variation. (210)

Within this microcosm of the Hawaiian racial and ethnic dynamic, identity is rhetorically structured and yet allows for a distinct kind of agency.

Asian American identity will need to maintain "this state of becoming," or "indeterminacy," which Mao and Young explain, "makes it possible for Asian Americans to be transformative," and engage new spaces of productivity (6). In the same way that Brummett describes our engagement with the rhetoric of popular culture as engendering a "creation of awareness in people of how culture rhetorically influences them" (xxi), so too does our engagement with Asian American representations in popular culture. In the specific case of Hawai'i, the increasing velocity of the racial and cultural population shift happening in contact zones throughout the U.S. exacerbates this kind of awareness.

UNRESOLVED QUESTIONS, FUTURE INQUIRIES, FURTHER RE/VISIONS, BY K. HYOEJIN YOON

The writings by Lee, Kaʻalele and Pak bring our attention to Hawaiʻi as a productive site of inquiry for questions about race, nationalism, and ethnic identity among other issues that emerge from the "alternative contact" of Asians/Asian Americans and Native Hawaiians. Paul Lai and Lindsey Claire Smith describe alternative contact as a way to de-center the primacy of "first contact" narratives that stage white Europeans against "others" (407-8). The framework of alternative contact allows us to zoom in on the relationships among those "others," and as Jody Byrd states, to examine the "horizontal struggles among peoples with competing claims to historical oppressions" (xxxiv). For example, in "Competition, Complicity, and (Potential) Alliance," Lisa King provides a vivid and exceptional analysis of the tensions among Asians and Native Hawaiians as represented in the exhibits in the Princess Bernice Pauahi Bishop Museum.

Lee, Kaʻalele, and Pak engage with this particular history through their experiences and scholarly lenses. A concept that runs throughout the three papers is the idea of "restored behaviors." Richard Schechner's term establishes the rhetorical aspects of self and its various roles and helps us to understand the seeming repetition of behaviors and expectations across time and place. Pak introduces this term in his discussion of the constructions of Asian masculinity that reinforce a model of a middle-class suburban East Asian male. Pak argues that the hybridity of race in Hawaiʻi complicates such easy narratives. Lee's discussion of local identities in Hawaiʻi implicitly connects to the idea of restored behaviors by seeing identities as being ascribed and constructed through stereotypes. In his discussion, Lee unearths even finer gradations of othering that he observes between Native Hawaiians and Asians through a status that accrues to becoming a "local." Even finer still, he brings to light the distinctions that are made between Asian locals and Asian immigrants, or "old" and "new" locals. Kaʻalele explores the iterations of various representations and conflations of Asians and Hawaiians in popular culture. All three writers highlight the particular kinds of tensions that can exist between the Native Hawaiian and the Asian immigrant, the native and the Local, and between the Locals and the "locals."

In addition to contributing these perspectives and analyses to broaden and complicate our understanding of race and national identity in the U.S., Lee, Kaʻalele, and Pak invite the reader to engage with "critical imagination" (Kirsch and Royster 648-56) to see how emerging scholars frame their concerns and enter the conversation. More specifically, reading with critical imagination allows us to see the writers grappling with the intersectionality of identity categories within the indigenous and colonial history of Hawai'i, the race and class issues within a context of immigrant and local dynamics, and the consequences of language and literacy.

Furthermore, the writers challenge us to use Kirsch and Royster's idea of "strategic contemplation" (656-9) to read with an openness to dialogue and self-awareness, and the ability to see what new and unfamiliar openings their contributions create in the dialogue. One concept that challenges me as a reader is Lee's use of the term "phenotypical." Lee names it explicitly in his piece, as a process of identification. In his use of the term, I see him grappling with how to work with the language of race.

The term is one way to name that which haunts the work of any project that groups people based on shared physical traits. As a biological term to denote the physical expression of genes, it hearkens back to 18th–19th century racialized medical and anthropological discourses, including phrenology and other fixations on anatomy as evidence of a hierarchy of races. Today's science debunks the myth that race has any basis in biology. Yet, as a group, Asians/Asian Americans, by virtue of physical, linguistic, and cultural characteristics, have been marked "forever foreign" and unassimilable by dominant groups (Tuan; Lee). Yet such categorizations have also been a source of resistance, solidarity, and empowerment for communities of color. Many Asians play the game of trying to guess the ethnic background of another "Asian." It is often assumed both by outsiders and insiders that Asians can "tell" the differences. However, this assumption is often thwarted; we often get it wrong.

This impulse to identify, claim, name, and perhaps to fix can be problematic. This is a point that all three presentations hint at. But as we saw in the work by Tran and Lee above, it can also be a necessary step if we want to clear a space from which to say some things about ourselves and our communities—a necessary essentialism, if not always sufficient. And this move is one that has been necessary to articulate and reimagine for Asian/Asian American communities, as Mao and Young made clear in their introduction to *Representations* (9) (also see Ditch in this collection). But pausing on the term, it becomes clear to me that phenotype is not as fixed a concept as one might, at first, think. Even in the language of biology, phenotype is an interpretation, an incomplete representation of genotype; in other words, what is coded in our genes is not always visible. Recent discoveries in epigenetics underline the importance of environment in what genes are turned on and off, and what might ultimately "show" up as a visible or measurable trait, condition, or attribute. And so I conclude that phenotype might actually be an apt word, the right word, to get at both the solid and visible, and the constructed and imagined, while also leaving room for what is encoded in some physical or biological reality that may or may not be seen or known—the interplay between fact and fiction and meaning and interpretation.

There are other ideas that, as often is the case in the genre of the conference presentation, are tested out and dropped, some elaborated, some not, some hinted at, some baldly stated, and some ideas simply juxtaposed to each other. What could happen if, rather than seeing these artifacts of the writing as gaps, incompletions, or inexperience, we looked for how they challenge, speak back to, and perhaps even offend sophisticated scholarly palates? I suspect we would see the buds of ideas and lines of inquiry that we could nurture or squash. As editors, we were confronted by the question of whether to remove the word "phenotypical" and to ask for more revisions to make the presentations "cleaner" or more "coherent," but we decided to maintain the original shape and texture, to leave the buds of the writers' ideas intact, and to deal with how they challenge us.

Recent research on writing pedagogy has helped us to see the work of graduate students as mirrors into the developmental process of writing, identity, and community (Micciche and Carr; Micciche; Herrington; also see Dietz, Kehler, and Yoon). Indeed, Joseph Harris's delineation of "writing moves" provides us a vocabulary with which we can talk about the ways we try to make our way into the scholarship discourse community. Rhetorical moves like "coming to terms," "forwarding," and "taking an approach" for example, provides readers and mentors a richer way of engaging ideas, rather than seeing only "incomplete" or "undeveloped" ideas (Harris). In the spirit of Shaughnessy, Smitherman, and indeed the foremothers of the AAAC profiled by Sano-Franchini, we are called to see the logic in the writing of others, and to explore the ways that writers of color, in particular, take a stance on ethnic/racial and gender identity in particular, as they also negotiate a scholarly voice and identity.

We can be guided by novel perspectives in these first forays and engagements, to "re/vision", in Adrienne Rich's version of the term, to re-see old terms and ideas. This does not mean that we forfeit our responsibility to mentor and develop emerging scholars and graduate students, or to empower them in the discourses of power in our fields, but it does mean seeing their contributions as real contributions, not simply grain for the grindstone, to be assimilated into the dominant narratives, orthodox and accepted lines of inquiry. True diversity is not to make "them" into "us," but to let "them" change "us." And in their ideas and grapplings, perhaps we can see glimpses of the future of our discipline.

In their 2010 publication *The Present State of Scholarship in the History of Rhetoric,* editors Lynée Lewis Gaillet and Winifred Bryan Horner discuss the future of Asian/Asian American rhetoric, and refer to Morris Young's bibliography in "Growing Resources in Asian American Literary Studies" and the areas he identified for future research:

> (1) hybrid rhetorical and discourse practices and forms; (2) Asian American diasporic and transnational rhetorical and discourse practices; (3) recuperation of Asian and Asian American rhetoric prior to the early twentieth century; (4) Asian and Asian American digital rhetorics; and (5) intersections of identity and rhetorical practices. (qtd. in Gaillet and Horner, 202)

I think that Young was prescient in looking forward to these directions. In the writings by Lee, Kaʻalele and Pak, I certainly see their potential contributions to the study of Asian American diasporic and transnational rhetorical and discourse practices, as well as to intersections of identity and rhetorical practices. Indeed, in their work, we see how these two categories might actually merge. Hawaiʻi is intimately enmeshed in and is a case study of the Asian diaspora; and given the history of the Pacific and of its Native peoples, it forces conversations of identity and race to move beyond national contexts. Certainly, work in and on Hawaiʻi can also easily contribute to the other areas that Young identifies: to explore hybridity in a unique testing ground and to revisit the history of pre-20th century Hawaiʻi and the Pacific, more broadly.

Finally, the presentations call us to examine how writing and research are also rhetorical practices of identity formation. As Stuart Hall writes:

> [p]erhaps instead of thinking of identity as an already accomplished face, which the new cultural practices then represent, we should think, instead, of identity as a "production which is never complete, always in process, and always constituted within, not outside representation." (qtd. in Mecenas 200)

Hall and Mecenas call us to take seriously the importance of nurturing and respecting the work of emerging writers; to consider the role of identity in our work and to make explicit its influence and processes; and to facilitate that process for others, making their work part of a larger, shared project, each of us "becoming," each of us a piece in the mosaic.

WORKS CITED

"Asian/Asian American Scholarship in Rhetoric and Composition: Risks and Rewards." Conference on College Composition and Communication. Tampa Marriott Waterside, Tampa, FL, 19 March 2015. Sponsored by the Asian/Asian American Caucus.

Brummett, Barry. *Rhetorical Dimensions of Popular Culture.* Tuscaloosa: U of Alabama, 1991. Print.

Buckley, Cara Louise, and Brian L. Ott. "Fashion(able/ing) Selves: Consumption, Identity, and Sex and the City" *It's Not TV: Watching HBO in the Post-Television Era.* Eds. Marc Leverette, Brian L. Ott, and Cara Louise Buckley. New York: Routledge, 2009. 209-26. Print.

Byrd, Jodi. *The Transit of Empire: Indigenous Critiques of Colonialism.* U of Minnesota P, 2011. Print.

Dietz, Gretchen L., Devon R. Kehler, and K. Hyoejin Yoon. "Together and Undone: Motion, Style, and Stance as Post/Graduate Research Literacies." *Research Literacies and Writing Pedagogies for Masters and Doctoral Writers.* Eds. Cecile Badenhorst and Cally Guerin. Leiden, The Netherlands and Boston, US: Koninklijke Brill NV, 2016. 149-65. Print.

Fujikane, Candace, and Jonathan Y. Okamura, eds. *Asian Settler Colonialism: From Local Governance to the Habits of Everyday Life in Hawaiʻi.* Honolulu: University of Hawaiʻi Press, 2008. Print.

Gaillet, Lynée Lewis, and Winifred Bryan Horner. *The Present State of Scholarship in the History of Rhetoric: A Twenty-first Century Guide.* Columbia: U of Missouri P, 2010. Print.

Hall, Stuart. "Cultural Identity and Diaspora." *Identity: Community, Culture, Difference.* Ed. J. Rutherford. London: Lawrence and Wishart, 1990. 222-37. Print.

Harris, Joseph. *Rewriting: How to Do Things with Texts.* Boulder: UP of Colorado, 2006. Print.

Hattori, Tomo and Stuart Ching. "Reexamining the Between-Worlds Trope in Cross-Cultural Composition Studies." *Representations: Doing Asian American Rhetoric.* Logan: Utah State UP, 2008. 41–61. Print.

Hauʻofa, Epeli. "Our Sea of Islands." *A New Oceania: Rediscovering Our Sea of Islands.* Ed. Eric Waddell, Vijay Naidu, and Epeli Hauʻofa. Suva, Fiji: U of the South Pacific P, 1993. 2–16. Print.

Herrington, Anne. "Composing One's Self in a Discipline: Students' and Teachers' Negotiations." *Constructing Rhetorical Education* (1992): 91–115. Print.

King, Lisa. "Competition, Complicity, and (Potential) Alliance: Native Hawaiian and Asian Immigrant Narratives at the Bishop Museum." *Native/Asian Encounters.* Spec. issue of *College Literature: A Journal of Critical Literary Studies* 4.1 (2014): 43–65. Print.

Kirsch, Gesa and Jacqueline J. Royster. "Feminist Rhetorical Practices: In Search of Excellence." *College Composition and Communications* 61.4 (2010): 640-72. Print.

Lai, Paul, and Lindsey Claire Smith, eds. *Alternative Contact: Indigeneity, Globalism, and American Studies.* Baltimore: Johns Hopkins UP, 2011. Print.

Lee, Rachel C. *The Americas of Asian American Literature: Gendered Fictions of Nation and Transnation.* Princeton: Princeton UP, 1999. Print.

Shaughnessy, Mina P. *Errors and Expectations: A Guide for the Teacher of Basic Writing.* New York, Oxford UP, 1977.

Mao, LuMing, and Morris Young, eds. *Representations: Doing Asian American Rhetoric.* Logan: Utah State UP, 2008. Print.

Mecenas, Jolivette. "Beyond ⸢Asian American ' and Back: Coalitional Rhetoric in Print and New Media." *Representations: Doing Asian American Rhetoric.* Ed. LuMing Mao and Morris Young. Logan: Utah State UP, 2008. 198–217. Print.

Micciche, Laura R. "Review Essay: Rhetorics of Critical Writing: Implications for Graduate Writing Instruction." *College Composition and Communication* 60.3 (2009): W35-W48. Print.

Micciche, Laura R., and Allison D. Carr. "Toward Graduate-Level Writing Instruction." *College Composition and Communication* 62.3 (2011): 477–501. Print.

Okamura, Jonathan Y. *Ethnicity and Inequality in Hawai'i.* Philadelphia: Temple UP, 2008. Print.

Rich, Adrienne. *A Human Eye: Essays on Art in Society, 1997–2008.* New York: W.W. Norton and Company, 2010. Print.

Rosa, John P. "Local Story: The Massie Case Narrative and the Cultural Production of Local Identity in Hawai'i." *Amerasia Journal* 26.2 (2000): 93–115. Print.

Schechner, Richard. *Performance Theory.* New York: Routledge, 2003. Print.

Smitherman, Geneva. *Talkin and Testifyin: The Language of Black America.* Detroit: Wayne State UP, 1977.

Trask, Haunani-Kay. "Settlers of Color and 'Immigrant' Hegemony: 'Locals' in Hawai'i." *Amerasia Journal* 26.2 (2000): 1–24. Print.

Tuan, Mia. *Forever Foreigners or Honorary Whites?: The Asian Ethnic Experience*

Today. New Brunswick: Rutgers UP, 1998. Print.

U.S. Census Bureau; Census 2010, "2010 Census Results: Hawaii." Web. www.census.gov/2010census/data. Accessed 30 August 2016.

Yamamoto, Eric K. "Rethinking Alliances: Agency, Responsibility and Interracial Justice." *UCLA Asian Pacific American Law Journal* 3 (1995): 33-74. Print.

Young, Morris. "Native Claims: Cultural Citizenship, Ethnic Expressions, and Rhetorics of Hawaiianness." *College English* 67.1 (2004): 83–101. Print.

—. "Growing Resources in Asian American Literary Studies." *College English* 69.1 (2006): 74-83. Print.

CHAPTER SIX

Globalization and the Teaching of Written English*†

Paul Kei Matsuda

REFLECTIONS ON "GLOBALIZATION AND THE TEACHING OF WRITTEN ENGLISH"

Asian and Asian American users of English have contributed to the richness of the English language and its varieties, but are constantly struggling to establish and reestablish our identity positions because of the linguistic and cultural differences, both perceived and real. The essay that follows addresses the issue of how identity, which is partly constructed by our discourse practices, can be negotiated. It is about how English became widespread and diversified as it came in contact with Asian peoples, languages, and cultures. It is also about teaching writing in English in ways that are sensitive to the individual needs of students and the societal needs of challenging the dominant linguistic and cultural practices. Many of the principles are applicable to any group of people who struggle in linguistic and cultural contact zones—"the social spaces where cultures meet, clash, and grapple with each other, often in contexts of highly asymmetrical relations of power, such as colonialism, slavery, or their aftermaths as they are lived out in many parts of the world today" (Pratt 34). But I wrote this piece especially with Asian and Asian American users of English in mind, including myself.

---

*   This piece has been previously published as follows: Matsuda, Paul Kei. "Globalization and the Teaching of Written English." Selected papers from 2011 PAC/The Twentieth International Symposium on English Teaching. Taipei, Taiwan: Crane Publishing, 2011. 109–18. Print.

†   I would like to express my gratitude to Aya Matsuda for her helpful comments and suggestions on this paper.

Abstract: *In an increasingly globalized world, where people, goods, services, and ideas flow freely across national boundaries, the ability to communicate in writing has become more important than ever. With the dominance of English as the ingua franca of business, political, and scientific communication, teaching English writing is inevitable not only for individual success but also to promote national interests. While users of English—both native and non-native English users alike—are often willing to overlook linguistic differences in spoken discourse to varying degrees, the same individuals seem less likely to accept differences when it comes to written discourse. In this paper, I discuss the diversity of English in today's world and discuss ways of addressing language differences in the context of written discourse use, development, and teaching.*

ENGLISH IN THE GLOBAL CONTEXT

The first decade of the 21st century can be characterized as the era of fluidity. We live in an increasingly globalized world, where people, goods, services and ideas seem to flow freely across national boundaries. In fact, the very term "globalized world" will likely fade away as people realize the redundancy inherent in it, which serves to expose just how parochial we all have been in dividing the world into us and them, "our" country and the rest of the world, citizens and foreigners, native speakers and non-native speakers, and so on. This is not to say that things that were completely rigid and static a decade ago suddenly became more fluid and dynamic. The transition from modernity to postmodernity was a gradual one; it was the collective consciousness of people that began to shift more drastically only in the last few decades. National boundaries still exist, of course, and they do still matter. In fact, they continue to create tension among nations. Yet, the limitations of the 18th century notion of the nation state with one language, one culture, and one ethnic group have become undeniably clear—as we continue to witness the dire consequences of the dominant ethno-linguistic group within each nation pursuing this untenable ideal by assimilating or eradicating other groups. As the ubiquity of transnational fluidity gains more recognition, many of the ideas and practices that were based on more rigid categories are now being contested and replaced by more complex and dynamic ways of understanding and interacting with reality.

Ironically, one of the most important forces that prompted the shift toward fluidity was the very nationalism that, in the late 19th and early 20th centuries, led to the global expansion of a few powerful countries that sought to impose the kinds of transnational flows that were advantageous to their own national interests, giving rise to imperialism and colonialism. Many industrialized countries, including Japan, joined this self-serving globalization movement that affected most of Asia, but the British Empire has been, by far, the most "successful" in this effort. The expansion of British colonies and the imposition of the English language have left a legacy that has come to be known as linguistic imperialism (Phillipson). The post–World War II rise of the English-dominant United States as the economic, political, military, and cultural superpower has further reinforced the dominance of English. Rather, I should say "Englishes," since the British and U.S. varieties of English continue to compete for attention with the financial and political backing of the British Council and the United States Agency for International Development (USAID), formerly known as the United States Information Agency (USIA). For these countries, the English language has become one of the most important commodities—a renewable resource, if you will.

At the same time, the English language turns out to be easily reproduced locally because no one can claim copyright on the English language itself. Indeed, the worldwide spread of the English language and the ensuing pluralization of "Englishes" do not end with the duel between the British and U.S. varieties. Braj B. Kachru's notion of the concentric circles of world Englishes (Kachru, "English") has helped to illuminate the historical development of the spread and diversification of the English language in three different contexts: inner-circle, outer-circle, and expanding-circle. Although Kachru's original formulation was nationalistic in nature, reflecting the zeitgeist of the 20th century, the concept still has some usefulness in highlighting the historical development of diverse Englishes in various contexts. The inner-circle refers to contexts where English has long been one of the dominant languages, including the United Kingdom and the United States as well as Canada, Australia and New Zealand. Outer-circle contexts are often postcolonial countries and states such as India, Singapore, and Hong Kong, where English was imposed by the ruling class of expats and their local "subjects," initially forming the state of diglossia; in those contexts, the language of privilege began to take a different shape as it interacted with local linguistic and cultural practices and became indigenized. While those "nativized" varieties were initially seen as the bastardization of the English language, they have gained some legitimacy as local languages as they became stabilized and the number of "native" users of those varieties increased. Then, there are outer-circle contexts, such as China, Japan, Korea, Taiwan, Thailand, and others, where English has been adopted as a dominant "foreign" language, predominantly for international communication.

That's right. Predominantly. As the English language became established in various parts of Asia, the diverse Asian Englishes have also come to take on different roles (McArthur; Kachru "English"; Kachru *Asian Englishes*). In some outer-circle contexts, such as India and the Philippines, local varieties of English have become the language of choice for intra-national communication over dominant local languages that are often tied to privileged ethnic groups. In expanding-circle contexts, English is often used for international communication among users of various Asian languages as it provides a compromise where the use of one Asian language or another would provide unfair advantage to the more experienced users of those languages. In this sense, English has become an Asian language with its linguistic forms and functions constantly being negotiated in the context of its use.

The impact of the spread of the English language is not limited to changes to linguistic features—i.e., morphology, phonology, syntax and lexicon. The uses of English in new contexts have also given rise to new discourse features and practices at the above-sentence level, affecting both formal (e.g., discourse organization) and functional (e.g., argument strategies) properties. While some of the changes may be due to the influence of local languages, others may represent innovative usage to suit the new situations. For example, James Stanlaw has documented various creative uses of English in Japan and argued that English in Japan is not merely borrowed but created by Japanese users for their own social and communicative purposes. The dominance of English in Asia has also influenced discourse practices in Asian languages, and some researchers have even argued the need to counterbalance the influence by promoting local discourse practices in English (Kubota).

TEACHING WORLD ENGLISHES?

As the diversity of Englishes has become undeniably clear, many people, including language teachers, have come to acknowledge their existence. Yet, the teaching implications of world Englishes has been less than clear—partly because the whole English language teaching profession has been deeply imbricated in the dominant language ideologies, such as the native speaker myth (i.e., the native speaker is the only possible model for language learners), and the monolithic view of the English language (i.e., there is a single privileged variety). Many well-intentioned teachers and researchers of English embrace these ideologies out of what they consider to be a pragmatic perspective (Santos). As Sarah Benesch and others have pointed out, however, the notion of pragmatism is often contrasted with critical approaches while ignoring its own ideological nature (Benesch "ESL"), thus reinforcing the dominant ideology while undermining the welfare of English language learners—who are positioned as perpetual learners—in the long run. To teach English in the global society that is increasingly transnational and translingual, English language teachers in all contexts need to adopt what Benesch has called "critical pragmatism" ("Critical Pragmatism" 161) that not only responds to the problems at hand but also seeks to address the issue of power and inequality surrounding the current situation. Specifically, we need to develop strategies for teaching that are conducive to both long- and short-term needs of the students who are going to be participating in the global society—where the presence of multiple languages and multiple varieties of English has become an undeniable reality.

Teaching English in the global context does not necessarily entail teaching all varieties of English—an impossible task—much less teaching multiple varieties thoroughly. While it is important to expose students to various Englishes so they can develop the flexibility to interact with users of non-dominant varieties, it is often necessary to choose a single target variety out of practical considerations. Although the idea of teaching a dominant variety has the danger of reifying the undue privilege these varieties currently enjoy, further marginalizing the users of non-dominant varieties, it would not be fair to require individual language users to bear the burden of social activism when their immediate goals are personal, academic, and economic success. The choice of the target variety needs to be based on the students' current and future communicative needs. If those needs happen to be communication in the dominant variety of English, so be it. But the chances are, students will be facing the challenge of communicating with users of different varieties of English, including non-dominant varieties.

Teaching the dominant forms and functions is also important even as the English language is diversifying, because the presence of diverse Englishes does not automatically erase the privilege that has been ascribed to the dominant varieties. For students who wish to acquire the dominant forms and functions in order to succeed in their studies, career, and other domains of life, it is important to make the dominant code available. It is also important to keep in mind, however, that the dominant code is not monolithic. Traditional approaches to describing the dominant code focused on native English users or the contrast between native and non-native English users, creating the false impression that the native English users somehow represent ideal language users (and, conversely, the false idea that non-native English users are always represent less-than-ideal language users). In reality, native English users come in different shapes and sizes (metaphorically speaking), and not all of them are effective writers. It is also important to recognize that some of the best writers are non-native English users who bring rich language awareness to communicate effectively with readers who come from various language backgrounds.

One of the most common approaches to the teaching of dominant varieties of written English has been to take the descriptive approach—to describe the forms and functions of successful written English and to present them to students. Although some students can figure out genre features intuitively without explicit instruction at least some of the time, it is not the case for many, if not most, students—and that is why they need language and writing classes in the first place. In order to facilitate the development of genre knowledge within a limited amount of time, writing teachers need to engage in the explicit teaching of genre features—along with exposure to realistic genres. Furthermore, for students who have not grown up reading and writing written English in a wide variety of contexts, being exposed to various genre examples and awareness-raising activities—in the forms of lectures, discussion, and genre analysis—constitute an important part of instruction.

The use of genre analysis for instruction does not necessarily mean students are given simple models to follow (although a simplistic application of genre pedagogy has the danger of teaching reductive forms without connecting them to the larger rhetorical contexts). Indeed, corpus-based descriptions of genres have become more sophisticated and realistic over the years. In the early years, the corpora that were used to generate the descriptions included a narrow range of samples written by native users of dominant Englishes. More recently, however, researchers have come to realize the importance of including samples from all competent users of English, including those who have learned the target language as an adult. This is an important trend because the readers of English texts are becoming increasingly multilingual; for example, with the internationalization of academic journals, it is no longer unusual to find non-native English users among the editorial board members. As a result, descriptions of the dominant language forms and functions are beginning to reflect the subtle changes that are taking place in the English language itself as a result of language contact among users who come from various language backgrounds. In terms of educational effectiveness, using examples of effective writing by someone who shares similar linguistic background as the students can provide a positive role model who can inspire students.

At the same time, it is also important to recognize that there are uses of English that are clearly not effective or that fail to get the message across to the intended audience. For students to understand the range of possibilities without falling into the trap of believing that anything goes, teachers of writing need to help students see that there are uses of language that are problematic. Even more important is to examine the gray area between acceptable differences (variations) and unacceptable differences (errors). In so doing, teachers can help students make informed decisions about when, how, and to what extent uses of different linguistic and discourse practices can be effective. In *Talkin and Testifyin: The Language of Black America*, rhetoric and composition scholar and sociolinguist Geneva Smitherman incorporated features of African American Vernacular English (AAVE)—such as contractions in gerund forms (e.g., "writin" rather than writing)—into her academic writing to make a point about valuing language differences. For example, she wrote:

> We have had pronouncements on black speech from the NAACP and the Black Panthers, from highly publicized scholars of the Arthur Jensen-William Shockley bent, from executives of national corporations such as Greyhound, and from housewives and community folk. I mean, really, it seem like everybody and they momma done had something to say on the subject! (1)

Here, the use of AAVE features such as—"folk," "they momma," "done had something to say"—in the last sentence seems to add strong emphasis on her reaction to how everyone seems to have an opinion about AAVE. It is important to note, however, that she did not write entirely in AAVE. Rather, she strategically embedded some of the features of AAVE into a dominant variety of English. Both her book and her use of AAVE in writing the book was—and still remains—controversial, but her work would not have had the impact on the field of rhetoric and composition that it did had she written the book entirely in AAVE or entirely in the dominant variety of English.

One of the implications that can be drawn from this example is that differences need to be strategic. The writer's intentions and the intended effects of using the alternative features should be apparent to the readers, and the writer needs to use those features judiciously in order to avoid overwhelming the readers. Furthermore, even when the differences are introduced in small doses, some readers will likely react negatively to it and eliminate those differences, citing ideas such as the dominant conventions of academic writing. The writer needs to know the risks involved in using alternative discourses and to be prepared to respond to possible questions and criticisms that are raised by potential readers.

The question, then, is how writing teachers can conceptualize and teach writing as negotiation. In "World Englishes and the Teaching of Writing," Aya Matsuda and I outlined the principles of writing instruction in light of the tension between standardization and diversification of Englishes (371–73):

- Teach the dominant language forms and functions.

- Teach the non-dominant language forms and functions.

- Teach the boundary between what works and what does not.

- Teach the principles and strategies of discourse negotiation.

- Teach the risks involved in using deviational features.

Teaching the dominant language forms and functions is important because doing so will provide students with the language of power that allows them to advance in society where the dominant varieties of English are highly valorized. At the same time, teaching the non-dominant language forms and functions allows students to understand the dominant discourses better by providing an understanding of what does not fit the dominant expectations. It also provides a broader repertoire that helps students to understand and articulate variations in dominant practices. Teaching the boundary between what works and what does not is also important not only because it can help students see where to draw the line between appropriate and inappropriate uses of language but also because it shows students the gray areas where negotiation of discourses becomes possible, if not necessary. To help students make sense of all these factors and navigate through the complex process of negotiation in producing written discourse, teaching the principles and strategies of discourse negotiation is also essential. Finally, students need to be informed about the risks involved in using deviational features so they can make appropriate decisions about when and how they negotiate or do not negotiate discourses.

A caveat is in order. These principles are intricately tied to one another, and it is not appropriate to adopt one or more of these principles selectively. Yet, teachers who are inclined toward one ideological position or another may be tempted to take one of these principles to justify the position they have always held. For example, teachers who have fully (and often unknowingly) submitted themselves to the dominant ideology often eagerly accept the first principle and ignore the rest. Conversely, teachers who are invested in challenging the status quo by, for example, encouraging students' individuality may take the second principle and ignore the rest. Neither of these responses is consistent with what I am advocating here—both of them end up reducing language and writing to simply a matter of form, which is counterproductive for both learning and use. In order to take writing for what it really is, teachers need to embrace the centripetal and centrifugal forces of writing to their fullest extent and convey the complexity of writing to students—rather than leaving students in the dark by continuing to strip writing of all its variations and rich contexts. To explore how these principles are intricately related with one another, the next section presents an example of discourse negotiation to show how these principles work together.

DISCOURSE NEGOTIATION IN ACTION

The notion of academic writing is often overgeneralized. Even though there are diverse practices even within an academic journal in the same field, people's judgments about what is appropriate and what is inappropriate is often based on crude generalizations that are based on a limited range of experience. Even in applied linguistics, where some (though not all) researchers focus on describing academic writing—ostensibly in all its variations—many still seem to fall into a fairly monolithic view of academic writing, which is dominated by the Introduction-Method-Results-Discussion (IMRD) structure. The IMRD structure (and its variations) is designed for reporting empirical research studies (including quantitative and some qualitative approaches). While this general structure is useful for straight empirical research reports, not all researchers practice this type of academic writing—at least not all the time. In academic journal articles that use other modes of inquiry, including philosophical, historical, and narrative articles, a significant part of knowledge construction happens through the act of writing (Bereiter and Scardamalia). For these reasons, conforming to formulaic structures actually prevents researchers from making significant new contributions to the field. Furthermore, the discursive construction of knowledge is not limited to these modes of inquiry; it happens in most qualitative research and, to some extent, even in quantitative research. As John Swales and others have amply demonstrated, article introductions in empirical sciences must construct research problems discursively, affecting the collection and interpretation of data and, ultimately, the conclusions drawn from the study.

Indeed, as Christine Pearson Casanave has pointed out, narrative permeates all aspects of second language writing research. Narratives include disciplinary metanarrative, research writing as narrative, the narrative construction of reality, and narrative as data. I have also written a fair share of narrative-based academic articles, including metadisciplinary history (e.g., "Situating ESL Writing"; "Composition Studies and ESL Writing"; "Coming to Voice"; "Process and Post-Process"), narrative inquiry into writing for scholarly publication ("Coming to Voice"), and the nature of PhD student mentoring (Simpson and Matsuda) and writing for publication. More recently, Dwight Atkinson and I have used dialogues to explore issues in contrastive rhetoric—which is now called intercultural rhetoric (Atkinson and Matsuda; Matsuda and Atkinson). In June 2011, we had a live dialogue at the 2011 Symposium on Second Language Writing in Taipei, Taiwan. The conversation was about strategies for finding a cutting edge in second language writing research. Since the use of dialogue as a form of academic publication represents our conscious effort to challenge the dominant mode of writing in the field, it may help illustrate some of the principles that have been mentioned above. For that reason, I am going to elaborate on it at length here.

Ever since we met at TESOL 1999 in New York, Dwight Atkinson and I have been having dialogues about various topics, academic and nonacademic. We have found our conversations helpful as we explore, challenge, question, and generate ideas. We also like to involve others, including both novice and experienced scholars, in our conversations. To us, academic conferences are our agora. To extend the Socrates metaphor, I tend to associate our dialogue with Socratic dialectic, where we question and challenge each other's ideas as we develop our thoughts further. Over the years, our conversations have influenced our individual works in various and profound ways, although not until recently did we find occasions to write collaboratively (partly because we tend to disagree on many issues).

When we were asked to write a chapter for an edited collection on intercultural rhetoric (Connor, Nagelhout, and Rozycki), we decided that having a dialogue and publishing it would help us explore the nuances of the topic—one that has a complex history filled with controversies—without being limited by the constraints imposed by more traditional genres of academic writing. A monologic writing, even a collaborative one, would force us to focus on a single theme and maintain coherence, thus imposing a superficial structure to reality that is often multifaceted and incoherent yet richly complex and insightful. We were, of course, aware that dialogues have their own constraints, but we reasoned that different sets of constraints allow for the kind of explorations that would not be possible with conventional genre constraints. That is, alternative discourses do not replace dominant discourses completely; rather, they augment dominant discourses by expanding the repertoire for performing intellectual work. Choosing the unconventional form would also help us make a point about how traditional approaches to contrastive rhetoric have focused on dominant practices within linguistic or cultural contexts, giving the false sense of consensus and stability to genre practices that are, in reality, often more complex, dynamic, and fluid. We also wanted to expose the occluded process of generating and exploring ideas—the part of intellectual work that is often invisible to novice researchers who only see the end result of the process in the form of conventional academic articles and book chapters.

To produce the dialogue, we sat by the fireplace at a small cottage on an island in Maine and turned on a tape recorder as we started our usual conversation with bottles of beer in our hands. (Now, that's an important part of the intellectual process that's definitely invisible in conventional academic publications.) We had a list of questions to guide our conversation, like an interview guide in qualitative interviews, but no part of the actual dialogue was scripted. Once we got started, we were having our conversation as always. After the conversation, we had the taped conversation transcribed by Steve Simpson, one of my doctoral students who later reflected on the experience in a book chapter about mentoring and professional development (Simpson and Matsuda). The outcome was more coherent than either of us had expected. We made minor cuts and edits, and added some citations, but we managed to develop the dialogue into a manuscript without making too many changes.

Our attempt to publish the first dialogue as a book chapter met with some resistance from some of the anonymous reviewers, who argued that our dialogue did not fit the conventions of academic writing—the very notion we were trying to challenge with the piece. We had to explain our intentions several times and respond to multiple layers of request to write something more conventional, which we were not willing to do. Yet, after some negotiation, we managed to publish it in the volume as planned while still keeping the integrity of our dialogue piece. Better yet, the dialogic approach was well-received, and we have been asked to perform our dialogues live at conferences. We performed our first live dialogue at the 2010 Conference on Intercultural Rhetoric and Discourse, which has been transcribed by Matthew Hammill, another doctoral student of mine, and the dialogue will soon appear in an edited collection (Atkinson and Matsuda). We have also been asked to return to the next Intercultural Rhetoric Conference in 2012 to continue our open conversation.

How does this example represent the principles of discourse negotiation mentioned earlier (Matsuda and Matsuda)? First, we had to know the dominant discourse practices to begin with in order to make it work. Both of us have published extensively in various top-tier journals on topics related to second language writing as well as broader areas of applied linguistics, composition studies, and TESOL, and many of our published articles use dominant forms of academic discourse. Therefore, people who know our work would not automatically assume that our choice is due to our inability to produce more traditional academic writing. In addition, in order to explain that using this alternative form is important, we had to know the dominant practices so we could explain their shortcomings as well as the contributions that alternative forms of writing might make. In fact, to persuade people who are themselves accomplished writers of traditional academic articles, we had to know the traditional genres as well as—if not better than—they did.

Likewise, to explain the merit of the alternative approach we were taking, we had to know the alternative forms of academic discourse inside out in order to demonstrate that the use of dialogue is not simply a whimsical choice but a deliberate and principled choice. We also had to make sure that the resulting dialogue actually provided new knowledge, new perspectives, or new interpretations that would make sense to experienced researchers and help new researchers gain intimate insights into the subject. The formal knowledge of dialogues is, of course, important, but it also had to be undergirded by an understanding of how knowledge is constructed and negotiated through dialogue. Having theoretical knowledge of the Bakhtinian dialogism (*The Dialogic Imagination*) and Socratic dialectic was therefore also important—not so much as explicit frameworks for our dialogue but as a way of assessing our dialogue after the fact to ensure that our conversation was performing the kind of intellectual work we thought we had always been accomplishing when we got together to talk.

It was also important for us to be able to gauge—and explain—where our dialogue fell on the continuum between acceptable and unacceptable discourse practices. To be able to explain when and how we were deviating from the norm as well as when and how we were using alternative discourse practices, we had to know the boundary between them. This is actually a tricky business because people draw different boundaries. Some members of the field may consider anything but traditional IMRD to be out of the question while others may be craving more narratives and dialogues. By having developed close relationships with many people in the field—through interactions at conferences and other social occasions—we have cultivated the sense of different individual preferences, which allows us to imagine our audience and a range of possible reactions.

Over the years, I have also developed different strategies for negotiating discourses both through experience and by researching discourse negotiation ("Contrastive Rhetoric"; "Voice in Japanese"; "Alternative Discourses"; Matsuda and Matsuda). One of the most important principles in negotiating discourses is to establish intentionality—to make clear to the readers that the features that deviate from the perceived norm are a result of our deliberate choices rather than random errors. Intentionality can be established through various strategies, including making the intention explicit through meta-discourse, through consistency both within and across texts, and through references to precedents. But being intentional is not enough; the intentions have to make some sense lest they be dismissed as "rampant alternative alternativisms" (Thaiss and Zawacki 81).

CODA

To teachers who work with students at a low proficiency level, this discussion may not seem immediately applicable. Yet, these principles and strategies are important especially in the early years of language learning because the texts they produce will contain many features and functions that deviate from the dominant discourses—both intentionally and unintentionally. Students need to continue to develop their language repertoire—including both dominant and alternative features and functions—while not being daunted by the thought of acquiring the dominant discourses completely. Given the complexity of the reality, both teachers and students have tended to take one extreme position (i.e., learn the dominant discourse and do not deviate from the norm) or the other extreme position (i.e., anything goes). Neither position is realistic or productive. An understanding of the diversity of Englishes and of the negotiation of languages and discourses helps put the experience of language learners and users into perspective.

WORKS CITED

Atkinson, Dwight, and Paul Kei Matsuda. "Intercultural Rhetoric: A Conversation—The Sequel." *Critical and Corpus-Based Approaches to Intercultural Rhetoric.* Ed. Diane Belcher and Gayle Nelson. Ann Arbor: U of Michigan P, 2013. Print.

Bakhtin, Mikhail. *The Dialogic Imagination: Four Essays by M. M. Bakhtin.* Trans. C. Emerson and M. Holquist. Austin: U of Texas P, 1981. Print.

Benesch, Sarah. "Critical Pragmatism: A Politics of L2 Composition." *On Second Language Writing.* Ed. Tony Silva and Paul Kei Matsuda. Mahwah: Lawrence Erlbaum Associates, 2001. 161-72. Print.

—. "ESL, Ideology and the Politics of Pragmatism." *TESOL Quarterly* 27 (1993): 601–26. Print.

Bereiter, Carl, and Marlene Scardamalia. "Surpassing Ourselves." *An Inquiry into the Nature and Implications of Expertise.* Chicago: Open Court, 1993. Print.

Casanave, Christine Pearson. "Uses of Narrative in L2 Writing Research." *Second Language Writing Research: Perspectives on the Process of Knowledge Construction.* Ed. Paul Kei Matsuda and Tony Silva. Mahwah: Erlbaum, 2005. 17–32. Print.

Connor, Ulla, Ed Nagelhout, and William Rozycki, eds. *Contrastive Rhetoric: Reaching to Intercultural Rhetoric.* Amsterdam: John Benjamins Publishing, 2008. Print.

Kachru, Braj B. *Asian Englishes: Beyond the Canon.* Hong Kong: U of Hong Kong P, 2005. Print.

—. "English as an Asian Language." *Links and Letters* 5 (1998): 89–108. Print.

Kubota, Ryuko. "Critical Approaches to Theory in Second Language Writing: A Case of Critical Contrastive Rhetoric." *Practicing Theory in Second Language Writing.* Ed. Tony Silva and Paul Kei Matsuda. West Lafayette: Parlor Press, 2010. 191–208. Print.

Matsuda, Aya, and Paul Kei Matsuda. "World Englishes and the Teaching of Writing." *TESOL Quarterly* 44.2 (2010): 369–74. Print.

Matsuda, Paul Kei. "Alternative Discourses: A Synthesis." *ALT DIS: Alternative Discourses and the Academy.* Ed. Christopher L. Schroeder, Helen Fox, and Patricia Bizzell. Portsmouth: Boynton/Cook Heinemann, 2002. 191–96. Print.

—. "Coming to Voice: Publishing as a Graduate Student." *Writing for Scholarly Publication: Behind the Scenes in Language Education.* Ed. Christine Pearson Casanave and Stephanie Vandrick. Mahwah: Lawrence Erlbaum Associates, 2003. 39–51. Print.

—. "Composition Studies and ESL Writing: A Disciplinary Division of Labor." *College Composition and Communication* 50.4 (1999): 699–721. Print.

—. "Contrastive Rhetoric in Context: A Dynamic Model of L2 Writing." *Journal of Second Language Writing* 6.1 (1997): 45–60. Print.

—. "Process and Post-Process: A Discursive History. *Journal of Second Language Writing* 12.1 (2003): 65–83. Print.

—. "Situating ESL Writing in a Cross-Disciplinary Context." *Written Communication* 15.1 (1998): 99–121. Print.

—. "Voice in Japanese Written Discourse: Implications for Second Language Writing." *Journal of Second Language Writing* 10.1–2 (2001): 35–53. Print.

Matsuda, Paul Kei, and Dwight Atkinson. "A Conversation on Contrastive Rhetoric: Dwight Atkinson and Paul Kei Matsuda Talk About Issues, Conceptualizations, and the Future of Contrastive Rhetoric. Ed. *Contrastive Rhetoric: Reaching to Intercultural Rhetoric.* Ulla Connor, Ed Nagelhout, and William Rozycki. Amsterdam: John Benjamins Publishing, 2008. 277–98. Print.

McArthur, Tom. "English as an Asian Language." *English Today* 19 (2003): 19–22. Print.

Phillipson, Robert. *Linguistic Imperialism.* Oxford: Oxford UP, 1992. Print.

Pratt, Mary Louise. "Arts of the Contact Zone." *Profession* 91 (1991): 33–40. Print.

Santos, Terry. "Ideology in Composition: L1 and ESL." *Journal of Second Language Writing* 1 (1992): 1–15. Print.

Simpson, Steve, and Paul Kei Matsuda. "Mentoring as a Long-Term Relationship: Situated Learning in a Doctoral Program. *Learning the Literacy Practices of Graduate School: Insiders' Reflections on Academic Enculturation.* Ed. Christine Pearson Casanave and Xiaoming Li. Ann Arbor: U of Michigan P, 2008. 90–104. Print.

Smitherman, Geneva. *Talkin and Testifyin: The Language of Black America.* Detroit: Wayne State UP, 1977. Print.

Stanlaw, James. *Japanese English: Language and Culture in Contact.* Hong Kong: U of Hong Kong P, 2004. Print.

Swales, John. *Genre Analysis: English in Academic and Research Settings.* Cambridge UP, 1990. Print.

Thaiss, Chris, and Terry Myers Zawacki. "Questioning Alternative Discourses: Reports from Across the Disciplines." *ALT DIS: Alternative Discourses and the Academy.* Ed. Christopher L. Schroeder, Helen Fox, and Patricia Bizzell. Portsmouth: Boynton/Cook Heinemann, 2002. 80–96. Print.

CHAPTER SEVEN
What Does the Field of Writing Assessment Need? Or, How Asian and Asian American Rhetoric Can Help Writing Assessments Work Better

Asao B. Inoue

Throughout my career, I've worked on many writing assessment projects: a book, *Antiracist Writing Assessment Ecologies* (2015); a co-edited collection (with Mya Poe), titled *Race and Writing Assessment* (2012); program assessment research at Fresno State and the University of Washington Tacoma for First Year Writing (FYW) and Directed Self-Placement (DSP) programs; and a number of smaller projects that amount to numerous chapters and articles in edited collections and journals, most of which are on topics that inquire about the effects of program or classroom assessment practices on particular racial formations. I use racial formation theory (Omi & Winant, 1994) because it defines race in a sociohistorical and contextualized manner, as historical processes. In our introduction to the collection, Mya Poe and I offer a way to understand the usefulness of this theory for writing assessment research:

> Racial formation . . . allows us to speak of black racial formations in a particular historical moment and location in a writing assessment technology without reducing that racial distinction to a static category because it acknowledges the social construction, the formation, of race by forces in history, local society, schools, and projects—such as writing programs. Part of what makes racial formations "local" is how

those formations are historically situated in particular communities with particular social, political, economic, and cultural histories. What makes racial formation useful for assessment purposes is that it allows researchers to account for race without essentializing racial identity in the conclusions they make about writing assessment outcomes. (6)

In this chapter, I reflect on my work on race and racial formations in writing assessment, and suggest future inquiries for writing assessment researchers and writing program administrators. Additionally, I hope that scholars who work in Asian and Asian American rhetoric will see how their own scholarly interests may offer insights to the field of writing assessment, which, in my view, would benefit greatly from such contributions.

The collection, *Race and Writing Assessment*, began as a conversation at a small table in a restaurant of the host hotel at CCCC in New York in 2007. Mya Poe and I met and considered how we could encourage others in the field of writing assessment to include explicit discussions of race in the scholarly work of validity, program assessment, assessment design, and in the dissemination of assessment results. In part, we felt (and still do) that many (perhaps most) writing assessments reported do not adequately address the ways that racial formations interact with those assessments. Another way to put this is that writing assessments might become more equitable and fairer for all students if researchers inquired more directly about how effective their curriculum is or how valid their assessment decisions are for the particular racial formations involved in their programs. Furthermore, there is a lack of theoretical and conceptual rigor around race in the literature on writing assessment. This makes complete sense given how the field of rhetoric and composition typically trains its specialists. If you're in a PhD program that focuses on writing assessment, likely you're not taking courses or studying the literature on race, racial formations, whiteness, colonial studies, or cultural studies (to name a few possible areas). You're likely studying writing assessment literature from journals like *College Composition and Communication*, *Assessing Writing*, or the *Journal of Writing Assessment*, or looking into research and scholarship from fields such as educational testing, psychological measurement, and validity studies. But you are reading particular scholarship that tends not to be informed by studies of race, racism, or cultural studies generally.

On top of this issue of training and what scholarship informs writing assessment research, there is also the question of who has historically done writing assessment and who gets heard by others in the larger communities of composition studies and writing program administration. Consider some of the most cited names in writing assessment over the last 20 years: Brian Huot, Richard Haswell, Michael Williamson, Peggy O'Neill, Ed White, William Condon, Liz Hamp-Lyons, and Bob Broad (we might include others who made portfolio assessment more prominent, like Peter Elbow, Pat Belanoff, and Kathleen Yancey). And then there are a few folks who work outside of writing assessment, but are often cited in writing assessment literature: Pamela Moss, Lee Cronbach, Samuel Messick, Sandra Murphy, Egon Guba, and Yvonne Lincoln. The point is, we don't have many (if any) scholars of color who can bring a sensitivity about being African American, Mexican American, Japanese American, Korean American, or Native American (to name a few racial formations) to writing assessment research, data, and decisions.

Encouraging scholars and researchers of color to do writing assessment work is crucial for a few important reasons. One, our students in community colleges and universities are becoming less white and getting assessed more often. Two, if students of color are being judged, placed, evaluated, graded, and assessed, then shouldn't faculty and scholars of color be a part of those decisions? If they are not right now, what does that say about where power relations in our schools and society are? White people still judging and controlling bodies of color? Don't we believe that being Japanese American, for example, offers something particular to judgments that a white colleague (as well intentioned as she may be) simply cannot provide? I'm thinking of Catherine Prendergast's and Victor Villanueva's discussions of colonialism in the academy, and in this case, in FYW programs and their assessments. I also wonder what a program portfolio assessment might look like if they considered seriously Paul Kei Matsuda's argument in "The Myth of Linguistic Homogeneity in U.S. College Composition." I don't think we have yet. Three, scholars of color tend to do work in rhetoric, not composition studies or writing assessment, but writing assessment, as Brian Huot has rightly argued, needs more carefully to incorporate our field's scholarship on literacy and rhetoric, and this includes most importantly the rhetorical work done on various racial formations. We need Asian and Asian American rhetoric (as well as other racial formation rhetorical work) in writing assessment theory and practice.

Thus there are two issues I'm identifying, and I've tried in my own research to address them: one, the field generally needs to have more robust notions of race and racism so that its scholarship, research, and practices can account better for racial formations in writing assessments; and two, the field needs more scholars and researchers of color to do this work alongside white scholars and researchers.

This is not to say that the folks mentioned above, and others, have not seriously considered race, class, gender, and other social factors in their work. They have, and often quite insightfully. I'm reminded of Haswell and Haswell's (1995; 1996) work on gender, or White and Thomas' (1981) early article on the results of a large-scale writing assessment on various racial groups in California, and Diane Kelly-Riley's (2006; 2011) work on race and validity. But all of the above scholars have done their work, out of necessity, from their own subject positions and histories, their own relations to education, the academic discourses used in assessments, and the decisions made by others like them. Victor Villanueva has argued "that a colonial sensibility remains . . . in the United States—in America—and that America's people of color are most affected by this sensibility" (184). This colonial sensibility may have its dark side, "internal colonialism," but it also offers academics of color a "colonial consciousness" (Villanueva 186, 187) that only occurs when cultures, languages, and histories clash both outside and inside the body. This colonial consciousness, I think, offers a "double consciousness," to use an often-cited concept from W.E.B. Du Bois, in which one's "two souls, two thoughts, two unreconciled strivings" (3) provide a way to see and feel the effects of writing assessments in particular and important, but often missed, ways.

My own colonial sensibility has allowed me as a WPA to recognize oppression in our writing program. As many readers of this collection can attest to, when you have been oppressed, when you have been colonized, it's easier to locate it when it happens to others. Several years ago, I introduced grading contracts into Fresno State's FYW program. These eliminate grades and points on assignments, and ask for students to do a certain amount of work or labor. If they do that labor, they receive a default grade, usually a "B," and if they do more labor, they get an "A" (no matter what anyone thinks of the writing). Quality is separated from the quantity of work. Quality is still the focus of feedback and activities, while quantity is used to calculate a course grade. After a few years of data collection, one thing became clear: the Hmong formation at Fresno State, unlike all other racial formations, find the contracts most helpful, prefer them at some of the highest rates, learn program outcomes at high levels, yet have some of the highest course failure rates (around 10%) (Inoue "Grading Contracts"). What Hmong students say in their end-of-program surveys is shocking to some of my colleagues, but not to me. Hmong students explain that the contracts allow them "freedom to write," whereas conventional grading does not. No other racial formation mentioned this at all. This isn't surprising to me because I was very much like our Hmong students—that is, I was similarly oppressed and misunderstood by educational systems and teachers attempting to evaluate my literacy as I was growing up. A colonial sensibility helped me see this issue in our program, when no one else seemed to even give our Hmong students a second thought. In short, I think students, programs, schools, and the field gain more when those who have been colonized, who have a colonial sensibility, become agents of writing assessments, when we can control writing assessment.

One of the goals of Poe's and my collection, then, beyond continuing a sustained discussion of race in writing assessment, was to gather research and voices that could carry such a burden. No collection published to date in the field of writing assessment has focused on this issue, so *Race and Writing Assessment* is a first of its kind. After several years, we found it difficult to get the kind of chapters we had first envisioned. We wanted some chapters to engage with theories of whiteness and race, then bring those ideas to bear on writing assessment theory and research, or we hoped for chapters that conducted writing assessments with an attention to race as it functions in the assessment or as it constructs or affects racial formations and their performances on those assessments. We also solicited chapters from key folks in the field, whom we felt others would listen to (I've named above some of those we asked). Unfortunately, few of the notable writing assessment scholars were able to contribute. Some did offer valuable anonymous readings for submitted chapters, but some did not. I will not guess at why they could not, nor do I suggest that they didn't see value in the project (all said they did). I'm sure there were good reasons for their non-participation; however, my sense is that the above issues of training and subject position may give some reason for why it has taken so long to publish such a collection and why the most-cited scholars in the field of writing assessment didn't feel it a top priority to participate in such an important project.

Race and Writing Assessment did produce some very interesting and insightful chapters. Chris Anson discussed the WAC/WID literature on assessment and finds that race is absent in just about all discussions. Diane Kelly-Riley discussed theoretically the effects of "shared evaluation approaches" on diverse populations, inquiring about the failure rates for African American students on the Washington State University portfolio exam. Anne Herrington and Sarah Stanley investigated *Criterion*, a computerized assessment of student writing designed for classroom-based instruction. They find that the program privileges one English dialect (no surprise), which may be affecting writers of nonstandard dialects of American English in negative ways. And of course, these English dialects occur in strong patterns in various U.S. racial formations. Zandra Jordan considered the impact that the "Students' Right to Their Own Language" statement has on classroom writing assessment, looking closely at one particular student in an HBCU at which Jordan taught. Kathleen Blake Yancey discussed admissions assessments and the way one assessment, Oregon State University's Insight Resume, has begun to transform access at that university for students of color.

Finally, my own chapter in *Race and Writing Assessment* investigated the effects of grading contracts on different racial formations at Fresno State, mentioned above. I considered two years of data, showing the effects of program-wide grading contracts on Asian, Black, and White students. Drawing on qualitative as well as quantitative data, I showed how contracts, as a particular institutionalized assessment technology, have different effects on different racial formations. In short, grading contracts are most effective at Fresno State for Asian Pacific Islanders, while only marginally effective for white students. While Asian Pacific Islanders, who are mostly Hmong at Fresno State, had the highest level of remedial status, lowest parental education levels, and more often spoke other languages at home, they performed statistically significantly higher in a key program outcome ("summary and conversation") in final portfolios, met workload expectations in their chosen courses at some of the highest rates among all racial formations, and were most satisfied with the grading contract. My own subject position as a Japanese American from a poor, working class family, who was tracked into remedial English and reading courses through elementary and middle school, has always made me particularly sensitive and interested in student populations like the Hmong formation at Fresno State. My sense that the contract would create such effects for the Hmong formation, among others, was part of the impetus for making the grading contract mandatory for some of the courses in the FYW program.

I also conducted program assessment work for Fresno State's FYW Program. This work shaped an article (Inoue "Self-Assessment") that argued for a culture of reflection and self-assessment at all levels in a writing program as a way to encourage good writing assessment practices and results (i.e., student learning). But mostly, this program assessment work has helped me understand the ways that a school, a writing program, even writing teachers, may find it very difficult to assess fairly when they have a racially diverse student population. There is no easy answer and no one-size-fits-all solution to this assessment situation (I resist calling it a "problem").

Finally, one project I'm particularly proud of is a chapter that Mya Poe and I wrote for *Writing Assessment in the 21st Century: Essays in Honor of Edward M. White*, edited by Norbert Elliot and Les Perelman. Our chapter, "Racial Formations in Two Writing Assessments" is a replication of Ed White and Leon Thomas' 1981 study, published in *College English*, "Racial Minorities and Writing Skills Assessment in the California State University and Colleges." Our chapter looks at the same EPT (English Placement Test) data for Fresno State students, just one of the schools included in the original study of all California State University students that White and Thomas compiled. We find interesting differences in performances on essentially the same writing assessment. Most notably, the Asian American students at Fresno State perform at the lowest levels compared to their peers, while technically the same students, "Asian" students, in the original 1978 CSU data performed at the highest levels relative to their peers. The difference? Lots of things.

As already mentioned, the population of Asian Americans at Fresno State currently consists mostly of Hmong students, who are often one or two generations (at most) removed from their families' immigration, and are tracked in local schools into ESL and ELL programs. Hmong have had a complex written language history, consisting of colonial and other influences. Many Hmong immigrants were farmers with no schooling in their native language (Duffy 21, 58–9), so many Fresno Hmong parents probably found learning English doubly difficult—English is a written and spoken language. Most Asian students in 1978, however, were not like this at all, and there were no Hmong in California to speak of. Many of the Asian Americans at CSU in the 1970s were born in the U.S. and often were high performers in schools. For instance, Japanese American families after WWII and internment often felt a need to be "more American" than their peers. In one sense, everything was sacrificed at the altar of scholastic success since doing well in school meant you were American, and this could shed the stigma of those internment experiences, even if one had not actually gone to camp.

We've all heard and read about the myth of the "model minority." The term "model minority" was coined in an article by William Peterson in his 1966 article, "Success Story: Japanese American Style." In 1978, the year of

White and Thomas' data, most Japanese American students taking the EPT in California were likely Sansei students (i.e., third generation, or second generation born in the U.S.). Most of their parents would not have spoken Japanese, but only English, since most *Issei* (first generation) immigrants made their children (*Nisei* and parents to the *Sansei*) speak only English. So there are many differences in the way the 1978 Asian American formation in California and the 2007 Asian American formation in Fresno are constituted, and these differences seem to translate to different results on the EPT, a literacy test. When placed next to my study of Hmong success with grading contracts in FYW courses, this replication study suggests contrary things about the Fresno Hmong, and complicates the concept of an "Asian" racial formation. While Fresno Hmong do poorer on standardized tests of literacy than all of their peers, they generally do better in FYW courses that do not use grading or ranking systems. Neither of these claims is true for the white populations at Fresno State.

In the process of editing *Race and Writing Assessment* and doing writing program assessment, I have theorized writing assessment as a technology which has racial validity implications (Inoue "The Technology"). Validity studies looks at the ways we confirm and prove what we say we are assessing when we assess a construct like "preparation for college writing," or "proficiency in college-level writing." This work on validity led me to consider how writing assessment is more than a collection of documents, prompts, people, or data, but an ecology. I worked mostly from scholars like Andrew Feenberg, who looks at the philosophy of technology, George Madaus, who considers the technology of education throughout history, Herbert Marcuse's critical social theories of technology as a mode of living, and of course, Michel Foucault's work on technologies that discipline bodies. While this project attempted to define in a productive way any writing assessment—from response, to grading, to placement, to proficiency "tests"—I was really thinking about the ways that current writing assessment technologies do not adequately account for diverse populations, and not just diverse in terms of race or class, but diverse in terms of intelligences, writing competencies and histories, and literacy practices. For instance, I imagine there are better ways to use writing assessment in classrooms and in placement processes that take advantage of the diverse students and diverse literacies that students bring with them. Most current models of writing assessment penalize diversity, penalize those who are not the same as the biases in the system, which in most cases amounts to promoting a version of a white, middle class, academic English language, one not used by the majority of those who use English on the planet. Part of this thinking comes from scholars who have thought carefully about creativity and education, such as Sir Ken Robinson and Howard Gardner. If we can understand better what writing assessment actually is, how it functions, and all that it produces (in students, in schools, and in society), we might better see the possibilities for equality and learning for all students. This work led to *Antiracist Writing Assessment Ecologies: Teaching and Assessing for a Socially Just Future* (2015).

If it is not clear already, allow me to conclude by stating the direction of future work in writing assessment that I find most important right now, and that I feel Asian and Asian American rhetorical scholarship can uniquely contribute to. I'll state these possibilities in the form of questions. How do we find ways to investigate racial formations in writing assessments, both in classrooms and large-scale assessments? What concepts and theories from other fields, such as cultural studies, colonial studies, feminist studies, and race studies, can be valuable to writing assessment researchers and WPAs, helping them collect and analyze race-based data? How do Asian and Asian American formations at local sites perform on writing assessments, placement assessments, or portfolio assessments? How does Asian and Asian American rhetorical scholarship help WPAs form better outcomes for their programs? How different are various historically and geographically situated Asian American formations and how do these differences play out in writing assessment technologies?

Finally, let me end with a personal anecdote that epitomizes some of the need for the kind of work in writing assessment and rhetorical studies that I'm asking for in this chapter:

> In the second grade, I won the school-wide reading contest. I read the most books in second grade. I wanted that trophy so badly that I recall staying up late each night reading books. Book after book, every night for months. When the day came, I got a trophy with a big smile on my face, so big I recall it hurting. I was honored in a formal ceremony after lunch. And after that ceremony was over, I put my trophy away and marched off to my remedial reading class, where the teacher awarded each of her charges with a goldfish cracker every time he (we were all boys) read a page from the books chosen for us. You see, I was judged by my white teacher to be a "slow" reader. I didn't know enough words. I couldn't read fast enough to keep up in class with others. I didn't talk

or say much in class. I remember her, my teacher, asking my mother, "what language does he speak at home?" He should speak English, she intimated. But I did speak English, only English. I just didn't talk in class. But when it came time to read on my own, I could put in the hours, the nights, the months—more than any of my peers. But that didn't seem to matter when one must be judged on other things. For years after elementary school, I searched for a teacher–mentor who was male and Japanese American, and strangely I did not understand why I wanted a mentor like that. I never found one.

WORKS CITED

Du Bois, W. E. B. *The Souls of Black Folk*. New York: Bantam Classic, 1903. Print.

Duffy, John. *Writing From These Roots: Literacy in a Hmong–American Community*. Honolulu: U of Hawai'i P, 2007. Print.

Haswell, Janis, and Haswell, Richard. "Gendership and the Miswriting of Students." *College Composition and Communication* 46.2 (1995): 223–54. Print.

Haswell, Richard, and Janis Haswell. "Gender Bias and Critique of Student Writing." *Assessing Writing* 3.1 (1996): 31–83. Print.

Huot, Brian. *(Re)Articulating Writing Assessment for Teaching and Learning*. Logan: Utah State UP, 2003. Print.

Inoue, Asao B. *Antiracist Writing Assessment Ecologies: Teaching and Assessing for a Socially Just Future*. Fort Collins and Anderson: WAC Clearinghouse and Parlor Press, 2015. Print.

—. "Grading Contracts: Assessing Their Effectiveness on Different Racial Formations." *Race and Writing Assessment*. Ed. Asao B. Inoue and Mya Poe. New York: Peter Lang Publishing, 2012. Print.

—. "Self-Assessment As Programmatic Center: The First Year Writing Program and Its Assessment at California State University, Fresno." *Composition Forum* 20. (2009). Web.

—. "The Technology of Writing Assessment and Racial Validity." *Handbook of Research on Assessment Technologies, Methods, and Applications in Higher Education*. Ed. Christopher Schreiner. Hershey: IGI Global, 2009. 97–120. Print.

Inoue, Asao B. and Mya Poe, eds. *Race and Writing Assessment*. New York: Peter Lang Publishing, 2012. Print.

—. "Racial Formations in Two Writing Assessments: Revisiting White and Thomas's Findings on the English Placement Test After 30 Years." *Writing Assessment in the 21st Century: Essays in Honor of Edward M. White*. New York: Hampton Press, 2012. 341-359.

Kelly-Riley, Diane. *A Validity Inquiry Into Minority Students' Performances in a Large-Scale Writing Portfolio Assessment*. Diss. Washington State University, 2006. Print.

Kelly-Riley, Diane. "Validity Inquiry of Race and Shared Evaluation Practices in a Large-Scale, University-Wide Writing Portfolio Assessment." *The Journal of Writing Assessment* 4.1 (2011). Web.

Matsuda, Paul Kei. "The Myth of Linguistic Homogeneity in U.S. College Composition." *College Composition and Communication* 68.6 (2006): 637–51. Print.

Omi, Michael, and Howard Winant. *Racial Formations in the United States: From the 1960s to the 1990s.* Second Edition. New York: Routledge, 1994. Print.

Peterson, William. "Success Story: Japanese American Style." *New York Times Magazine* 9 January 1966: 20–43. Print.

Prendergast, Catherine. "Race: The Absent Presence in Composition Studies." *College Composition and Communication* 50.1 (1998): 36–53. Print.

Villanueva, Victor. "Maybe A Colony: And Still Another Critique of the Comp Community." *JAC: A Journal of Rhetoric, Culture, and Politics* 17.2 (1997): 183–90. Print.

White, Edward M., and Leon Thomas. "Racial Minorities and Writing Skills Assessment in the California State University and Colleges." *College English* 43.3 (1980): 276–83. Print.

CIRCULATION ESSAY

Building on Recent Research from AAAC Members to Advocate for Second Language International Students

Jolivette Mecenas

The short-lived and informal women of color faculty group at my university began, like many feminist gatherings before us, as a reading group. Fired up by *Presumed Incompetent*, a 2012 collection of narratives and research by women of color in academia, our small group of faculty members intended to open a friendly discussion space for Latina, African American, Asian American, and mixed-race academics. At the time, it was daunting for me to articulate my own challenges as an Assistant Professor, even as I admired how the book's contributors offered their detailed testimonies. By the end of the meeting we had gravitated back to talking about our students, and how we could make college better for them, even as we recognized the need to foster a much-needed space for us to prioritize our own needs and experiences in academia. What I learned from our few meetings inevitably influenced my current research in writing program administration. In order to navigate our own experiences as academics and as women of color, we needed to speak publicly about our observations of race, class, gender, and structural forms of inequality in higher education. As a result of these conversations, I am better grounded not just in my field of rhetoric and composition, but also in my personal and work communities. They are interrelated.

For these same reasons, I make sure that I attend presentations and the roundtables organized by fellow members of the Asian/Asian American Caucus whenever I'm at CCCC, which are most years. This has also led me to read recent research of fellow caucus members, particularly on the responsibilities of writing program administrators concerning second language students, and on racial formation theory as a methodology for writing assessment research. This essay highlights recent presentations and publications by AAAC members in these areas, providing insight into some of the critical race-conscious research produced by caucus members who connect sociopolitical realities with structured inequities in U.S. higher education. Though my sense of advocacy is influenced by various personal and professional communities, my scholarship on writing program administration and linguistically and racially diverse student populations is informed and inspired by my CCCC community, the Asian/Asian American Caucus.

Returning briefly to my reading group: at the first meeting, one of my colleagues, an Asian American psychology professor, informed us that several second language international students—many of whom were Chinese—felt segregated from the larger university community. In particular, first-year international students wondered why they were placed into a learning community separate from other first-year students. Were they evaluated as "different" from other students because of their language, culture, or race? The counseling center received many international students distraught about the pressures and stresses that they faced far from home. Our reading group wondered if these students' perceived and experienced segregation contributed to their stressful experience. We also wondered, what was our responsibility as faculty members, and what was the university's responsibility, to support these students?

Several in rhetoric and composition have acknowledged the increased presence of multilingual students in writing classes and contemplated the responsibility of WPAs to address language diversity in their writing programs (Horner, Lu and Matsuda; Matsuda; Miller-Cochran). My campus, a private university, has seen a ten-fold enrollment increase of Chinese students over the past five years, in addition to students from Taiwan, Thailand, Japan, and Vietnam. This is not unique, as the majority of international students pay full tuition, providing a vital revenue stream for both public and private universities across the U.S. In his 2014 article, "Where Are They Now? The Presence and Importance of International Students to Universities in the United States," Niall Hegarty cites a study conducted by economists that predicts a future decline in the number of U.S. domestic students enrolling in U.S. universities (226). Hegarty provides statistics that illustrate the intense recruitment efforts of higher education institutions across the U.S., vying to bring international students to their campuses to compensate for this projected decline in enrollment and tuition (226). Hegarty also provides statistics that demonstrate that three of the top four countries of origin for international students are Asian (China, India, and South Korea); Chinese students represented over half of all students from Asia studying in the U.S. in 2013, with 233,992 students out of 437,000 (226). With the push to enroll more international students—specifically, more Asian students—in colleges and universities across the U.S., WPAs face the impact upon their writing programs when enrollment efforts are not accompanied with support for curriculum and faculty development. Particularly vulnerable are faculty-driven assessment, placement, and curricula for multilingual writers, especially for international students for whom English is a foreign language. At my campus, increased enrollment of second language writers impacted our writing program and writing center immediately. The impact on writing across the curriculum and writing in the disciplines is less clear, but faculty in other departments have voiced concerns about teaching second language students, most vocally about Asian students; some believe that they are irreformable plagiarizers, disinclined to participate in class discussion, and cannot comprehend course requirements due to cultural and linguistic differences.

These concerns voiced by faculty nationwide reflect what AAAC members Tanita Saenkhum and Paul Kei Matsuda identify as "an undeniable reality in writing programs across North America": the increasing presence of diverse populations of second language writers (199). In his 2012 article, "Let's Face It: Language Issues and the Writing Program Administrator," Matsuda further exhorts WPAs to align instruction with intended outcomes and assessment in writing programs, particularly in how we teach grammar to second language students so that they may reach stated learning outcomes for grammar in writing courses. Matsuda also observes, critically, that "institutions aggressively recruit ethnic minority students (who contribute to the visible diversity of the student population) and international students (who pay out-of-state tuition and, at an increasing number of institutions, thousands of dollars in additional fees)" ("Let's Face It" 142).

Matsuda's insights on the state of writing instruction for second language students reflect issues that likewise have been addressed by other members of the Asian/Asian American Caucus, who presented on Asian/Asian American disciplinary history and scholarship at the 2014 CCCC meeting in Indianapolis. Linh Dich's presentation, "The United States of Ambivalence: International Students as Sources of Income and Difference," raised issues surrounding the increased recruitment of international students from Asia, focusing on resident students' perceptions of Asians and Asian Americans as "competition, inassimilable, and socially awkward." Dich argues that these are the same stereotypes that maintain the image of Asians as "ambivalent, racialized figures: they are welcomed for their financial contributions, but remain outliers to the University culture and community." In her talk, she critiques the lack of effort on behalf of colleges to create meaningful intercultural exchanges between resident students and international students in order to mediate negative perceptions and experiences of Asian students. Dich's description of the flattened and neglected experiences of Asian students as the status quo demands that faculty and university administration consider how second language international students are racially organized in their everyday lives in U.S. colleges.

My own research extends Dich's critique of higher education's increased recruitment and enrollment of Asian students as profit-oriented, which I analyze as a *racial project*, a term from the racial formation theory of sociologists Michael Omi and Howard Winant. *Racial projects* serve to "reorganize and redistribute resources along particular racial lines" while *racial formation* is "a process of historically situated projects in which human bodies and social structures are represented and organized" within the hierarchal social structure (Omi and Winant 56). First-year writing placement, for example, can be analyzed as a racial project that determines student placement into their first-year writing courses. Using racial formation as an analytic tool, we may ask, for example: over time, how has the racial project of first-year writing placement constructed the cultural identities of college students from low-income, urban neighborhoods, and how are resources distributed to students as a result? By examining first-year placement technologies through the social construct of racial projects, we may examine how first-year students become a racial formation that intertwines testing performance with racial identity. Thus, we may examine racial groups that are disproportionately placed into basic writing as a social construct—a result more of socioeconomic forces than of essentialist and static ways of thinking about race.

So what does it mean when campuses flatten second language international students from Asia into one racial formation: "international students"? How do they fit into the social structure of the American university, and how are they culturally represented? More importantly, how does this representation influence the distribution of resources, such as tutoring support for second language international students in writing programs, and ongoing professional development for faculty who teach writing in the disciplines? These are questions that guide my study of faculty perceptions of multilingual college writers at a private university, which I presented at the AAAC-sponsored roundtable at the 2015 meeting of CCCC in Tampa.

The AAAC-sponsored roundtable was titled "Asian/Asian American Scholarship in Rhetoric and Composition: Risks and Rewards." My presentation was titled "Racial Formations of Second Language International Students and the Responsibility of the WPA," in which I discussed past and ongoing research of AAAC members whose work directly influences my current project on writing program administration. One influential text is the 2012 edited collection of caucus member Asao B. Inoue and his colleague Mya Poe, *Race and Writing Assessment,* which builds upon Omi and Winant's racial formation theory to consider the potential impact of race and class in large-scale writing assessment, and how biased interpretations of assessment outcomes are often structured into assessment practices. Inoue and Poe's work helped me articulate my objective for studying faculty perceptions of second language international students, which is to seek insight into how students may or may not be racialized in ways that bias both large-scale and individual assessment of student writing in WAC/WID courses. In a more recent article published in *Research in the Teaching of English,* Inoue asserts that writing assessments have naturalized failure for some students, particularly for students of color and low-income students designated as "remedial" (334). Inoue's study prompted me to inquire in my own project: In what ways are the cultural representations of "international student" and "Asian" conflated to naturalize failure for students designated as "second language," much like the remedial designation? These questions remind me of Paul Kei Matsuda's argument that "the field of rhetoric and composition has dismissed language pedagogy based on the assumption of linguistic homogeneity" ("The Myth" 157).[1] I agree with Matsuda's suggestion that writing instructors and faculty in other disciplines may be setting up second language students for failure by failing to teach metalinguistic awareness of grammar and sentence-level strategies, yet focusing writing evaluation on error production. My project investigates these concerns by gathering qualitative information on instructors' perceptions of the needs of second language writers, and instructors' de-

---

1   In his article "The Myth of Linguistic Homogeneity in US College Composition," Matsuda defines linguistic homogeneity as the belief that all college students should have native fluency in "Standard American Edited English," and therefore should be evaluated primarily by the "correctness" of their language usage (641).

scriptions of their teaching practices with second language writers in WAC/WID courses. The impact of teachers' perceptions of ESL/EFL students and their preparation to teach them must be examined in order for first-year writing and WAC/WID program administrators to understand how race and linguistic diversity may be factors in campus-wide writing assessment.

My own study is a conceptual replication of an institutional case study by caucus members Matsuda and Tanita Saenkhum, with their colleague Steven Accardi, as discussed in their 2013 article published in the *Journal of Second Language Writing*. With permission from the authors, I adapted their survey instrument for my research questions and at the time of writing this essay, I am still collecting data. Matsuda, Saenkhum, and Accardi studied writing instructors' perceptions of second language students at their institution, Arizona State University, by distributing a survey to writing program faculty. In the original study, survey results indicated that few instructors have received formal training to teach writing to second language students, even amongst writing program faculty. Still, instructors' attitudes toward and perceptions of second language students were positive, recognizing the need and desire for professional development in this area, and for shared curriculum and materials for teaching second language writers. Writing instructors in that study also identified reasons why they felt limited in addressing writing issues specific to second language writers, including "the need for more time and attention on the part of the teachers; the perception that those issues were outside the scope of the first-year composition curriculum; the limitation of professional preparation opportunities; [and] the lack of instructional materials that are suitable for L2 writers" (Matsuda, Saenkhum, and Accardi 82). Interestingly, preliminary findings from my own study show that faculty in other disciplines seem to echo these reasons given by writing instructors in the Matsuda, Saenkhum, and Accardi study. This indicates to me a lack of clarity for faculty in writing programs and in other disciplines regarding instructor responsibilities for language instruction and support for second language international students, in first-year writing and in WAC/WID courses. I hope that survey results provide more insight into these and related issues in second language writing pedagogy.

Preliminary findings of my study have helped inform a professional development workshop that I recently co-organized and co-facilitated on my campus, on supporting second language writers in the disciplines, which was open to all university faculty members. My co-organizer/facilitator is a university librarian who was herself an international student from China, before completing her library science graduate degree and securing a tenure track position as an Assistant Professor. Speaking of her own experiences as illustrative examples, my colleague bestowed upon our workshop the title, "The Learning Journey of the International Student"—a simple, yet accurate reminder that we meet students at different stages of a long process. The arguments and research discussed in this essay are also reminders that the critical, relevant, race-conscious works produced by AAAC members have a real and positive impact on students during their journeys.

WORKS CITED

Dich, Linh. "The United States of Ambivalence: International Students as Sources of Income and Difference," Conference on College Composition and Communication. JW Marriott, Indianapolis, IN, 20 March 2014. Sponsored by the Asian/Asian American Caucus.

Gutiérrez y Muhs, Gabriella, Yolanda Flores Niemann, Carmen G. González, and Angela P. Harris, eds. *Presumed Incompetent: The Intersections of Race and Class for Women in Academia.* Boulder: UP of Colorado, 2012. Print.

Hegarty, Niall. "Where Are They Now? The Presence and Importance of International Students to Universities in the United States." *Journal of International Students* 4.3 (2014): 223–35. Print.

Horner, B., Min-Zhan Lu, and Paul Kei Matsuda, eds. *Cross-Language Relations in Composition.* Carbondale: Southern Illinois UP, 2010. Print.

Inoue, Asao B. "Theorizing Failure in U.S. Writing Assessments." *Research in the Teaching of English* 48.3 (February 2014): 330–52. Print.

Inoue, Asao B. and Mya Poe, eds. *Race and Writing Assessment.* New York: Peter Lang Publishing, 2012. Print.

Matsuda, Paul Kei. "The Myth of Linguistic Homogeneity in US College Composition." *College English* 68.6. (July 2006): 637–51. Print.

—. "Let's Face It: Language Issues and the Writing Program Administrator." *WPA: Writing Program Administration* 36.1 (Fall/Winter 2012): 141–63. Print.

Matsuda, Paul Kei, Tanita Saenkhum, and Steven Accardi. "Writing Teachers' Perceptions of the Presence and Needs of Second Language Writers: An Institutional Case Study." *Journal of Second Language Writing* 22 (2013): 68–86. Print.

Miller-Cochran, Susan. "Language Diversity and the Responsibility of the WPA." *Cross-Language Relations in Composition.* Ed. Bruce Horner, Min-Zhan Lu, and Paul Kei Matsuda. Carbondale: Southern Illinois UP, 2010. 212-20. Print.

Omi, Michael and Howard Winant. *Racial Formation in the United States, 2nd Edition.* New York, NY: Routledge, 1994. Print.

Saenkhum, Tanita and Paul Kei Matsuda. "Second Language Writers in College Composition Programs: Toward Awareness, Knowledge and Action." *WPA: Writing Program Administration* 35.1 (Fall/Winter 2011): 199–203. Print.

CIRCULATION ESSAY

Risks and Affordances: The Naming of the Asian/Asian American Caucus

Lehua Ledbetter

This paper was inspired by LuMing Mao's talk at Michigan State University in the spring of 2014. At the time, I was a graduate student. I remember, vividly, Mao explaining his approach to comparative rhetoric. It seemed that Mao was laying a conceptual groundwork that was not only an approach to comparative rhetoric, but also a way of thinking and being that creates space for that which either goes unnamed or unacknowledged in the Western rhetorical tradition—what Malea Powell refers to as the "absent present" in her work on rhetorics of survivance. In his talk, Mao argued that "understanding textual effects and their excess requires attention to places where rhetoric is unrecognizable or barely acknowledged: the traces and the gaps." In his 2013 article "Beyond Bias, Binary, and Border: Mapping Out the Future of Comparative Rhetoric," Mao discusses incongruities between systems of meaning-making and interpretation and their generative possibilities. As we continue to cross borders in our work and in our lives, Mao argues that such incongruities will continue to arise, and serve as an opportunity to think about rifts between "what we think we know about and can speak for the other and what has to happen in order for us to begin to know about and speak for the other" ("Beyond" 211). Such incongruities and rifts can also arise in the naming practices in which we engage, perhaps at times unknowingly, in an institutional or professional context.

Mao's logic provides a guiding framework for asking the question, what are the risks and affordances of naming the Asian/Asian American Caucus? Naming as a rhetorical practice can and has served to construct and deconstruct canons and, as a result, the curricula that take shape around them (e.g., the naming of the *Rhetorical Tradition* and the texts within this canon, and its subsequent impression on the Euro–Western bias of many rhetoric and composition courses and programs). Powell argues that in the academy, it is vital to "make visible the fact that some of us read and listen from a different space, and to suggest that, as a discipline, it is time we all learned to hear that difference" (398). In keeping with this framework of hearing that difference, I ask, in a similar vein: what do we think we know about ourselves, and who do we speak for, as members of the caucus? What has to happen in order for us to begin to know about and speak for this group? Moreover, how can we hear the differences within the space(s) that are impacted by the caucus and its scholarship and teaching? In thinking about these questions, I have encountered, for example, quite a few incongruities within myself, between my own meaning-making systems as a person of half Japanese and half Caucasian descent, a woman of color, an academic, a first-generation college student, and a feminist. Many of the questions that I propose in this piece stem from my own experiences of these incongruities. In fact, all caucus members have (and recognize) these multiplicities, and it is my hope that we will continue to draw on them generatively in the dialogue that we began at the CCCC.

With that, I want to draw some parallels to Mao's arguments by proposing the following questions, to which I don't yet have clear answers, but which I hope will provide an opportunity for continuing the important dialogue that began at the 2014 CCCC—and perhaps future action—amongst members of the caucus as we examine what it means to name ourselves:

- In what other ways, contexts, and places do we name ourselves, individually and as members of this caucus?

- What other experiences, identities, ways of being, and forms of meaning-making do we as members of this organization bring with us to the organization? What risks do we take in bringing them with us?

- What systems of meaning-making are involved in naming the AAAC?

- What systems of meaning-making are involved in our institutional situatedness? What is included and excluded in this naming?

- In what ways do we represent the diversity within our organization? What is left out?

- What are the risks and affordances of either representation or non-representation?

- What boundaries do we draw around ourselves in our everyday lives, and do we bring those boundaries with us?

- How do we define ourselves amongst, for, and outside of the other?

- What practices do we enable and constrain in doing so?

Exploring these questions can provide some insight into the boundaries, experiences, and systems of meaning-making that shape the caucus, but also potentially open up possibilities to expose the incongruences that exist within the larger institutional systems in which we live and work. The resulting dialogue might offer our caucus, and perhaps other groups like ours, insight into where, why, and how we name and organize ourselves within institutional systems, the ways we resist and also reinforce those systems, what is left out and what made visible, and what is made possible for marginalized groups within institutional systems.

In her 2014 address to the Rhetoric Society of America, Linda Martín Alcoff argued that racial identities are "often but not always visible features of our material worlds—a meaningful organization of our materiality." This approach to understanding identity offers one possible way to understand, with better granularity, the implications of naming practices (and, therefore, rhetorical incongruities) that shape and are shaped by the caucus, as not all rhetorical incongruities are experienced and understood in the same way by every individual in a given situation. Seeking out and accounting for the stories of current, potential, or prospective members of the AAAC will shed light on new directions for the caucus, particularly in regards to the questions above, as well as create possibilities for connections with other organizations like ours.

WORKS CITED

Alcoff, Linda Martín. "The Rhetoric of Whiteness." Rhetoric Society of America Conference, Marriott River Center, San Antonio, TX. 23 May 2014. Keynote Address.

Mao, LuMing. "Beyond Bias, Binary, and Border: Mapping Out the Future of Comparative Rhetoric." *Rhetoric Society Quarterly* 43.3 (2013): 209–25. Print.

—. "Facts of Usage and Nonusage: Yin and Yang of Rhetoric." Writing, Rhetoric, and American Cultures Speaker Series. Michigan State University. The Writing Center, East Lansing, MI. 4 April 2014.

Powell, Malea. "Rhetorics of Survivance: How American Indians *Use* Writing." *College Composition and Communication* 53.3 (2002): 396–434. Print.

APPENDIX A
Asian/Asian American Caucus, 2016

PAST AND PRESENT CO-CHAIRS

1999–2005	LuMing Mao and Morris Young
2005–2010	Haivan V. Hoang and Nancy Linh Karls
2010–2012	Stuart Ching and Terese Guinsatao Monberg
2012–2015	Terese Guinsatao Monberg and K. Hyoejin Yoon
2015–2016	Jennifer Sano-Franchini and K. Hyoejin Yoon
2016–present	Iswari Pandey and Jennifer Sano-Franchini

CURRENT MEMBERSHIP

Based on subscriptions to the AAAC listserv, updated March 2016.

Chanon	Adsanatham
Dominic	Ashby
Jada	Augustine
Florence	Bacabac
Lamiyah	Bahrainwala
Angela	Castillo
Cara	Chang
Stuart	Ching
Karen	Ching Carter
Elaine	Cho
Tammy	Conard-Salvo
Linh	Dich
Tom	Do

Qi	Feng
Shreelina	Ghosh
Anam	Govardhan
Terese	Guinsatao Monberg
Al	Harahap
Tomo	Hattori
Haivan	Hoang
Chenchen	Huang
Shereen	Inayatulla
Asao	Inoue
Bo	Jimenez
Fify	Juliana
Scott	Ka'alele
Vani	Kannan
Nancy Linh	Karls
Soyeon	Kim
Kyung Min (Kay)	Kim
Eileen	Lagman
Lehua	Ledbetter
Jerry Won	Lee
Helen	Lee
Edward	Lee
Jasmine	Lee
Eunjeong	Lee
Jennifer Lin	LeMesurier
LuMing	Mao
Paul Kei	Matsuda
Peter	Mayshle
Jolivette	Mecenas
Madhu	Narayan
Stella	Oh
Ryan	Omizo
Andrea	Osteen-Chinn
Iswari P.	Pandey
Michael	Pak
Patti	Poblete

Tanita	Saenkhum
Jennifer	Sano-Franchini
Charlyne	Sarmiento
Ling	Shi
Mira	Shimabukuro
Priya	Sirohi
Tim	Smith
Sarah	Snyder
Larry	Su
Marie-Therese	Sulit
Reid	Sunahara
Robyn	Tasaka
Data	Tolentino-Canlas
Phuong Minh	Tran
Maria	Turnmeyer
David	Uedoi
G. Chris	Villanasco
Amy	Wan
Bo	Wang
Margaret	Wong
Hui	Wu
Belle	Xiaobo Wang
K. Hyoejin	Yoon
Morris	Young
Yuko	Ztatsu

APPENDIX B
Timeline of Scholarship and Accomplishments

Below is a working timeline of moments relevant to, and produced collaboratively by, the Asian/Asian American Caucus. The moments listed below—of featured sessions at CCCC, of awards in the discipline of rhetoric and composition won by AAAC members and others affiliated with the AAAC; of changes in AAAC leadership; and of notable publications in Asian American rhetoric—have been collected through calls to the AAAC listserv and responses from members, individual conversations with AAAC members, and past CCCC convention programs. Thus, note that this timeline is limited and not comprehensive; rather, this list is intended to highlight moments not reflected in the previous narratives—moments that present some of the achievements for which members of the caucus as well as Asian and Asian American scholars in NCTE more generally have been recognized, and that acknowledge some of the important contributions that Asians/Asian Americans have made to the field of rhetoric and composition more broadly. For instance, the CCCC featured sessions not only show that Asian/Asian American concerns in rhetoric and composition have been recognized and that Asian/Asian American scholars' voices have been included at the convention, but also how members of the caucus have been integral to conversations that engage the broader discipline with regards to such concerns as literacy studies, writing assessment, access, and historiography.

Yet, it is worth noting as well as problematizing the fact that disciplinary awards are heavily represented in the timeline below, likely because they are the most visible kinds of accomplishments in the discipline and in our profession, where particular kinds of knowledge work are valued over others. While it is important to celebrate that the work of Asian/Asian American scholars has been recognized in the discipline, there is also the risk that these individual awards may detract from the collective spirit of the caucus and reinforce traditional understandings of success in the profession. Thus, we suggest that readers approach this timeline while keeping in mind the larger message of this book: that mentorship, support, and collaboration are crucial to the making of a field. This timeline, furthermore, is a work in progress that has much room for expansion, to include dissertations relevant to Asian/Asian American rhetoric and literacy, courses that have been taught on Asian/Asian American rhetoric, the kinds of community work that has being done by caucus members, and the numerous publications that have emerged on Asian/Asian American rhetoric and literacy practices.

2016 AAAC Sponsored Session at CCCC: "New Directions in Transnational Asian/Asian American Rhetoric and Composition: Issues for Historiography, Digital Rhetoric, Racial Justice, and Writing Center Research," with Chanon Adsanatham, Vani Kannan, Patty Poblete, Priya Sirohi, Xiaobo Wang, and Morris Young presenting, Jolivette Mecenas as chair, and Jennifer Sano-Franchini as respondent.

CCCC Rhetoric's Histories, Theories, Pedagogies Special Interest Group Session: "What Can Scholarship and Teaching in Rhetorical Studies Contribute to Current Debates about the Changing Landscape of Higher Education," with Suzanne Bordelon, Ralph Cintron, Jack Selzer, Jeffrey Walker, and Bo Wang presenting.

2015 Jennifer Sano-Franchini and K. Hyoejin Yoon take on role of AAAC co-chairs.

AAAC Sponsored Session at CCCC: "Asian/Asian American Scholarship in Rhetoric and Composition: Risks and Rewards," with Linh Dich, Scott Kaʻalele, Lehua Ledbetter, Edward Lee, Jolivette Mecenas, Michael Pak, Phuong Minh Tran, and K. Hyoejin Yoon presenting, Terese Guinsatao Monberg as convener and chair, and Hui Wu as respondent.

Bo Wang is elected to the Executive Committee of the Conference on College Composition and Communication.

A. Suresh Canagarajah receives the MLA Mina P. Shaughnessy Prize for *Translingual Practice: Global Englishes and Cosmopolitan Relations.*

Symposium on Comparative Rhetoric in *Rhetoric Review*, co-edited by LuMing Mao and Bo Wang (34.3), including essays by Arabella Lyon, Bo Wang, Susan Jarratt, C. Jan Swearingen, Susan Romano, Peter Simonson, Steven Mailloux, and Xing Lu.

Cara M. Chang receives Scholars for the Dream Award.

Xiaobo Wang receives MLA Travel Grant and Michael Leff Award at RSA Summer Institute.

Chanon Adsanatham receives CCCC James Berlin Memorial Outstanding Dissertation Award for *"Civilized" Manners and Bloody Splashing: Recovering Conduct Rhetoric in the Thai Rhetorical Tradition*, directed by LuMing Mao.

2014 A. Suresh Canagarajah receives the BAAL (British Association of Applied Linguistics) Book Award for *Translingual Practice: Global Englishes and Cosmopolitan Relations.*

RSA Supersession: "Speaking for and with Each Other: Crossing Borders in the Company of Comparative Rhetoric," with LuMing Mao, Arabella Lyon, Bo Wang, C. Jan Swearingen, Steven Mailloux, Susan Jarratt, and Xing Lu presenting.

AAAC Sponsored Session at CCCC: "Voices from the Asian/Asian American Caucus: Opening up our Disciplinary History and Scholarship" with Linh Dich, Terese Guinsatao Monberg, Jennifer Sano-Franchini, and K. Hyoejin Yoon presenting, and Asao B. Inoue as respondent.

Bo Wang and K. Hyoejin Yoon elected to the Advisory Board of the Coalition of Women Scholars in the History of Rhetoric and Composition.

Asao B. Inoue and Mya Poe receive CCCC Outstanding Book Award for their edited collection, *Race and Writing Assessment.*

Jerry Won Lee receives CCCC Chairs' Memorial Scholarship.

Linh Dich recognized with honorable mention for the James Berlin Outstanding Dissertation Award for *Technologies of Racial Formation: Asian-American Online Identities*, directed by Haivan V. Hoang.

2013 Special Issue on Comparative Rhetoric in *Rhetoric Society Quarterly*, with Guest Editor LuMing Mao (43.3), including articles by Bo Wang, Mary Garrett, Dominic Ashby, Carol Lipson, Keith Lloyd, with a response by C. Jan Swearingen.

CCCC Featured Session: "Writing and Working for Change: Agenda for a New Generation," with Matt Cox, Qwo-Li Driskill, Tracey Flores, Austin Jackson, Kendra Mitchell, Pamela Roeper, and Jennifer Sano-Franchini presenting, Cristina Kirklighter as chair, and Stephen Parks as respondent.

Huatong Sun receives CCCC Best Book in Technical or Scientific Communication award for *Cross-Cultural Technology Design: Creating Culture-Sensitive Technology for Local Users*.

Karen Ching Carter publishes "Public Sphere, Theater and the Rhetoric of Re-Imaging an Identity: Oriental to Asian American," in *Re/Framing Identifications*.

Amy Wan receives the Richard Ohmann Award for her article "In the Name of Citizenship: The Writing Classroom and the Promise of Citizenship," published in *College English*.

2012 Terese Guinsatao Monberg and K. Hyoejin Yoon take on role of AAAC co-chairs.

CCCC Featured Session: "Legacies, Gateways, and the Future of Literacy Studies," with Harvey J. Graff, Morris Young, and Deborah Brandt presenting, and John Duffy, Rhea Lathan, and Kate Vieira as respondents.

CCCC Featured Session: "Race, Writing Assessment, and Failure: Confronting Language Attitudes, Testing Legacies, and Technologies," with Zandra L. Jordan, Mya Poe, and Asao B. Inoue presenting, Norbert Elliot as chair, and Min-Zhan Lu as respondent.

CCCC Featured Session: "Access Happening," with Samantha Blackmon, Qwo-Li Driskill, Paul Kei Matsuda, Margaret Price, Cynthia L. Selfe, Melanie Yergeau, and Amy Vidali presenting, and Jay Dolmage as chair.

RSA Supersession: "How Women's Rhetorical History Shapes Our Rhetorical Present/Presence," including speakers Katherine Adams, Gwendolyn Pough, Jessica Enoch, Hui Wu, and chair Shirley Wilson Logan.

Bruce Horner, Min-Zhan Lu, and Paul Kei Matsuda receive CCCC Outstanding Book Award for *Cross-Language Relations in Composition*.

Tanita Saenkhum receives CCCC Chairs' Memorial Scholarship.

Karen Ching Carter and Eileen Lagman receive CCCC Scholars for the Dream Award.

Jennifer Sano-Franchini receives *Kairos* Award for Scholarship/Research by a Graduate Student or Adjunct Faculty Member.

Chanon Adsanatham receives the Outstanding Teacher Award from the Department of English at Miami University.

Asao B. Inoue and Mya Poe publish *Race in Writing Assessment*, the first edited collection on race in writing assessment.

College English includes a "Comment and Response" exchange where Kathleen Yancey responded to Mira Shimabukuro's "'Me Inwardly, Before I Dared': Japanese Americans Writing-to-Gaman."

2011 CCCC Featured Session: "Contesting and Constructing Asian American Rhetorics: Reflections and Possibilities," with Morris Young, Terese Guinsatao Monberg, Mira Shimabukuro, and LuMing Mao presenting.

CCCC Featured Session: "'Gathering up our Multiple Participations': Exploring Intersections/Interferences within and outside Rhetoric and Writing," with Donnie Sackey, Marilee Brooks, Madhu Narayan, and Daisy Levy presenting, and Terese Guinsatao Monberg as respondent.

CCCC Featured Session: "We are 113!" with Rochelle (Shelley) Rodrigo, Paul Kei Matsuda, Kathleen Blake Yancey, Cynthia L. Selfe, Chris Anson, Greg Glau, Jay Dolmage, Kati Fargo, Kevin Brock, and Lamiyah Bahrainwala presenting.

CCCC Featured Session: "New Directions from Feminist Rhetorical Studies: Charting the Future of Rhetoric, Composition, and Literacy Studies," with Shirley Rose, Beverly Moss, Gail Hawisher, Joyce I. Middleton, Hui Wu, and Shirley Wilson Logan presenting, Jacqueline Jones Royster as chair and Gesa E. Kirsch as respondent.

CCCC Panel: "South Asian and Asian Rhetorical Histories," with K. Hyoejin Yoon, Stacey Sheriff, and Danielle Nielsen presenting.

CCCC Coalition of Women Scholars in the History of Rhetoric and Composition Keynote: "Women in the Profession: Disciplinary and Institutional Relations Past, Present, Future," with Erika Lindemann, Hui Wu, Rhea Estelle Lathan, and Michelle T. Johnson presenting, and Nancy Myers as chair.

Xiaoye You receives Outstanding Book Award for *Writing in the Devil's Tongue: A History of English Composition in China.*

Lehua Ledbetter receives CCCC Scholars for the Dream Award.

Gail Y. Okawa publishes "Putting Their Lives on the Line: Personal Narrative as Political Discourse among Japanese Petitioners in American World War II Internment" in *College English.*

Mira Shimabukuro publishes "'Me Inwardly, Before I Dared': Japanese Americans Writing-to-Gaman" in *College English.*

2010 Terese Guinsatao Monberg and Stuart Ching take on role of AAAC co-chairs.

CCCC Featured Session: "Octalog III: The Politics of Historiography in 2010," with Vicki Tolar Burton, Ralph Cintron, Jay Dolmage, Jessica Enoch, Ronald L. Jackson, LuMing Mao, Malea Powell, Arthur E. Walzer, and Victor Vitanza presenting, and Lois Agnew as chair. Subsequently published in *Rhetoric Review* 30.2 (2011).

AAAC Sponsored Session at CCCC: "Re/Presenting Asian American Texts as Rhetoric," with Bo Wang, Mira Shimabukuro, Haivan V. Hoang, Peiling Zhao, Morris Young, Stella Oh, and Stuart Ching presenting, and LuMing Mao as chair.

RSA "Supersession on Conflict, Community, and Creativity: Identifying Asian American Rhetorical Texts," with Chanon Adsanatham, Kent Ono, Dominic Ashby, Stuart Ching, Stella Oh, and LuMing Mao presenting, and Morris Young as director.

Special Issue of *College English* on Chinese rhetoric, with Guest Editor LuMing Mao (72.4), including articles by Arabella Lyon, Xiaoye You, Bo Wang, Hui Wu, and a response by C. Jan Swearingen.

2009 CCCC Featured Session: "Voice in Written Discourse: Implications for Multilingual Writers," with Peter Elbow, Paul Kei Matsuda, and Christine Tardy presenting, and LuMing Mao as chair.

CCCC Featured Session: "Multigenerational, Intersectional Coalitions," with Dora Ramirez-Dhoore, Aneil Rallin, and Renee Moreno presenting, Angela Haas as discussant, and Asao B. Inoue as respondent.

CCCC Panel: "Making Asian American Rhetoric," with Haivan V. Hoang, Morris Young, Terese Guinsatao Monberg, and Stuart Ching presenting.

CCCC Panel: "Diasporic Asian Rhetorics: Investigating Strategies, Identity, and Representation in Classroom and Online Environments," with Robyn Tasaka, Fify Juliana, Peiling Zhao, and Jolivette Mecenas presenting.

Feminisms and Rhetorics Featured Speaker: Terese Guinsatao Monberg, "Pinay Peminists: Listening for New Locations and Re/visions of Rhetorical Theory."

John M. Duffy receives Outstanding Book Award for *Writing from These Roots: Literacy in a Hmong–American Community*.

LuMing Mao and Morris Young receive honorable mention for the MLA 2009 Mina P. Shaughnessy Prize for *Representations: Doing Asian American Rhetoric*. (Reviewed in *Journal of Language, Identity, and Education* 9.)

Hui Wu receives Theresa J. Enos 25th Anniversary Award, recognizing the best article in *Rhetoric Review* for "Lost and Found in Transnation: Modern Conceptualization of Chinese Rhetoric."

2008 CCCC Featured Session: "The Shape of Things to Come: Higher Education in the Aftermath of the Spellings Commission Report," with Paul Bodmer, Vickie Schray, Linda Adler-Kassner, Howard Tinberg, Asao B. Inoue, and Jeffrey Andelora presenting.

RSA "Supersession on Doing Asian American Rhetoric" with LuMing Mao, Morris Young, Stuart Ching, Tomo Hattori, Rory Ong, Bo Wang, Mary Louise Buley-Meissner, Mira Shimabukuro, and Terese Guinsatao Monberg presenting, LuMing Mao as chair, and Min-Zhan Lu as respondent.

2007 CCCC Featured Session: "Double Trouble: Misunderstanding Chinese Rhetorics," with C. Jan Swearingen, Hui Wu, Xiaoye You, and Lu Liu presenting, and LuMing Mao as chair.

CCCC Coalition of Women Scholars in the History of Rhetoric and Composition Keynote: "The Future of the History of Rhetoric and Composition," with Linda Ferreira-Buckley, Kate Adams, Bo Wang, and Mary Hocks presenting, and Lynée Gaillet Lewis as chair.

Feminisms and Rhetorics Featured Speaker: Hui Wu, "Whose Feminism Is It?: The Rhetoric of Post-Mao Chinese Women Writers."

A. Suresh Canagarajah receives Braddock Award: Best *CCC* Article of the Year for "The Place of World Englishes in Composition: Pluralization Continued."

LuMing Mao receives Richard Ohmann Award for "Studying the Chinese Rhetorical Tradition in the Present: Re-presenting the Native's Point of View." *College English* 69.3.

Ryan Masaaki Omizo receives CCCC Scholars for the Dream Award.

2006 CCCC Featured Session: "On the Margins of Citizenship: Tests, Texts, and Spaces in the (re)Making of Literate Americans," with Amy Wan, Morris Young, and Connie Kendall presenting, and Peter Mortensen as chair.

CCCC All-Day Workshop sponsored by Language Policy Committee, and American Indian, Asian/Asian American, Black, and Latinx Caucuses: "Race, Space, Place: Language, Identity and Students of Color in the Composition Classroom" with Terry Carter, Rashidah J. Muhammad, Elaine Richardson, Denise Troutman, Itzcoatl T. Meztli, Jaime A Mejía, Luisa Rodriguez Connal, Damián Baca, Bo Wang, Christine Faith Law, Fify Juliana, Joyce Rain Anderson, Qwo-Li Driskill, Malea Powell, Mindy Morgan, Ellen Cushman, and Angela M. Haas facilitating, and Geneva Smitherman as chair.

Morris Young receives Outstanding Book Award for *Minor Re/Visions: Asian American Literacy Narratives as a Rhetoric of Citizenship*.

Paul Kei Matsuda receives Richard Ohmann Award for "The Myth of Linguistic Homogeneity in U.S. College Composition," published in *College English.*

Huatong Sun receives Nell Ann Pickett Award for the Best Article of *Technical Communication Quarterly* for "The Triumph of Users: Achieving Cultural Usability Goals With User Localization."

Iswari P. Pandey receives CCCC Chairs' Memorial Scholarship.

Jolivette Mecenas receives CCCC Scholars for the Dream Award.

LuMing Mao publishes *Reading Chinese Fortune Cookie: The Making of Chinese American Rhetoric*. (Reviewed in *Composition Studies* 35.1; *College Composition and Communication* 59:1; *Rhetoric Review* 26:4; *Rhetoric Society Quarterly* 38:1; and *Quarterly Journal of Speech* 95:1.)

2005 Haivan V. Hoang and Nancy Linh Karls take on role of AAAC co-chairs.

CCCC Featured Session: "The Rhetoric of Rememory: Archival Research among Researchers of Color," with speakers Victor Villanueva, Malea Powell, David G. Holmes, and Gail Okawa presenting.

Haivan V. Hoang receives CCCC James Berlin Outstanding Memorial Dissertation Award for *"To Come Together and Create a Movement": Solidarity Rhetoric in the Vietnamese American Coalition (VAC)*.

Huatong Sun receives CCCC Outstanding Dissertation Award in Technical Communication for *Expanding the Scope of Localization: A Cultural Usability Perspective on Mobile Text Messaging Use in American and Chinese Contexts*.

CCCC All Day Workshop sponsored by Language Policy Committee; American Indian, Asian/Asian American, Black, and Latinx Caucuses; Second Language Writing Committee; and SIG on Language, Linguistics and Writing: "Language Diversity in the Composition Classroom with facilitators including Rashidah Muhammad, Terry Carter, Denise Troutman, Elaine Richardson, Malea Powell, Joyce Rain Anderson, Angela M. Haas, Paul Kei Matsuda, Victor Villanueva, Gail Okawa, Cristina Kirklighter, Susan Miller, Michelle Hall Kells, Kim Brian Lovejoy, C. Jan Swearingen, Arthur Palacas, LuMing Mao, Nancy Linh Karls, Haivan V. Hoang, Eleanor Kutz, MaryAnn K. Crawford, and Katherine K. Sohn, and Geneva Smitherman as chair.

CCCC Roundtable by the Progressive SIG/Caucus Coalition and the CCCC Diversity Committee: "Affirming Action," with Harriet Malinowitz, Damián Baca, Scott Lyons, Akua Duku Anokye, James McDonald, Morris Young, Jonathan Alexander, and Luisa Rodriguez Connal presenting, and Stephen Parks as chair.

CCCC Panel: "Accessing Asian American Rhetoric(s): Locations, Movements, Actions," with Terese Guinsatao Monberg, Morris Young, Hai-van V. Hoang, and Stuart Ching presenting, and LuMing Mao as chair.

Linh Dich and Robyn Tasaka receive CCCC Scholars for the Dream Award.

K Hyoejin Yoon receives the Elizabeth A. Flynn award for the most outstanding article in feminist rhetoric and composition presented by *JAC: A Journal of Rhetoric, Culture, and Politics* and the Association of Teachers of Advanced Composition for her article, "Affecting the Transformative Intellectual: Questioning 'Noble' Sentiments in Critical Pedagogy and Composition," published in *JAC* 25.4.

2004 CCCC Featured Session: "Cross-Language Relations in Composition," with A. Suresh Canagarajah, Bruce Horner, Min-Zhan Lu, Paul Kei Matsuda, and John Trimbur presenting.

Morris Young receives W. Ross Winterowd Award for the most outstanding book on composition theory published that year for *Minor Re/Visions: Asian American Literacy Narratives as a Rhetoric of Citizenship*.

2003 Wendy S. Hesford and Theresa A. Kulbaga receive the Elizabeth A. Flynn award for the most outstanding article in feminist rhetoric and composition presented by *JAC: A Journal of Rhetoric, Culture, and Politics* and the Association of Teachers of Advanced Composition for their article, "Labored Realisms: Geopolitical Rhetoric and Asian American and Asian (Im)migrant Women's (Auto)biography," published in *JAC* 23.1.

A. Suresh Canagarajah wins the Gary Olson Award for *A Geopolitics of Academic Writing*.

2002 CCCC Featured Session: "Borderlands, Histories, Politics: Returning Asian American Rhetorics to the Street," with Morris Young, LuMing Mao, and Terese Guinsatao Monberg presenting, and Keith Gilyard and Gail Okawa as respondents.

Haivan V. Hoang and Asao B. Inoue receive CCCC Scholars for the Dream Award.

1997 First meeting of the AAAC in Atlanta, Georgia, with LuMing Mao and Morris Young as co-chairs.

A. Suresh Canagarajah receives Mina P. Shaughnessy Prize for *Resisting Linguistic Imperialism in English Teaching*.

1996 K. Hyoejin Yoon receives CCCC Scholars for the Dream Award.

1995 Terese Guinsatao Monberg receives CCCC Scholars for the Dream Award.

APPENDIX C
Bibliography of Asian/Asian American Rhetoric and Composition*

Adams, Heather, Holly Hassel, Jessica Rucki, and K. Hyoejin Yoon. "Key Concept: Service." "The Next 25 Years: Scholarship in Celebration of the Coalition of Women Scholars in the History of Rhetoric and Composition." Spec. issue of *Peitho* 18.1 (2015): 45-50. Print.

Adsanatham, Chanon. *"Civilized" Manners and Bloody Splashing: Recovering Conduct Rhetoric in the Thai Rhetorical Tradition.* Diss. Miami University. 2014. Print.

Agnew, Lois, Laurie Gries, Zosha Stuckey, Vicki Tolar Burton, Jay Dolmage, Jessica Enoch, Ronald L. Jackson II, LuMing Mao, Malea Powell, Arthur E. Walzer, Ralph Cintron, and Victor Vitanza. "Octalog III: The Politics of Historiography in 2010." *Rhetoric Review* 30.2 (2011): 109–34. Print.

Ashby, Dominic J. *Enacting a Rhetoric of Inside-Outside Positionalities: From the Indexing Practice of Uchi/Soto to a Reiterative Process of Meaning-Making.* Diss. Miami University. 2013. Print.

Canagarajah, A. Suresh. *A Geopolitics of Academic Writing.* Pittsburgh: U of Pittsburgh P, 2002. Print.

—. *Critical Academic Writing and Multilingual Students.* Ann Arbor: U of Michigan P, 2002. Print.

—. "Multilingual Strategies of Negotiating English: From Conversation to Writing." *JAC: A Journal of Rhetoric, Culture, and Politics* 29 (2009): 711-43. Print.

---

*   See also the bibliography of works listed in Appendix D: Asian/Asian American Publications in *College Composition and Communication* (1950–2010), which was compiled by Phuong Minh Tran, whose research is included in this collection.

—. "The Place of World Englishes in Composition: Pluralization Continued." *College Composition and Communication* 57.4 (2006): 586–619. Print.

—. *Resisting Linguistic Imperialism in English Teaching*. Oxford: Oxford UP, 1999. Print.

—. "Toward a Writing Pedagogy of Shuttling between Languages: Learning from Multilingual Writers." *College English* 68.6 (2006): 589–604. Print.

—. *Translingual Practice: Global Englishes and Cosmopolitan Relations*. New York and Abingdon: Routledge, 2013. Print.

Canagarajah, A. Suresh, ed. *Literacy as Translingual Practice: Between Communities and Classrooms*. New York: Routledge, 2013. Print.

Carpenter, Cari M. and K. Hyoejin Yoon, eds. *Native Asian Encounters*, Spec. issue of *College Literature* 4.1 (Winter 2014). Print.

Carpenter, Cari M. and K. Hyoejin Yoon. Introduction. "Rethinking Alternative Contact in Native American and Chinese Encounters: Juxtaposition in Nineteenth-Century US Newspapers." *College Literature* 4.1 (Winter 2014). 7-42. Print.

Carroll, Jeffrey, Brandy Nālani McDougall, and Georganne Nordstrom. *Huihui: Navigating Art and Literature in the Pacific*. Honolulu: University of Hawaiʻi Press, 2015. Print.

Chin, Frank and Jeffery Paul Chan. "Racist Love." *Seeing Through Shuck*. Ed. Richard Kastalanetz. New York: Ballantine Books. 65-79. Print.

Ching, Doris Camvone. "Effects of a Six Month Remedial English Program on Oral, Writing, and Reading Skills of Third Grade Hawaiian Bilingual Children." *The Journal of Experimental Education* 32.2 (1963): 133–45. Print.

Ching, Doris C. "Methods for the Bilingual Child." *Elementary English* (1965): 22–27. Print.

Ching, Doris C. *Reading and the Bilingual Child*. Newark: International Reading Association, 1976. Print.

Combs, Steven C. *The Dao of Rhetoric*. Albany: State U of New York P, 2005. Print.

Cushman, Ellen, and Shreelina Ghosh. "The Mediation of Cultural Memory: Digital Preservation in the Cases of Classical Indian Dance and the Cherokee Stomp Dance." *Journal of Popular Culture* 45.2 (2012): 264-83. Print.

Dich, Linh L. *Technologies of Racial Formation: Asian–American Online Identities*. Diss. University of Massachusetts Amherst, 2012. Ann Arbor: UMI, 2012. Print.

Ding, Huiling. "Confucius' Virtue-Centered Rhetoric: A Case Study of the *Analects* with Mixed Research Methods." *Rhetoric Review* 26 (2007): 142–59. Print.

—. "Technical Communication Instruction in China: Localized Programs and Alternative Models." *Technical Communication Quarterly* 19 (2010): 300–17. Print.

Duffy, John. *Writing from These Roots: Literacy in a Hmong–American Community*. Honolulu: U of Hawai'i P, 2007.

Gale, Xin Liu. "Historical Studies and Postmodernism: Rereading Aspasia of Melitus." *College English* 63.3 (2000): 361–86. Print.

Garrett, Mary. "Pathos Reconsidered from the Perspective of Classical Chinese Rhetorical Theories." *Quarterly Journal of Speech* 79.1 (1993): 19–39. Print.

—. "Some Elementary Methodological Reflections on the Study of the Chinese Rhetorical Tradition." *International and Intercultural Communication Annual* 22 (1999): 53–63. Print.

—. "Women and the Rhetorical Tradition in Pre-modern China: A Preliminary Sketch." *Chinese Communication Studies: Contexts and Comparisons*. Ed. Xing Lu, Wenshan Jia, and D. Ray Heisey. Westport: Ablex, 2002. 87–100. Print.

Ghosh, Shreelina. *Dancing Without Bodies: Pedagogy and Performance in Digital Spaces*. Diss. Michigan State University, 2012. Print.

—. "Modern Rendition of Ancient Arts: Negotiating Values in Traditional Odissi Dance." *Rupkatha: On Interdisciplinary Studies in Humanities* 5.2 (Oct. 2013): 76-88. Web.

—. "Sculptures and Avatars: Mediating of the Memory of Odissi Dance." *Currents in Electronic Literacy: Memories, Technologies, Rhetorics* (Spring 2012). Web.

—. "Technological Mediation in Odissi Dance: A Transnational Perspective of Digitized Practice and Pedagogy in a Traditional Artistic Community." *Emerging Pedagogies in the Networked Knowledge Society: Practices Integrating Social Media and Globalization*. Ed. Marohang Limbu and Binod Gurung. Hershey, PA: IGI Global, 2013. 100-18. Print.

Hesford, Wendy S., and Theresa A. Kulbaga. "Labored Realisms: Geopolitical Rhetoric and Asian American and Asian (Im)migrant Women's (Auto)biography." *JAC: A Journal of Rhetoric, Culture, and Politics* 23.1 (2003): 77-107. Print.

Hirata-Knight, Penny. *Building a Mystery, Moving Beyond Masks: Gender, Race, and Teacher Authority in the Composition Classroom*. Diss. University of Hawai'i, 2009. Print.

Hoang, Haivan V. "Asian American Rhetorical Memory and 'A Memory that is Only Sometimes Our Own.'" *Representations: Doing Asian American Rhetoric*. Ed. LuMing Mao and Morris Young. Logan: Utah State UP, 2008. 62–82. Print.

—. "Campus Racial Politics and a 'Rhetoric of Injury.'" *College Composition and Communication* 61.1 (2009): W385–W408. Print.

—. "To Come Together and Create a Movement: Solidarity Rhetoric in the Vietnamese American Coalition (VAC)." Diss. Ohio State University, 2004. Print.

—. *Writing against Racial Injury: The Politics of Asian American Student Rhetoric*. Pittsburgh: U of Pittsburgh P, 2015. Print.

Hoang, Haivan V., and LuMing Mao. "Conversation with Haivan V. Hoang and LuMing Mao." Interview with Keith Gilyard and Victor E. Taylor. *Conversations in Cultural Rhetoric and Composition Studies*. Aurora, CO: The Davies Group, 2009. 105–24. Print.

Horner, Bruce, Min-Zhan Lu, and Paul Kei Matsuda, eds. *Cross-Language Relations in Composition*. Carbondale, IL: Southern Illinois UP, 2010. Print.

Hum, Sue. "Articulating Authentic Chineseness: The Politics of Reading Race and Ethnicity Aesthetically." *Relations, Locations, Positions: Composition Theory for Writing Teachers*. Ed. Peter Vandenberg, Sue Hum, and Jennifer Clary-Lemon. Urbana: National Council of Teachers of English, 2006. 442–70. Print.

—. "Idioms as Cultural Commonplaces: Corporeal Lessons from Hokkien Idioms." *The Journal of the Assembly for Expanded Perspectives on Learning* 11.1 (2005): 42–51. Print.

—. "'Yes, We Eat Dog Back Home': Contrasting Disciplinary Discourse and Praxis on Diversity." *JAC: A Journal of Rhetoric, Culture, and Politics: A Journal of Rhetoric, Culture, and Politics* 19:4 (1999): 569–87. Print.

—. "Zen and Writing: Anglo-American Interpretations, Revolutionary Possibilities: A Review Article." Rev. of *Wild Mind: Living the Writer's Life* by Natalie Goldberg, *Writing Down the Bones: Freeing the Writer Within* by Natalie Goldberg, and *Zen in the Art of Rhetoric: An Inquiry Into Coherence* by Mark Lawrence McPhail. *Journal of Teaching Writing* 15:2 (1996): 295–310. Print.

Hum, Sue, and Arabella Lyon. "Recent Advances in Comparative Rhetoric." *The Sage Handbook of Rhetorical Studies*. Ed. Andrea A. Lunsford, Kirt H.

Wilson, and Rosa A. Eberly. Thousand Oaks: Sage Publications, Inc., 2009. 153–65. Print.

Inoue, Asao B. "Articulating Sophistic Rhetoric as a Validity Heuristic for Writing Assessment." *Journal of Writing Assessment* 3.1 (2007): 31–54. Web.

—. "Community-Based Assessment Pedagogy." *Assessing Writing* 9.3 (2004): 208–38. Print.

—. *Antiracist Writing Assessment Ecologies: Teaching and Assessing Writing for a Socially Just Future.* Perspectives on Writing. Fort Collins, Colorado: The WAC Clearinghouse and Parlor Press, 2016. Print.

Inoue, Asao B., and Mya Poe. *Race and Writing Assessment.* New York: Peter Lang, 2012. Print.

Jarratt, Susan, and Rory Ong. "Aspasia: Rhetoric, Gender, and Colonial Ideology." *Reclaiming Rhetorica: Women in the Rhetorical Tradition.* Ed. Andrea A. Lunsford. Pittsburgh: U of Pittsburgh P, 1995. 9–24. Print.

Jenks, Christopher J., and Jerry Won Lee. "Heteroglossic Ideologies in World Englishes: An Examination of the Hong Kong Context." *International Journal of Applied Linguistics* (2016): n.p. Print.

Jon, Sun-Gi. "Towards a Rhetoric of Communication, with Special Reference to the History of Korean Rhetoric." *Rhetorica* 28.3 (2010): 313–29. Print.

Lee, Jerry Won. "Legacies of Japanese Colonialism in the Rhetorical Constitution of South Korean National Identity." *National Identities* 16.1 (2014): 1–13. Print.

—. "Re/Framing Transnational Collective Memories: Dokdo/Takeshima, Korea/Japan." *Re/Framing Identifications.* Ed. Michelle Ballif. Long Grove: Waveland, 2013. 142–47. Print.

Lin, San-su C. "A Developmental English Program for the Culturally Disadvantaged." *College Composition and Communication* (1965): 273–76. Print.

—. "An Experiment in Changing Dialect Patterns: The Claflin Project." *College English* (1963): 644–47. Print.

—. "Disadvantaged Student? Or Disadvantaged Teacher?" *English Journal* (1967): 751–56. Print.

Liu, Yameng. "'Nothing Can Be Accomplished If the Speech Does Not Sound Agreeable:' Rhetoric and the Invention of Classical Chinese Discourse." *Rhetoric Before and Beyond the Greeks.* Ed. Carol S. Lipson and Roberta A. Binkley. Albany: SUNY P, 2012. 147-64. Print.

Liu, Yameng. "To Capture the Essence of Chinese Rhetoric: An Anatomy of a

Paradigm in Comparative Rhetoric." *Rhetoric Review* 14 (1996): 318–35. Print.
Lu, Min-Zhan. "From Silence to Words: Writing as Struggle." *College English* 49 (April 1987): 437–48. Print.
—. "Professing Multiculturalism: The Politics of Style in the Contact Zone." *College Composition and Communication* 45.4 (1994): 442–58. Print.
Lu, Min-Zhan, Bruce Horner, and Paul Kei Matsuda, eds. "Composing Across Language Differences." Spec. issue of *College English* 68.6 (2006). Print.
Lu, Shujiang. "Let Wen Shine Forth: The Chinese Poetic Tradition and the English Composition Course." *Composition Forum* 14.2 (Fall 2005). Web.
Lu, Xing. *Rhetoric in Ancient China, Fifth to Third Century B.C.E.: A Comparison with Greek Rhetoric.* Columbia: U of South Carolina P. Print.
—. *Rhetoric of the Chinese Cultural Revolution: Impacts on Chinese Thought, Culture, and Communication.* Columbia: U of South Carolina P. Web.
Lyon, Arabella. "Confucian Silence and Remonstration: A Basis for Deliberation?" *Rhetoric Before and Beyond the Greeks*. Ed. Carol S. Lipson and Roberta A. Binkley. Albany: SUNY P, 2012. 131-46. Print.
—. *Deliberative Acts: Democracy, Rhetoric, and Rights.* University Park: Pennsylvania State UP, 2013. Print.
—. "Misrepresentations of Missing Women in the U.S. Press: The Rhetorical Uses of Disgust, Pity, and Compassion." *Just Advocacy?: Women's Human Rights, Transnational Feminisms, and the Politics of Representation*. Ed. Wendy S. Hesford and Wendy Kozol. New Brunswick: Rutgers UP, 2005. 173–92. Print.
—. "Rhetorical Authority in Athenian Democracy and the Chinese Legalism of Han Fei." *Philosophy and Rhetoric* 41.1 (2008): 51–71. Print.
—. "'Why do the Rulers Listen to the Wild Theories of Speech-Makers?' Or *Wuwei, Shi*, and Methods of Comparative Rhetoric." *Ancient Non-Greek Rhetorics*. Ed. Carol S. Lipson, and Roberta A. Binkley. West Lafayette: Parlor Press, 2009. 176-96. Print.
—. "Writing an Empire: Cross-Talk on Authority, Act, and Relationships with the Other in the *Analects*, *Daodejing*, and *HanFeizi*." *College English* 72.4 (2010): 350–66. Print.
—. "'You Fail': Plagiarism, the Ownership of Writing, and Transnational Conflicts." *College Composition and Communication* 61:2 (2009): 222–39. Print.

Mao, LuMing. Comparative Rhetoric. Spec. issue of *Rhetoric Society Quarterly* 43.3 (2013). Print.

—. "Doing Comparative Rhetoric Responsibly." *Rhetoric Society Quarterly* 41.1 (2011): 64–69. Print.

—. "Economies of Writing Writ Large: The Rhetoric of Cultural Nationalism." *JAC: A Journal of Rhetoric, Culture, and Politics* 32.3–4 (2012): 513–39. Print.

—. "Illustrating Comparative Rhetoric through a Socratic Parable." *Contemporary Rhetoric* 164.2 (2011): 1–7. Print.

—. *Reading Chinese Fortune Cookie: The Making of Chinese American Rhetoric.* Logan: Utah State UP, 2006. Print.

—. "The Rhetoric of Responsibility: Practicing the Art of Recontextualization." *Rhetoric Review* 30.2 (2011): 119–20; 131–32. Print.

—. "Re-clustering Traditional Academic Discourse: Alternating with Confucian Discourse." *ALT DIS: Alternative Discourses and the Academy.* Ed. Helen Fox, Christopher Schroeder, and Patricia Bizzell. Portsmouth, NH: Boynton, 2002. 112–25. Print.

—. "Reflective Encounters: Illustrating Comparative Rhetoric." *Style* 37 (Winter 2003): 401–25. Print.

—. "Rhetorical Borderlands: Chinese American Rhetoric in the Making." *College Composition and Communication* 56.3 (2005): 426–69. Print.

—. "Searching for the Way: Between the Whats and the Wheres of Chinese Rhetoric." *College English* 72: 4 (2010): 329–49. Print.

—. "Studying the Chinese Rhetorical Tradition in the Present: Re-presenting the Native's Point of View." *College English* 69.3 (2007): 216–37. Print.

—. Symposium on Comparative Rhetoric. *Rhetoric Review* 34.3 (Summer 2015): 239–43. Co-editor. Print.

—. "Uniqueness or Borderlands? The Making of Asian–American Rhetorics." *Rhetoric and Ethnicity.* Ed. Keith Gilyard and Vorris Nunley. Portsmouth, NH: Boynton/Cook, 2004. 46–55. Print.

—. "Writing the Other into Histories of Rhetorics: Theorizing the Art of Recontextualization." *Theorizing Histories of Rhetoric.* Ed. Michelle Ballif. Carbondale: Southern Illinois UP, 2013. 41–57. Print.

Mao, LuMing, and Morris Young, eds. *Representations: Doing Asian American Rhetoric.* Logan: Utah State UP, 2008.

Mao, LuMing, Bo Wang, Arabella Lyon, Susan C. Jarratt, C. Jan Swearingen, Susan Romano, Peter Simonson, Steven Mailloux, and Xing Lu.

"Symposium: Manifesting a Future for Comparative Rhetoric." *Rhetoric Review* 34.3 (Summer 2015): 239–74. Print.

Matsuda, Paul Kei. "Composition Studies and ESL Writing: A Disciplinary Division of Labor." *College Composition and Communication* 50.4 (1999). 699–721. Print.

—. "The Myth of Linguistic Homogeneity in U.S. College Composition." *College English* 68.6 (2006): 637–51. Print.

—. "Negotiation of Identity and Power in a Japanese Online Discourse Community." *Computers and Composition* 19.1 (2002): 39–55. Print.

Mecenas, Jolivette. "A Career of Acting 'Ill-Mannered'": Jeffery Paul Chan on Reviewing Textbooks for NCTE and Teaching Ethnic Studies (Because It's Good For People)." *Listening to Our Elders: Writing and Working For Change.* Ed. Samantha Blackmon, Cristina Kirklighter, and Steve Parks. Logan: Utah State UP, 2012. 28–44. Print.

—. "Beyond 'Asian American' and Back: Coalitional Rhetoric in Print and New Media." *Representations: Doing Asian American Rhetoric.* Ed LuMing Mao and Morris Young. Logan: Utah State UP, 2008. 198–217. Print.

—. *Teaching for Transnational Literacy: Reading and Composing Civic Discourse Publics.* Diss. University of Hawai'i, 2009. Print.

Monberg, Terese Guinsatao. "Listening for Legacies, or How I Began to Hear Dorothy Laigo Cordova, the Pinay Behind the Podium Known as FANHS." *Representations: Doing Asian American Rhetoric.* Ed. LuMing Mao and Morris Young. Logan: Utah State UP, 2008. 83–105. Print.

—. "Reclaiming Hybridity: How One Filipino American Counterpublic Hybridizes Academic Discourse." *Rhetorical Agendas: Political, Ethical, Spiritual.* Ed. Patricia Bizzell. New York: Routledge, 2005. Print.

—. *Re-positioning Ethos: Rhetorics of Hybridity and the Filipino American National Historical Society.* Diss. Rensselaer Polytechnic University, 2002. Print.

—. "Writing Home or Writing *As* the Community: Toward a Theory of Recursive Spatial Movement for Students of Color in Service-Learning Courses." *Reflections* 8.3 (2009): 21–51. Print.

Okawa, Gail. "Diving for Pearls: Mentoring as Cultural and Activist Practice Among Academics of Color." *College Composition and Communication* 53.3 (2002): 507–32. Print.

—. "Multi-Cultural Voices: Peer Tutoring and Critical Reflection in the Writing Center." *Writing Center Journal* 12.1 (1991): 11–33. Print.

—. "Putting Their Lives on the Line: Personal Narrative as Political Discourse among Japanese Petitioners in American World War II Internment."

College English 74.1 (2011): 50–68. Print.

—. "'Resurfacing Roots': Developing a Pedagogy of Language Awareness from Two Views." *Language Diversity in the Classroom: From Intention to Practice.* Ed. Geneva Smitherman and Victor Villanueva. Carbondale: Southern Illinois UP, 2003. Print.

—. "Unbundling: Archival Research and Japanese American Communal Memory of U.S. Justice Department Internment, 1941–45." *Beyond the Archives: Research as a Lived Process.* Ed. Gesa Kirsch and Liz Rohan. Carbondale: Southern Illinois UP, 2008. 93-106. Print.

Oliver, Robert T. *Communication and Culture in Ancient India and China.* Syracuse: Syracuse UP, 1971. Print.

Ouchi, Shizuko. "Elementary English Language Arts Program in Transition." *Hawaii Schools* 5.2 (1968): 6–9. Print.

Ouyang, Huining. "Rewriting the Butterfly Story: Tricksterism in Onoto Watanna's A Japanese Nightingale and Sui Sin Far's 'The Smuggling of Tie Co.'" *Alternative Rhetorics: Challenges to the Rhetorical Tradition.* Ed. Laura Gray-Rosendale and Sibylle Gruber. Carbondale: Southern Illinois UP, 2001. 203–19. Print.

Pandey, Iswari. "Literate Lives Across the Digital Divide." *Computers and Composition* 23.2 (2006): 246–57. Print.

—. *South Asian in the Mid-South: Migrations of Literacies.* Pittsburgh: U of Pittsburgh P, 2015. Print.

Pham, Vincent. *Mobilizing "Asian American": Rhetoric and Ethnography of Asian American Media Organizations.* Diss. University of Illinois at Urbana-Champaign, 2011. Print.

Powell, Pegeen Reichert. "Facing the Audience: Reconsidering 'Audience' Through the Chinese Concept of Face." *Rhetoric, the Polis, and the Global Village: Selected Papers from the 1998 Thirtieth Anniversary Conference of the Rhetoric Society of America.* Ed. C. Jan Swearingen and Dave Pruett. Mahwah: Erlbaum, 1999. 139-46. Print.

Powers, John H., and Gwendolyn Gong. "East Asian Voice and the Expression of Cultural Ethos." *Voices on Voice: Definitions, Perspectives, Inquiry.* Ed. Kathleen Blake Yancey. Urbana, IL: National Council of Teachers of English, 1994. 202–25. Print.

Saenkhum, Tanita. *Investigating Agency in Multilingual Writers' Placement Decisions: A Case Study of The Writing Programs at Arizona State University.* Diss. Arizona State University, 2012. Print.

Sano-Franchini, Jennifer. "Cultural Rhetorics and the Digital Humanities: Toward Cultural Reflexivity in Digital Making." *Rhetoric and the Digital Humanities*. Ed. Jim Ridolfo and William Hart-Davidson. University of Chicago Press, 2015. 49-64. Print.

—. *The Rhetorical Making of the Asian/Asian American Face: Reading and Writing Asian Eyelids*. Diss. Michigan State University, 2013. Print.

Sano-Franchini, Jennifer, Robyn Tasaka, and Lehua Ledbetter. "Toward a Reflexive Approach to Remix, or, What Hawai'i Creole English and Tourism Can Teach Us About Copyright." *Cultures of Copyright: Contemporary Intellectual Property*. Ed. Dànielle Nicole DeVoss and Martine Courant Rife. New York: Peter Lang International Academic Publishers, 2014. 226–42. Print.

Schonberg, Jeff. "When Worlds Collide: Rhetorics of Profit, Rhetorics of Loss in Chinese Culture." *Alternative Rhetorics: Challenges to the Rhetorical Tradition*. Ed. Laura Gray-Rosendale and Sibylle Gruber. Carbondale: Southern Illinois UP, 2001. 235–56. Print.

Shen, Fan. "The Classroom and the Wider Culture: Identity as a Key to Learning English Composition." *College Composition and Communication* 40.4 (December 1989): 459–66. Print.

Shimabukuro, Mira. "'Me Inwardly Before I Dared': Japanese Americans Writing to Gaman." *College English*. 73.6 (2011): 648–71. Print.

—. *Relocating Authority: Japanese Americans Writing to Redress Mass Incarceration*. Boulder: UP of Colorado, 2015. Print.

—. *Relocating Authority: Japanese Americans Writing to Redress Mass Incarceration*. Diss. University of Wisconsin-Madison, 2009. Print.

Sun, Huatong. *Cross-Cultural Technology Design: Crafting Culture-Sensitive Technology for Local Users*. Oxford: Oxford UP, 2012. Print.

—. "The Triumph of Users: Achieving Cultural Usability Goals with User Localization." *Technical Communication Quarterly* 15.4 (2006): 457–81. Print.

Swearingen, C. Jan. "Originality, Authenticity, Imitation, and Plagiarism: Augustine's Chinese Cousins." *Perspectives on Plagiarism and Intellectual Property in a Postmodern World*. Ed. Lise Buranen and Alice M. Roy. Albany: State U of New York P, 1999. 19–30. Print.

—. "Rhetoric in Cross-Cultural Perspectives." *Handbook of Communication History*. Ed. Peter Simonson, Janice Peck, Robert T. Craig, and John P. Jackson, Jr. New York: Routledge, 2013. 109–21. Print.

—. "Song to Speech: The Origins of Early Epitaphia in Ancient Near Eastern Women's Lamentations." *Rhetoric Before and Beyond the Greeks.* Ed. Carol S. Lipson and Roberta A. Binkley. Albany, NY: SUNY, 2004. 213–25. Print.

—. "Tao Trek: One and Other in Comparative Rhetoric, A Response." *Rhetoric Society Quarterly* 43.3 (2013): 300–309. Print.

Swearingen, C. Jan and LuMing Mao. "Afterword: A Dialogue on Dialectic and Other Double Matters." CCC Special Symposium on East-West Comparative Rhetorical Studies. Ed. C. Jan Swearingen and LuMing Mao. *College Composition and Communication* 60.4 (June 2009): W99–W106. Print.

—. "Introduction: Double Trouble: Seeing Chinese Rhetoric through Its Own Lens." *College Composition and Communication* 60.4 (2009): 831–38. Print.

Swearingen, C. Jan, and Dave Pruett. "Language Diversity and the Classroom: Problems and Prospects, a Bibliography." *Language Diversity in the Classroom: From Intention to Practice.* Ed. Geneva Smitherman and Victor Villanueva. Carbondale: Southern Illinois UP, 2003. 134-50. Print.

Tasaka, Robyn. *Challenges and Privileges, Entanglement and Appropriation: Rhetorical Practices of Asian Americans from Hawai'i.* Diss. Michigan State University, 2009. Print.

Tsien, Tsuen-Hsuin. *Written on Bamboo and Silk: The Beginnings of Chinese Books and Inscriptions.* Chicago: U of Chicago P, 2004. Print.

Wan, Amy. "In the Name of Citizenship: The Writing Classroom and the Promise of Citizenship." *College English* 74.1 (2011): 28–49. Print.

Wang, Bo. "A Survey of Research in Asian Rhetoric." *Rhetoric Review* 23.2 (2004): 171–81. Print.

—. "'Breaking the Age of Flower Vases': Lu Yin's Feminist Rhetoric." *Rhetoric Review.* 28.3 (2009): 246–64. Print.

—. "Comparative Rhetoric, Postcolonial Studies, and Transnational Feminisms: A Geopolitical Approach." *Rhetoric Society Quarterly.* 43.3 (Summer 2013): 226–42. Print.

—. "Engaging 'Nüquanzhuyi': The Making of a Chinese Feminist Rhetoric." *College English* 72.4 (2010): 385–405. Print.

—. "Rereading Sui Sin Far: A Rhetoric of Defiance." *Representations: Doing Asian American Rhetoric.* Ed. LuMing Mao and Morris Young. Logan: Utah State UP, 2008. Print.

—. "Rethinking Feminist Rhetoric and Historiography in a Global Context: A Cross-Cultural Perspective." *Advances in the History of Rhetoric* 15.2 (2012): 28–52. Print.

—. "Transrhetorical Practice." *Rhetoric Review* 34.3 (Summer 2015): 246–49. Print.

—. "Writing to Connect Minds: Bing Xin as a Feminist Rhetorician." *College Composition and Communication* 60.4 (June 2009). W66–76. Print.

Wang, Xiaobo. "Huang Zongxi's and John Locke's Rhetoric Toward Modernity." *International Research and Review* 2. (2012): 49-56. Web.

Wexler, Steven. "Rhetoric, Literacy, and Social Change in Post-Mao China." *College Composition and Communication* 60.4 (2009): 808–26. Print.

Wu, Hui. "An Academic Career Built on Hybrid Feminist Rhetorics: From China to the U.S." *Peitho: A Publication of Coalition of Women Scholars in the History of Rhetoric and Composition* 13.1 (Spring 2011): 4–5. Print.

—. "The Alternative Feminist Discourse of Post-Mao Chinese Writers: A Perspective from the Rhetorical Situation." *Alternative Rhetorics: Challenges to the Rhetorical Tradition*. Ed. Laura Gray-Rosendale and Sibylle Gruber. Carbondale: Southern Illinois UP, 2001. 219–34. Print.

—. "A Comment on 'Historical Studies and Postmodernism: Rereading Aspasia of Miletus." *College English* 63.1 (2000): 102–105. Print.

—. "Historical Studies of Rhetorical Women Here and There: Methodological Challenges to Dominant Interpretive Frameworks. *Rhetoric Society Quarterly* 32.1 (2002): 81–97. Print.

—. "Lost and Found in Transnation: Modern Conceptualization of Chinese Rhetoric." *Rhetoric Review* 28.2 (2009): 148–66. Print.

—. trans. and ed. *Once Iron Girls: Essays on Gender by Post-Mao Chinese Literary Women*. Lexington Books, 2010. Print.

—. "The Paradigm of Margaret Cavendish: Reading Women's Rhetorics in a Global Context." *Calling Cards: Theory and Practice in Studies of Race, Gender, and Culture*. Ed. Jacqueline Jones Royster and Ann Marie Mann Simpkins. SUNY P. March 2005. 171–85. Print.

—. "Post-Mao Chinese Literary Women's Rhetoric Revisited: A Case for an *Enlightened* Feminist Rhetorical Theory." *College English* 72.4 (2010): 406–23. Print.

—. "Writing and Teaching behind Barbed Wire: An Exiled Composition Class in a Japanese–American Internment Camp." *College Composition and Communication* 59.2 (2007): 233–58. Print.

—, and Emily Standridge. *Reading and Writing about the Disciplines: A Rhetorical Approach*. Southlake: Fountainhead Press, 2015. Print.

—, and C. Jan Swearingen. *Guiguzi, China's First Treatise on Rhetoric: A Critical Translation and Commentary*. Carbondale: Southern Illinois UP, 2016. Print.

Xu, George Q. "The Use of Eloquence: The Confucian Perspective." *Rhetoric Before and Beyond the Greeks*. Ed. Carol S. Lipson and Roberta A. Binkley. Albany: SUNY P, 2012. 115-30. Print.

Yancey, Kathleen, and Mira Shimabukuro. "Comment and Response." *College English* 74.5 (2012): 486–89. Print.

Yoon, K. Hyoejin. "Affecting the Transformative Intellectual: Questioning 'Noble' Sentiments in Critical Pedagogy and Composition." *JAC: A Journal of Rhetoric, Culture, and Politics* 25.4 (2005): 717–59. Print.

—. "Afong Moy: Reframing Gentility in the Early Nineteenth Century." *Re/Framing Identifications*. Ed. Michelle Ballif. Long Grove, IL: Waveland Press Inc., 2013. 297-306. Print.

—. "The 'Good Teacher' of Composition: Towards a Genealogy of Emotion." *JAC: A Journal of Rhetoric, Culture, and Politics* 33.3–4 (2013): 688–711. Print.

—. "Learning Asian American Affect." *Representations: Doing Asian American Rhetoric*. Ed LuMing Mao and Morris Young. Logan: Utah State UP, 2008. 293–322. Print.

—. *The Subjects of Critical Pedagogy and Composition: The Asian–American Teacher–Intellectual and Affect*. Diss. State University of New York at Albany, 2003. Ann Arbor: UMI, 2003. Print.

You, Xiaoye. "Building Empire through Argumentation: Debating Salt and Iron in Western Han China." *College English* 72.4 (2010): 367–84. Print.

—. "Conflation of Rhetorical Traditions: The Formation of Modern Chinese Writing Instruction." *Rhetoric Review* 24.2 (2005): 150–69. Print.

—. *Writing in the Devil's Tongue: A History of English Composition in China*. Carbondale: Southern Illinois UP, 2010. Print.

Young, Morris. "Growing Resources in Asian American Literary Studies." *College English* 69.1 (2006): 74–83. Print.

—. *Literacy, Legitimacy, and the Composing of Asian–American Citizenship*. Diss. University of Michigan, 1997. Ann Arbor: UMI, 1997. Print.

—. *Minor Re/Visions: Asian American Literacy Narratives as a Rhetoric of Citizenship*. Carbondale: Southern Illinois UP, 2004. Print.

—. "Native Claims: Cultural Citizenship, Ethnic Expressions, and the Rhetorics of 'Hawaiianness.'" *Rhetorics from/of Color.* Spec. issue of *College English* 67.1 (September 2004): 83–101. Print.

—. "Standard English and Student Bodies: Institutionalizing Race and Literacy in Hawai'i." *College English* 64.4 (2002): 405–31. Print.

APPENDIX D
Asian/Asian American Publications in *College Composition and Communication* (1950–2010)

Phuong Minh Tran

No.	Year	Author	Title of Publication	Type of Publication	Keywords	General or A/AA Rhet/Comp Issues?
1	1962, No. 1	S. I. Hayakawa	Learning to Think and to Write: Semantics in Freshman English (pp. 5–8)	Article	Semantics; Grammar; Teaching pedagogy	General Rhet/Comp
2	1965, No. 5	San-su C. Lin	A Developmental English Program for the Culturally Disadvantaged (pp. 273–276)	Staffroom Interchange	Structured heuristic; Teaching pedagogy	General Rhet/Comp
3	1968, No. 2	San-su C. Lin	Review of *English and the Disadvantaged* by Edward R. Fagan (pp. 178)	Book Review		
4	1982, No. 2	Irwin Hashimoto (with Donald M. Murray)	Review of *Writing with Power: Techniques for Mastering the Writing Process* by Peter Elbow (pp. 208–212)	Book Review		
5	1984, No. 4	King Kok Cheung	Drawing out the Silent Minority (pp. 452–454)	Staffroom Interchange	ESL students; ESL writing; Minority students; Literacy practices	General Rhet/Comp

6	1985, No. 1	Irvin Hashimoto	Structured Heuristic Procedures: Their Limitations (pp. 73–81)	Article	Structured heuristic; Teaching pedagogy	General Rhet/Comp
7	1985, No. 2	Irvin Hashimoto	Review of *Helping Students Write Well: A Guide for Teachers in All Disciplines* by Barbara E. Fassler Walvoord (pp. 246–247)	Book Review		
8	1987, No. 1	Irvin Hashimoto	Voice as Juice: Some Reservations about Evangelic Composition (pp. 70–80)	Article	Voice; Style	General Rhet/Comp
9	1989, No. 2	Irvin Hashimoto	Writers on Writing by Tom Waldrep (pp. 245–246)	Book Review		
10	1989, No. 4	Fan Shen	The Classroom and the Wider Culture: Identity as a Key to Learning English Composition (pp. 459–66)	Staffroom Interchange	Chinese ESL writing; Identity; Translingual writing; Transnational culture; Literacy practices	A/AA Rhet/Comp

11	1992, No. 3	Marian M. Sciachitano	Introduction: Feminist Sophistics Pedagogy Group (pp. 297–300)	Introduction for Symposium on Feminist Experiences in the Composition Classroom	Feminist composition	General Rhet/Comp
12	1994, No. 4	Min-Zhan Lu	Professing Multiculturalism: The Politics of Style in the Contact Zone (pp. 442–458)	Article	Multiculturalism; Style; Chinese ESL writing; Errors	General Rhet/Comp; A/AA Rhet/Comp
13	1999, No. 4	Paul Kei Matsuda	Composition Studies and ESL Writing: A Disciplinary Division of Labor (pp. 699–721)	Article	ESL writing	General Rhet/Comp
14	1999, No. 1	Min-Zhan Lu (with Elizabeth Robertson)	Life Writing as Social Acts (pp. 119–131)	Book Review		
15	1999, No. 2	Min-Zhan Lu	Redefining the Literate Self: The Politics of Critical Affirmation (pp. 172–194)	Article	Literacy practices; Racial legacies; Asian Immigrants; Identity	General Rhet/Comp; A/AA Rhet/Comp

16	2001, No. 3	Johnson Cheu (with Brenda Jo Brueggemann, Linda Feldmeier White, Patricia A. Dunn, Barbara A. Heifferon)	Becoming Visible: Lessons in Disability (pp. 368–98)	Article	Disability; Teaching pedagogy	General Rhet/Comp
17	2002, No. 3	Gail Y. Okawa (with Marilyn M. Cooper)	From the Editor (pp. 393–395)	Editor's letter		
18	2002, No. 3	Gail Y. Okawa	Diving for Pearls: Mentoring as Cultural and Activist Practice among Academics of Color (pp. 507–532)	Article	Latinx American Composition; Ethnic rhetorics	General Rhet/Comp (not particularly about A/AA rhetorics)
19	2002, No. 1	Chikako D. Kumamoto	Bakhtin's Others and Writing as Bearing Witness to the Eloquent "I" (pp. 66–87)	Article	Rhetorical strategies in discourse; Style in Freshman Composition; Teaching Pedagogy	General Rhet/Comp

20	2004, No. 1	Min-Zhan Lu	An Essay on the Work of Composition: Composing English against the Order of Fast Capitalism (pp. 16–50)	Article	World Englishes	General Rhet/Comp; A/AA Rhet/Comp
21	2005, No.3	LuMing Mao	Rhetorical Borderlands: Chinese American Rhetoric in the Making (pp. 426–469).	Article	Chinese American Composition; Comparative rhetorics	A/AA Rhet/Comp
22	2005, No.4	Xiaoye You	Ideology, Textbooks, and the Rhetoric of Production in China (pp. 632–53)	Article	Chinese Rhetorics; EFL writing; Teaching pedagogy	A/AA Rhet/Comp
23	2005, No. 4	Susan Miller	Review of *Minor Re/Visions: Asian American Literacy Narratives as a Rhetoric of Citizenship* by Morris Young (pp. 688–700)	Book Review		
24	2006, No. 4	A. Suresh Canagarajah (Sri Lanka)	The Place of World Englishes in Composition: Pluralization Continued (pp. 586–619)	Article	World Englishes	General Rhet/Comp

25	2007, No. 2	Hui Wu	Writing and Teaching behind Barbed Wire: An Exiled Composition Class in a Japanese–American Internment Camp (pp. 237–62)	Article	Race; Immigrants; Teaching Pedagogy; Rhetorical strategies in A/AA discourse	A/AA Rhet/Comp
26	2008, No. 3	Matthew Abraham (Palestine)	Academic Freedom as a Rhetorical Construction: A Response to Powers and Chaput (pp. 512–18)	Interchanges	Academic freedom	General Rhet/Comp
27	2009, No. 3	Joseph Jeyaraj	Modernity and Empire: A Modest Analysis of Early Colonial Writing Practices (pp. 468–92)	Article	Teaching pedagogy; Indian colonial composition; Ethnic rhetorics	General Rhet/Comp (not particularly about A/AA rhetorics)
28	2009, No. 1	Haivan V. Hoang	Campus Racial Politics and a "Rhetoric of Injury" (p. 188) Print. Published in its entirety online at www.ncte.org/cccc/ccc, "The Extended CCC" (W385-W408). Web.	Article	Race; Asian Immigrants; Rhetorical strategies in A/AA discourse; A/AA identity	A/AA Rhet/Comp

| 29 | 2009, No. 4 | C. Jan Swearingen, LuMing Mao, Xiaoye You, Yichun Liu, Bo Wang, Weiguo Qu, Hui Wu and Liu Lu | Symposium: Comparative Rhetorical Studies in the New Contact Zone: Chinese Rhetoric Reimagined [Excerpt] (pp. 831–38) | Symposium | Comparative rhetorics; Chinese rhetorics | A/AA Rhet/Comp |

Contributors

**Chanon Adsanatham** is an Assistant Professor of English (writing and rhetoric) at the University of Maryland, where he researches and teaches comparative rhetoric, multimodality, and digital writing pedagogy. His works have appeared in *Computers and Composition* and an edited collection, *Multimodal Literacies and Emerging Genres*. Chanon is working on a book-length study of Thai conduct rhetoric, building upon his dissertation, which received the James Berlin Memorial Outstanding Dissertation Award from the Conference on College Composition and Communication in 2015.

Dominic Ashby is an Assistant Professor of English (Composition and Rhetoric) at Eastern Kentucky University. He teaches courses in Composition Theory, Technical and Professional Writing, Rhetorical Theory, and Pop Culture. His comparative work on Japanese rhetoric has appeared in a special issue of *Rhetoric Society Quarterly*. His current research focuses on nostalgia and its relationship to the rhetoric of place-based identities and inside–outside positionalities.

Holly Bruland's dissertation presented research conducted on the University of Hawai'i Mānoa Writing Mentors Program. Her work documents and analyzes the roles played by writing mentors across one hundred sections of first-year composition that were configured according to a "trinary" classroom arrangement involving teachers, students, and writing mentors. The dissertation also considers how participants understood their approaches to mentoring to be inflected by specific traditions from their home cultures, such as *senpai-kohai* relationship in Japanese culture and the *mo'o* deity in Hawaiian culture, as well as the place of Hawai'i more generally.

Karen Ching Carter is a PhD candidate in English with a concentration in rhetoric, composition, and linguistics at Arizona State University. She holds an MA in writing, rhetoric and discourse from DePaul University and a JD from the University of Denver. Her primary interests lie in the intersection between law, narrative, and rhetoric and how social meaning is created in diverse populations. More specifically, she is interested in analyzing how legal discourses in different social and political contexts transform social perceptions of marginalized and minority populations.

Stuart Ching has taught English in the Hawai'i public schools and in southern California at Loyola Marymount University, where he is Associate Professor of English. He is both a fiction writer and a long-time advocate of multicultural causes in K–college literacy education. His stories have appeared in anthologies such as *Growing Up Local*, *The Best of Honolulu Fiction*, and *A Voice for Earth: American Writers Respond to the Earth Charter,* and he has published scholarship on K–college literacy issues in journals such as *The New Advocate*, *Language Arts*, and *English Journal*.

Linh Dich is an Assistant Professor of English at Miami University of Ohio. Her scholarship interrogates the relationship between race, digital contexts, and public theories. She is currently investigating transnational publics and language practices emerging from the relationship between Vietnam and the United States. Her article, "Community Enclaves and Public Imaginaries: Formations of Asian American Online Identities," was published in *Computers and Composition* in 2016. She has been a member of the Asian/Asian American Caucus since 2005.

Haivan V. Hoang is Associate Professor of English and Director of the Writing Program at the University of Massachusetts Amherst. Her research and teaching interests include literacy studies and race, qualitative research methodologies, and composition pedagogy. She is the author of *Writing against Racial Injury: The Politics of Asian American Student Rhetoric* (University of Pittsburgh Press, 2015). The Asian/Asian American Caucus has been a professional home for her since 2002, and with Nancy Linh Karls, she served for several years as caucus co-chair (2005–2009).

Lawson Fusao Inada is a third-generation Japanese American from Fresno, California. As a child during World War II, he was imprisoned in California, Arkansas, and Colorado. A graduate of Fresno State University and the University of Oregon, he is an emeritus professor at Southern Oregon University. His books of poetry are *Before the War*, *Legends from Camp*, and *Drawing the Line*. He is the editor of *Only What We Could Carry: The Japanese American Internment Experience*. His honors include an Oregon Book Award, American Book Award, fellowships from the National Endowment for the Arts, and a Guggenheim Fellowship in Poetry. He has served as Steinbeck Chair of the National Steinbeck Center, and as Poet Laureate of Oregon.

Asao B. Inoue is an Associate Professor of Interdisciplinary Arts and Sciences and the Director of University Writing at the University of Washington Tacoma. He has published in the areas of writing assessment, validity studies, racism, and classroom assessment, with articles appearing in various edited collections as well as in *Assessing Writing*, the *Journal of Writing Assessment*, and *Composition Forum*. He co-edited *Race and Writing Assessment* (Lang, 2012), which won the CCCC Outstanding Book Award, and authored *Antiracist Writing Assessment Ecologies: Teaching and Assessing for a Socially Just Future* (WAC Clearinghouse/Parlor, 2015). Currently, he is co-editing a special issue of *College English* on writing assessment as social justice, and working on a new book project that theorizes labor for the writing classroom.

Scott Kaʻalele is a PhD student in the English Department at the University of Hawaiʻi at Mānoa, with interests in Pacific literature, Renaissance literature, and composition pedagogy.

Lehua Ledbetter is an Assistant Professor of Writing and Rhetoric at the University of Rhode Island with specializations in technical and professional communication as well as digital, cultural, and feminist rhetorics. She writes about the ways in which women use digital platforms to do rhetorical and entrepreneurial work in and for online communities. Her research also focuses on the effects of place and locality on programmatic development.

Edward Lee is a PhD student in the English Department at the University of Hawai'i at Mānoa. He received his B.A. in English/creative writing from Emory University, an M.M. in piano performance from Northwestern University, and an M.A in English (with a concentration in composition and rhetoric) from the University of Hawai'i at Mānoa. Edward's research interests include technical/professional writing, composition pedagogy, digital rhetorics, and Asian/Asian American life writing.

Jerry Won Lee is Assistant Professor of English and faculty affiliate in Asian American Studies at the University of California, Irvine. His other publications appear or are forthcoming in journals such as *College Composition and Communication, Critical Inquiry in Language Studies,* and *National Identities.* He earned his PhD from the University of Arizona in 2014.

LuMing Mao is a professor of English and chair of the Department of English at Miami University of Ohio. His teaching and research center on Asian/Asian American rhetoric, comparative rhetoric, Chinese rhetoric, and writing and discourse analysis in translingual contexts. He is author of, among other works, *Reading Chinese Fortune Cookie: The Making of Chinese American Rhetoric* and co-editor of *Representations: Doing Asian American Rhetoric* (with Morris Young). He is currently working on a book project, *Searching for a Tertium Quid: Studying Chinese Rhetoric in the Present,* and co-editing *The Norton Anthology of Rhetoric and Writing.*

Paul Kei Matsuda is Professor of English and Director of Second Language Writing at Arizona State University, where he works closely with master's and doctoral students in rhetoric and composition, applied linguistics, and Teaching English to Speakers of Other Languages (TESOL). He has published widely on issues related to language differences and writing in such journals as *College Composition and Communication, Composition Studies, College English, Journal of Basic Writing, Journal of Second Language Writing, TESOL Quarterly, Writing Program Administration,* and *Written Communication.* His research interests

include second language writing, intercultural rhetoric, identity and writing, technology and writing, and writing program administration. He has been involved in the Asian/Asian American Caucus since its inception in the mid-1990s. Born and bred in Japan, Paul learned English in Japan primarily through reading and writing, and he has been negotiating his personal and academic identities and discourse practices in English ever since.

Peter Mayshle is Assistant Professor of Writing and Rhetoric at Hobart and William Smith Colleges. He has a PhD in composition and rhetoric from the University of Wisconsin-Madison, and an MFA in creative writing from the University of Michigan-Ann Arbor. His interests include spatial rhetoric, postcolonial studies, narrative, and ethnography. With the help of a Vilas Travel Grant and a UW-Mellon Summer Fellowship, he conducted his dissertation research in Manila, Philippines on Intramuros, the walled city of Old Manila.

Jolivette Mecenas is Associate Professor and the Director of the Writing Program at the University of La Verne, in La Verne, CA. Her research focuses on writing program administration at minority-serving universities. She has been a member of the CCCC Asian/Asian American Caucus since 2007.

Terese Guinsatao Monberg is Associate Professor and a founding faculty member of the Residential College in the Arts and Humanities at Michigan State University, where she also serves as core faculty in Writing, Rhetoric, and American Cultures and affiliated faculty in Asian Pacific American Studies. Her work focuses on methodologies for uncovering, documenting, mobilizing, and sustaining Asian Pacific American and Filipinx American rhetorical and historical legacies. Her current book project examines Asian Pacific American notions of dwelling and listening—and how those notions can inform civic engagement and undergraduate curricula in rhetorical studies. Publications representative of her work include articles/book chapters in *Rhetorical Agendas: Political, Ethical, and Spiritual*, *Representations: Doing Asian American Rhetoric*, *Reflections: A Journal of Writing, Service-Learning, and Community Literacy,* and a special issue on cultural rhetorics with *enculturation: a journal of rhetoric, writing, and*

culture. She has been a member of the CCCC Asian/Asian American Caucus since 1999 and served as a co-chair of the caucus (2010–15).

Michael Pak is a PhD student in the English Department at the University of Hawai'i at Mānoa, with interests in popular culture, African American literature, and composition pedagogy.

Iswari Pandey serves on the faculty of English at California State University, Northridge, where he directs its program in Business and Professional Communication. He is the author of *South Asian in the Mid-South: Migrations of Literacies* (University of Pittsburgh Press, 2015), a multi-year qualitative research on the literacy practices of South Asian Hindu and Muslim immigrants in the U.S. Mid-South. His in-progress work, *Global English, Remedial English: Caste, Class, Nation* (forthcoming, Routledge), examines the teaching and learning of "remedial' English in Indian higher education in relation to local caste and class politics as well as to the forces of globalization. Iswari was born and raised in Nepal. He learned English from fourth grade and worked as a journalist and college lecturer there before beginning his graduate studies in the U.S.

Patti Poblete (@voleuseCK) is the Assistant Director of the Writing and Media Center at Iowa State University. Her research investigates writing program administration, public rhetorics, and communication through digital spaces.

Jennifer Sano-Franchini is Assistant Professor of Professional and Technical Writing in the Department of English at Virginia Tech, where she teaches courses on professional writing and intercultural communication. Her research interests are at the intersection of cultural rhetorics and digital rhetoric, information design, and Asian American rhetoric. Her scholarship has been published in

Computers and Composition, Present Tense, and the *International Journal for the Scholarship on Teaching and Learning.*

Charlyne Sarmiento is a PhD student in the Department of Education at the University of California, Santa Barbara. She received her MA in English from the University of Illinois, Chicago where she conducted an ethnography on two Chicago neighborhoods and explored how neoliberal ideology shaped community activists' arguments against gentrification and local educational reform. She also has a BA in Asian American Studies and participated in the student movement for an Asian American Studies minor at UIC. Charlyne is interested in genre theory, contemporary rhetorical theory, writing research across the disciplines and communities, and civic engagement in the teaching of writing.

Mira Shimabukuro is a lecturer in the School of Interdisciplinary Arts and Sciences at University of Washington Bothell, where she teaches first year composition and classes on the politics of literacy, language, and Japanese American incarceration. Her composition and rhetoric scholarship can be found in *College English, Representations: Doing Asian American Rhetoric* (co-edited by LuMing Mao and Morris Young), and in her book, *Relocating Authority: Japanese Americans Writing to Redress Mass Incarceration* (2015). In addition to her scholarship, Mira is also currently finishing a book-length poem titled *The Winter Drafts.* She lives in Seattle.

Robyn Tasaka is a Tutor Coordinator in the Noʻeau Center for Writing, Math, and Academic Success at the University of Hawaiʻi-West Oʻahu. Her essay "Rhetoric of the Asian American Self: Influences of Region and Social Class on Autobiographical Writing" was published in *Representations: Doing Asian American Rhetoric.*

Phuong Minh Tran is a Master's student in Teaching English to Speakers of Other Languages (TESOL) and a graduate assistant at Ball State University. She received a Bachelor's degree in Business English at Foreign Trade University in Hanoi, Vietnam. Her research interests include composition studies, reading and writing connections, and teaching composition to ESL students.

Bo Wang is Associate Professor of English and Co-Director of the Writing Program at California State University, Fresno. Her research interests include Asian/Asian American rhetoric and writing, comparative rhetoric, feminist rhetoric and historiography, and global/transnational rhetorical studies. She has published in such journals as *Advances in the History of Rhetoric, College Composition and Communication, College English, JAC, Rhetoric Review,* and *Rhetoric Society Quarterly*. Her co-edited symposium "Manifesting a Future for Comparative Rhetoric" appeared in *Rhetoric Review* in 2015. Currently she is at work on a book project on translated feminism and writing women in early-twentieth-century China.

Hui Wu is Professor of English and Chair of the Department of Literature and Languages at the University of Texas at Tyler. Her research interests encompass history of rhetoric, comparative studies of rhetoric, global feminist rhetorics, and archival research in rhetoric and composition. Her article, "Lost and Found in Transnation: Modern Conceptualization of Chinese Rhetoric" won the 2010 Theresa Enos award for the best article published in 2009 in *Rhetoric Review*. Her book, *Once Iron Girls: Essays on Gender by Post-Mao Literary Women* (Lexington Books, 2010) is a critical edition of Chinese feminist thought. More recently, she translated and studied China's earliest treatise on rhetoric, *Guiguzi*, published in 2016 with Southern Illinois University Press.

K. Hyoejin Yoon became full professor of English at West Chester University of Pennsylvania in 2014. Currently, she is Associate Dean of Humanities and Liberal Arts in the College of Arts and Sciences, also at WCU. She is co-chair of the Asian/Asian American Caucus and the CCCC Committee on the Status of Women in the Profession. Her research interests include emotion studies, feminist studies, Asian/American studies, graduate writing pedagogy, women's professional development, and leadership and higher education. She has published in *JAC, College Literature, Peitho*, as well as chapters in *Representations: Doing Asian American Rhetoric* (2008), edited by Mao and Young, and *Research Literacies and Writing Pedagogies for Masters and Doctoral Writers*, edited by

Badenhorst and Guerin. She co-edited a special issue of *College Literature* with Cari Carpenter called "Native/Asian Encounters" (2014).

Morris Young is Director of English 100, professor of English, and faculty affiliate in Asian American Studies at the University of Wisconsin, Madison. His book, *Minor Re/Visions: Asian American Literacy Narratives as a Rhetoric of Citizenship* (2004) received the 2004 W. Ross Winterowd Award and the 2006 CCCC Outstanding Book Award. His co-edited collection (with LuMing Mao), *Representations: Doing Asian American Rhetoric* (2008), received honorable mention for the 2009 MLA Mina P. Shaughnessy Prize.

www.ingramcontent.com/pod-product-compliance
Lightning Source LLC
Chambersburg PA
CBHW030525230426
43665CB00010B/768